Athol Fugard

Athol Fugard's work includes: *The Island, Sizwe Bansi is Dead, Arrest Under the Immorality Act, Playland, My Children! My Africa!, A Place with the Pigs, The Road to Mecca, Master Harold and the Boys, A Lesson from Aloes, The Drummer, Dimetos, The Coat, Boesman and Lena, Hello and Goodbye, People are Living There, The Blood Knot, Nongogo, No Good Friday* and *Valley Song*.

ATHOL FUGARD

Plays One

The Road to Mecca

A Place with the Pigs

My Children! My Africa!

Playland

Valley Song

Introduced by
the Author

faber and faber
LONDON · BOSTON

This collection first published in 1998
by Faber and Faber Limited
3 Queen Square London WC1N 3AU

Typeset by Country Setting, Woodchurch, Kent TN26 3TB
Printed in England by Mackays of Chatham plc, Chatham, Kent

Introduction © Athol Fugard, 1998
This collection © Athol Fugard, 1998

The Road to Mecca © Athol Fugard, 1985
A Place with the Pigs © Athol Fugard, 1988
My Children! My Africa! © Athol Fugard, 1990
Playland © Athol Fugard, 1992
Valley Song © Athol Fugard, 1996

Athol Fugard is hereby identified as author of this
work in accordance with Section 77 of the Copyright,
Designs and Patents Act 1988

All rights whatsoever in these plays are strictly reserved and
application for permission to perform them must be made in advance,
before rehearsals begin, to William Morris Agency, 31/32 Soho Square,
London W1V 5DG

A CIP record for this book
is available from the British Library

ISBN 0–571–19093–6

Contents

Foreword

The private and the public, the personal and the political . . . the two safe platforms at opposite ends of the tightrope on which I have spent my writing life. If there is one thing I know about writing it's that being 'safe' is not a good idea, so I have tried to stay out there on the wire. The five plays in this volume represent my attempt over the past fifteen years at that very precarious balancing act. Inevitably, as the circumstances in my life changed, there has been a bias in one direction or the other. In this sense *The Road to Mecca* and *A Place with the Pigs* are very personal plays. At the heart of the first one is an attempt on my side to understand the genesis, nature and consequences of a creative energy . . . an attempt which produced no answers. But I am also aware that in examining the predicament of the artist in a hostile environment I was saying something about my country. *A Place with the Pigs* is based on a three-inch news item in the *New York Times*. The story of Pavel's cowardly self-incarceration in a pig-sty also gave me a perfect metaphor for my struggle with alcoholism.

Moving to the other end of the wire, *My Children! My Africa!* was written out of the darkest decade in my country's history. It was a time when the prophecies of a bloodbath seemed to be coming true, when to have any hope in the future seemed the height of idiocy. But even in a play as overtly political as this one, the personal statement is still there. If the embattled sculptress Helen in *The Road to Mecca* is Athol Fugard in drag, then Mr. M in *My Children! My Africa!* is Athol Fugard in a black skin and threadbare suit. And then at the end of that decade, South Africa's famous political miracle. I saw it coming and I knew that the extraordinary opportunity to build a just and decent society would depend on our capacity for Truth and Forgiveness. *Playland* is my recognition of that.

And then, finally, *Valley Song*. Possibly my most successful attempt at balancing the personal and the political in its examination of the inevitability of change, of loss and renewal. It is a play which ends like all the others with a note of hope and affirmation.

Athol Fugard
September 1997

THE ROAD TO MECCA

For S.H.

A Note on Miss Helen

It was a drive into the Karoo to spend a holiday on a friend's farm and the route I drove that took me for the first time through what had only been a name on a map until then: New Bethesda, a small village in what turned out to be an absolutely magnificent setting. As I drove through it, I couldn't help responding to it, because I'm actually born in that part of the world – as a matter of fact, I was born fifteen miles away from New Bethesda in a place called Middelburg. Driving to my friend's farm I was struck by its isolation and thought to myself, hell, this would be quite a nice place to have a house, and escape from the city if ever I felt like getting away from the world. I mentioned this to my friend who said, 'Well, you know, the houses are dirt-cheap in New Bethesda because there has been a move from the rural areas into the cities. You could pick up a house there very cheaply.' So on the way back to Port Elizabeth, I in fact stopped and inquired and looked around and discovered there were houses for sale very, very cheaply.

I returned three months later with the express purpose of buying a house, which I still own. In the course of looking at various houses and getting to know a few of the locals, reference was made to a rather strange character who lived in the village. Her name was Helen Niemand and the people were kind of apologetic about her because they regarded her as a little crazy. They said that her craziness took the form of rather silly statues and sculpture that she made and had all around her house. I obviously couldn't resist the temptation of strolling in the direction of her house and seeing Miss

Helen's 'Mecca' for the first time. She was still alive
at that point but had become virtually a total recluse.
So, apart from seeing her in the distance once or twice,
and nodding at her when she was among her statues and
I happened to be walking past, I never got to know her
personally.

About two years after I bought my house and started
visiting the village regularly, Miss Helen committed
suicide. Obviously, as a writer I couldn't help responding
to this very eccentric character in this strange little community – a community which was in a sense hostile to her
life and her work because it was a deviation from what
they considered to be the way a life should be lived –
and thinking: there's a damn good story. Over the next
few years thoughts about Miss Helen occurred with
some frequency in my notebooks.

I also began to discover more about the real Miss
Helen. For example, up until the age of fifty, when her
husband died, there was nothing about her that gave
any hint of what was going to happen. Then her life
suddenly erupted in this remarkable way in terms of
her sculpture. Suddenly there was the first statue in the
garden, and then over the next fifteen or seventeen years
she worked away, with obsessive dedication, at what
must have been a personal vision. After her death I went
on to discover what she had done inside her house as
well – as remarkable a feat as what she had done outside
with the sculptures. Those seventeen years of creative
activity ended, and there was a period of about eighteen
months or two years during which she made nothing,
did nothing and became very paranoid, very depressed.
One night she killed herself by drinking caustic soda (the
Americans would call it lye): she burned away her insides.

Though obviously in a sense provoked by Miss Helen's
story, I've never quite been hooked by it. I'm a fisherman
and I know the difference between a fish that's just

playing with your bait and one that says, 'WRITE! I'M IT!' and takes your rod down and you sit back and put the hook deep in. I wasn't hooked.

The hooking came through a coincidence of factors. At a personal level, I began to realize, a provocation had been thrown at me four years previously by an actress who was doing *A Lesson from Aloes* in Amsterdam (she had also done *Boesman and Lena*). In the course of a conversation at the Rijksmuseum she said to me, 'Those are marvellous roles you have created for women. I'm very grateful to you for that, but, looking back at your work, I can't help being struck by the fact that you have never had two women together. When are you going to do that?'

And I suddenly registered for the first time that although I had created an interesting gallery of women's portraits over the years, I'd never put two women together on a stage as the focus of the whole event. Other personal factors in my life helped give the provocation more of an edge, more of a demand that I think about it, try to do something about it.

While this was happening to me, I discovered another fact about Miss Helen: that in the last years of her life, the last period of nothing until her death, there had been one very significant friendship – a friendship with a young woman, a social worker, from Cape Town. I'd rather not mention her name, because I've taken every liberty I felt necessary in writing the play. I've done my own thing; I've not written a documentary. I discovered that the friendship had been very, very meaningful. I accidentally happened to meet the young woman. I was struck by her because she was very strong, a very remarkable person, with a strong social conscience, a strong sense of what South Africa was about, a strong outrage at what was wrong with it. I couldn't help thinking of the anomaly of this sort of stern decency encountering the almost feudal world of New Bethesda – a South Africa which disappeared from the rest of the country a hundred years ago. Obviously, that young person had had quite a confrontation with the village.

Because of my respect for Miss Helen the young woman gave me, as a gesture, a little memento of the occasion when we met, a photograph of herself and Miss Helen. I took one look at the photograph – it's a brilliant, beautiful photograph – and there was the play. There was the coincidence. I was hooked. That was the moment when I swallowed the bait.

ATHOL FUGARD

from an interview with Gitta Honegger, 1984
first printed in Yale Reports

Characters

Miss Helen
Elsa
Marius Byleveld

The time: Autumn 1974

The Road to Mecca opened at the Lyttelton Theatre, London, on 22 February 1985. The cast was as follows:

Miss Helen Yvonne Bryceland
Elsa Charlotte Cornwell
Marius Byleveld Bob Peck

Directed by Athol Fugard
Designed by Douglas Heap

The soul selects her own society –
Then – shuts the door –
On her divine majority –
Present no more.

Emily Dickinson

Act One

The lounge and, leading off it, the bedroom alcove of a house in the small Karoo village of New Bethesda. An extraordinary room by virtue of the attempt to use as much light and colour as is humanly possible. The walls – mirrors on all of them – are all of different colours, while on the ceiling and floor are solid, multi-coloured geometric patterns. Yet the final effect is not bizarre but rather one of light and extravagant fantasy. Just what the room is really about will be revealed later when its candles and lamps – again, a multitude of them of every size, shape and colour – are lit. The late afternoon light does, however, give some hint of the magic to come.

Miss Helen is in the bedroom alcove. A frail, bird-like little woman in her late sixties. A suggestion of personal neglect, particularly in her clothes which are shabby and were put on with obvious indifference to the final effect. She is nervously fussing around an old-fashioned washstand, laying out towels, soap, etc., etc., and from time to time directs her attention to the lounge and a door leading from it to the rest of the house. In the course of moving around she sees an overnight bag and a briefcase on the floor near the lounge entrance. She fetches these and carries them into the alcove.

Elsa enters, a strong young woman in her late twenties dressed in a tracksuit or something else suitable for a long motorcar ride.

Elsa Not cold enough yet for the car to freeze up, is it?

Helen No. No danger of that. We haven't had any frost yet.

Elsa I'm too exhausted to put it away. (*Collapses on the bed.*) Whew! Thank God that's over. Another hour and I would have been wiped out. That road gets longer and longer every time.

Helen Your hot water is nearly ready.

Elsa Good. (*Starts to unpack her overnight bag.*)

Helen Nice clean towels . . . and I've opened that box of scented soaps you brought me last time.

Elsa What? Oh, those. Haven't you used them yet?

Helen Of course not! I was keeping them for a special occasion.

Elsa And this is it?

Helen Yes. An unexpected visit from you is a *very* special occasion. Is that all your luggage?

Elsa When I said a short visit I really meant it.

Helen Such a long way to drive for just one night.

Elsa I know.

Helen You don't think you could . . .?

Elsa Stay longer?

Helen Even just two nights?

Elsa Impossible. We're right in the middle of exams. I've got to be in that classroom at eight-thirty on Monday morning. As it is I should be sitting at home right now marking papers. I've even brought a pile of them with me just in case I get a chance up here. (*Starts to undress . . . tracksuit top, sneakers and socks.*)

Helen Put anything you want washed on one side and I'll get a message to Katrina first thing in the morning.

Elsa Don't bother her with that. I can do it myself.

Helen You can't leave without seeing Katrina! She'll never forgive me if I don't let her know you're here. Please . . . even if it's only for a few minutes.

Elsa I won't leave without seeing Katrina, Miss Helen! But I don't need her to wash a pair of pants and a bra for me. I do my own washing.

Helen I'm sorry . . . I just thought you might . . . There's an empty drawer here if you want to pack anything away.

Elsa (*an edge to her voice*) Please stop fussing, Miss Helen! I know my way around by now.

Helen It's just that if I'd known you were coming, I would have had everything ready for you.

Elsa Everything is fine just the way it is.

Helen No, it isn't! I don't even know that I've got enough in the kitchen for a decent supper tonight. I did buy bread yesterday, but for the rest . . .

Elsa Please, Miss Helen! If we need anything, I'll get old Retief to open his shop for us. In any case, I'm not hungry. All I need at this moment is a good wash and a chance to unwind so that I can forget I've been sitting in a motorcar for twelve hours.

Helen Be patient with me, Elsie. Remember the little saying: 'Patience is a virtue, virtue is a grace, and . . .'

Elsa (*unexpectedly sharp*) For God's sake, Helen! Just leave me alone for a few minutes!

Pause.

Helen (*timidly*) I'll get your hot water.

Miss Helen exits. Elsa slumps down on the bed, her head in her hands. Miss Helen returns a few seconds later with a large kettle of hot water. She handles it with difficulty.

I've got the small one on for tea.

Elsa Let me do that!

She jumps up and takes the kettle away from Miss Helen. The two women stand staring at each other for a few seconds. Elsa puts down the kettle and then puts her hands on Miss Helen's shoulders.

My turn to say sorry.

Helen You don't need to do that.

Elsa Please! It will help. Sorry, Miss Helen. I also need to hear you say you forgive me.

Helen To tell you the truth, I was getting on my own nerves.

Elsa (*now smiling*) Come on.

Helen Oh, all right . . . But I promise you it isn't necessary. You're forgiven.

Elsa (*leading Miss Helen over to a chair*) Now sit down and stop worrying about me. We're both going to close our eyes, take a deep breath and start again. Ready?

Helen Ready.

Elsa One, two, three . . . (*closed eyes and deep breaths*) And now?

Helen (*with the sly, tongue-in-cheek humour we will come to recognize as characteristic of the relaxed Miss Helen*) Well, if you really mean it, I think the best thing is for you to get back into your car, drive around the block and arrive again. And this time I want you, please, to hoot three times the way you usually do, so that I don't think a ghost has walked in through the front door when you appear.

Elsa (*calling Miss Helen's bluff*) Right. Where are the car keys? (*Finds them and heads for the front door.*)

Helen Where are you going?

Elsa To do what you said. Drive around the block and arrive again.

Helen Like that?

Elsa Why, what's wrong?

Helen Elsie! Sterling Retief will have a heart attack if he sees you like that.

Elsa But I wear less than this when I go to the beach. Oh, all right then, you old spoilsport, let's pretend.

Elsa runs into the other room, revs up her motorcar, grinds through all its gears and 'arrives'. Three blasts on the horn. The two women play the 'arrival game' (specifics to be determined in rehearsal). At the end of it they come together in a good laugh.

If my friends in Cape Town were to have seen that! You must understand, Miss Helen, Elsa Barlow is known as a 'serious young woman'. Bit of a blue-stocking, in fact. Not much fun there! I don't know how you did it, Helen, but you caught me with those stockings down from the first day we met. You have the rare distinction of being the only person who can make me make a fool of myself . . . and enjoy it.

Helen You weren't making a fool of yourself. And any-way what about me? Nearly seventy and behaving as if I were seven!

Elsa Let's face it, we've both still got a little girl hidden away in us somewhere.

Helen And they like to play together.

Elsa Mine hasn't done that for a long time.

Helen And I didn't even know that mine was still alive.

Elsa *That* she most certainly is. She's the one who comes running out to play first. Feeling better?

Helen Much better.

For the moment all tensions are gone. Elsa cleans herself as thoroughly as a basin of water, a face cloth and a bar of scented soap will allow.

Elsa God, this Karoo dust gets right into your pores. I can even taste it. That first mouthful of tea is going to be mud. I'll fill up all the kettles tomorrow and have a really good scrub. When did you last have one?

Miss Helen has to think about that.

Right, settled. Your name is down for one as well.

A few seconds of industrious scrubbing. Miss Helen watches her.

What are you thinking?

Helen So many things! About the way you *did* arrive. I wasn't joking. For a few seconds I did think I was seeing a ghost. I heard the front door open . . . I thought it was little Katrina, she also never knocks . . . but instead there you were. (*She wants to say more but stops herself.*)

Elsa Go on.

Helen It was so strange. Almost as if you didn't really see me or anything else at first . . . didn't want to. And so cross! I've never seen you like that before.

Elsa This isn't quite like the other times, Miss Helen.

Helen That's a pity. They were all good times. (*Pause.*)
So what sort of time is this going to be? A bad one?

Elsa (*evenly*) I hope not. Doesn't have to be. It depends
on you.

*Miss Helen avoids Elsa's eyes. The young woman
looks around the room.*

But you're right. I hadn't really arrived until now.

Helen Where were you, Elsie?

Elsa (*she thinks about the question before answering*)
Way back at the turn-off to the village from the National
Road . . . or maybe a few miles further along it now . . .
walking to Cradock.

Helen I don't understand.

Elsa I gave a lift to a woman outside Graaff-Reinet.
That's most probably where she is now. I dropped her
at the turn-off to the village.

Helen Who was she?

Elsa (*shrugging with apparent indifference*) An African
woman.

Helen Cradock! That's a long walk.

Elsa I know.

Helen It's about another eighty miles from the turn-off.
(*She waits for Elsa to say more.*)

Elsa I nearly didn't stop for her. She didn't signal that
she wanted a lift or anything like that. Didn't even look
up when I passed . . . I was watching her in the rear-view
mirror. Maybe that's what told me there was a long walk

17

ahead of her . . . the way she had her head down and just kept on walking. And then the baby on her back. It was hot out there, Miss Helen, hot and dry and a lot of empty space . . . There wasn't a farmhouse in sight. She looked very small and unimportant in the middle of all that. Anyway, I stopped and reversed and offered her a lift. Not very graciously. I'd already been driving for ten hours and all I wanted was to get here as fast as I could. She got in and after a few miles we started talking. Her English wasn't very good, but when I finally got around to understanding what she was trying to tell me it added up to a good old South African story. Her husband, a farm labourer, had died recently, and no sooner had they buried him when the *Baas* told her to pack up and leave the farm. So there she was . . . on her way to the Cradock district, where she hoped to find a few distant relatives and a place to live. (*trying to remember the woman as clearly as possible*) About my age. The baby couldn't have been more than a few months old. All she had with her was one of those plastic shopping bags they put your groceries in at supermarkets. I saw a pair of old slippers. She was barefoot.

Helen Poor woman.

Elsa So I dropped her at the turn-off. Gave her what was left of my food and some money. She carried on walking and I drove here.

Pause.

Helen Is there something else?

Elsa No. That's all.

Helen I'm sure somebody else will give her a lift.

Elsa (*too easily*) Hope so. If not, she and her baby are in for a night beside the road. There's eighty miles of the

Karoo ahead of her. Shadows were already stretching out across the veld when she got out of the car. The Great Karoo! And just when I thought I was getting used to it, beginning to like it, in fact. Down in Cape Town I've actually caught myself talking rubbish about its vast space and emptiness, its awesome stillness and silence! Just like old Getruida down the road. It's that all right, but only because everything else has been all but damned out of existence. It's so obvious where you Afrikaners get your ideas of God from. Beats me how you've put up with it so long, Miss Helen. Nearly seventy years? My God, you deserve a medal. I would have packed up and left it at the first opportunity . . . and let's face it, you've had plenty of those.

Helen I was born here, Elsa.

Elsa I sympathize, Miss Helen. Believe me, I truly sympathize.

Helen It's not really as bad as you make it sound. The few times I've been away, I've always ended up missing it and longing to be back.

Elsa Because you wanted to get back to your work?

Helen (*shaking her head*) No. Even before all that started. It grows on you, Elsa.

Elsa Which is just about the only growing it seems to allow. For the rest, it's as merciless as the religion they preach around here. Looking out of the car window this afternoon I think I finally understood a few things about you Afrikaners . . . and it left me feeling just a little uneasy.

Helen You include me in all you're saying.

Elsa Yes. You might not go to church any more, but you're still an Afrikaner, Miss Helen. You were in there

19

with them, singing hymns every Sunday, for a long, long time. Bit of a renegade now, I admit, but you're still one at heart.

Helen And that heart is merciless?

Pause.

Elsa No. That you aren't. A lot of other things maybe, but certainly not that. Sorry, sorry, sorry . . .

Helen You're still very cross, aren't you? And something else as well. There's a new sound in your voice. One I haven't heard before.

Elsa What do you mean?

Helen Like the way you talked about that woman on the road. Almost as if you didn't care, which I know isn't true.

Elsa Of course I cared. I cared enough to stop and pick her up, to give her money and food. But I also don't want to fool myself. That was a sop to my conscience and nothing more. It wasn't a real contribution to her life and what she is up against. Anyway, what's the point in talking about her? She's most probably curling up in a stormwater drain at this moment – that's where she said she'd sleep if she didn't get a lift – and I feel better for a good wash.

Helen There it is again.

Elsa Well, it's the truth.

Helen It was the way you said it.

Elsa You're imagining things, Miss Helen. Come on, let's talk about something else. It's too soon to get serious. We've got enough time, and reasons, for that later on. What's been happening in the village? Give me the news. Your last letter didn't have much of that in it.

*Elsa gets into clean clothes. Miss Helen starts to fold
the discarded tracksuit. Elsa stops her.*

I can do that.

Helen I just wanted to help.

Elsa And you can do that by making a nice pot of tea
and giving me the village gossip.

*Miss Helen goes into the lounge. She takes cups and
saucers, etc., from a sideboard and places them on
the table.*

Helen I haven't got any gossip. Little Katrina is the only
one who really visits me any more, and all she wants to
talk about these days is her baby. There's also Marius,
of course, but he never gossips.

Elsa He still comes snooping around, does he?

Helen Don't put it like that, Elsa. He's a very old friend.

Elsa Good luck to him. I hope the friendship continues.
It's just that *I* wouldn't want him for one. Sorry, Miss
Helen, but I don't trust your old friend, and I have a
strong feeling that Pastor Marius Byleveld feels the same
way about me. So let's change the subject. Tell me about
Katrina. What has she been up to?

Helen She's fine. And so is the baby. As prettily dressed
these days as any white baby, thanks to the clothes you
sent her. She's been very good to me, Elsa. Never passes
my front door without dropping in for a little chat. Is
always asking about you. I don't know what I would do
without her. But I'm afraid Koos has started drinking
again. And making all sorts of terrible threats about her
and the baby. He still doesn't believe it's his child.

Elsa Is he beating her?

Helen No. The warning you gave him last time seems to have put a stop to that.

Elsa God, it makes me sick! Why doesn't she leave him?

Helen And then do what?

Elsa Find somebody else! Somebody who will value her as a human being and take care of her and the child.

Helen She can't do that, Elsie. They're married.

Elsa Oh, for God's sake, Helen. There's the Afrikaner in you speaking. There is nothing sacred about a marriage that abuses the woman! I'll have a talk to her tomorrow. Let's make sure we get a message to her to come around.

Helen Don't make things more difficult for her, Elsa.

Elsa How much more difficult can 'things' be than being married to a drunken bully? She *has* got a few rights, Miss Helen, and I just want to make sure she knows what they are. How old is she now?

Helen Seventeen, I think.

Elsa At that age I was still at school dreaming about my future, and here she is with a baby and bruises. Quick, tell me something else.

Helen Let me see . . . Good gracious me! Of course, yes! I have got important news. Old Getruida has got the whole village up in arms. Brace yourself, Elsa. She's applied for a licence to open a liquor store.

Elsa A what?

Helen A liquor store. Alcoholic beverages.

Elsa Booze in New Bethesda?

Helen If you want to put it that bluntly . . . yes.

Elsa Now that is headline material. Good for old Gerty. I always knew she liked her sundowner, but I never thought she'd have the spunk to go that far.

Helen Don't joke about it, Elsie. It's a very serious matter. The village is very upset.

Elsa Headed, no doubt, by your old friend Pastor Marius Byleveld.

Helen That's right. I understand that his last sermon was all about the evils of alcohol and how it's ruining the health and lives of our Coloured folk. Getruida says he's taking unfair advantage of the pulpit and that the Coloureds get it anyway from Graaff-Reinet.

Elsa Then tell her to demand a turn.

Helen At what?

Elsa The pulpit. Tell her to demand her right to get up there and put her case . . . and remind her before she does that the first miracle was water into wine.

Helen (*trying not to laugh*) You're terrible, Elsie! Old Getruida in the pulpit!

Elsa And you're an old hypocrite, Miss Helen. You love it when I make fun of the Church.

Helen No, I don't. I was laughing at Gerty, not the Church. And you have no right to make me laugh. It's a very serious matter.

Elsa Of course it is! Which is why I want to know who you think is worse: the Dominee deciding what is right and wrong for the Coloured folk or old Getruida exploiting their misery?

Helen I'm afraid it's even more complicated than that, Elsa. Marius *is* only thinking about what's best for them, but on the other hand Getruida has offered to donate part of her profits to their school-building fund. And what about Koos? Wouldn't it make things even worse for Katrina if he had a local supply?

Elsa They are two separate issues, Miss Helen. You don't punish a whole community because one man can't control his drinking. Which raises yet another point: has anybody bothered to ask the Coloured people what they think about it all?

Helen Are we going to have that argument again?

Elsa I'm not trying to start an argument. But it does seem to me right and proper that if you're going to make decisions which affect other people, you should find out what those people think.

Helen It is the same argument. You know they don't do that here.

Elsa Well, it's about time they started. I don't make decisions affecting the pupils at school without giving them a chance to say something. And they're children! We're talking about adult men and women in the year 1974.

Helen Those attitudes might be all right in Cape Town, Elsa, but you should know by now that the Valley has got its own way of doing things.

Elsa Well, it can't cut itself off from the twentieth century for ever. Honestly, coming here is like stepping into the middle of a Chekhov play. While the rest of the world is hoping the bomb won't drop today, you people are arguing about who owns the Cherry Orchard. Your little world is not as safe as you would like to believe, Helen. If you think it's going to be left alone to stagnate in the nineteenth century while the rest of us hold our

breath hoping we'll reach the end of the twentieth,
you're in for one hell of a surprise. And it will start with
your Coloured folk. They're not fools. They also read
newspapers, you know. And if you don't believe me,
try talking about something other than the weather
and her baby next time Katrina comes around. You'll
be surprised at what's going on inside that little head.
As for you Helen! Sometimes the contradictions in you
make me want to scream. Why do you always stand up
and defend this bunch of bigots? Look at the way
they've treated you.

Helen (*getting nervous*) They leave me alone now.

Elsa That is not what you said in your last letter!

Helen My last letter?

Elsa Yes.

Pause. Helen has tensed.

Are you saying you don't remember it, Helen?

Helen No . . . I remember it.

Elsa And what you said in it?

Helen (*trying to escape*) Please, little Elsie! Not now.
Let's talk about it later. I'm still all flustered with you
arriving so unexpectedly. Give me a chance to collect my
wits together. Please? And while I'm doing that, I'll make
that pot of tea you asked for.

*Miss Helen exits into the kitchen. Elsa takes stock
of the room. Not an idle examination; rather, she
is trying to see it objectively, trying to understand
something . . . She spends a few seconds at the
window, staring out at the statues in the yard. She sees
a cardboard box in a corner and opens it – handfuls
of coloured ceramic chips. She also discovers a not*

very successful attempt to hide an ugly burn mark on one of the walls. Miss Helen returns with tea and biscuits.

Elsa What happened here?

Helen Oh, don't worry about that. I'll get Koos or somebody to put a coat of paint over it.

Elsa But what happened?

Helen One of the lamps started smoking badly when I was out of the room.

Elsa And new curtains.

Helen Yes. I got tired of the old ones. I found a few Marie biscuits in the pantry. Will you be mother?

Light is starting to fade in the room. Elsa pours the tea, dividing her attention between that and studying the older woman. Miss Helen tries to hide her unease.

Do I get a turn now to ask for news?

Elsa No.

Helen Why not?

Elsa I haven't come up here to talk about myself.

Helen That's not fair!

Elsa It's boring.

Helen Not to me. Come on Elsie, fair is fair. You asked me for the village gossip and I did my best. Now it's your turn.

Elsa What do you want to know?

Helen Everything you would have told me about in your letters if you had kept your promise and written them.

26

Elsa Good and bad news?

Helen I said everything . . . but try to make the good a little bit more than the bad.

Elsa Right. The *Elsa Barlow Advertiser*! Hot off the presses! What do you want to start with? Financial, crime or sports page?

Helen The front-page headline.

Elsa How's this? 'Barlow to appear before School Board for possible disciplinary action.'

Helen Not again!

Elsa Yep.

Helen Oh dear! What was it this time?

Elsa Wait for the story. 'Elsa Barlow, a twenty-eight-year-old English language teacher, is to appear before a Board of Enquiry of the Cape Town School Board. She faces the possibility of strict disciplinary action. The enquiry follows a number of complaints from the parents of pupils in Miss Barlow's Standard Nine class. It is alleged that in April this year Miss Barlow asked the class, as a homework exercise, to write a five-hundred-word letter to the State President on the subject of racial inequality. Miss Barlow teaches at a Coloured School.'

Helen Is that true?

Elsa Are you doubting the accuracy and veracity of the *Advertiser*?

Helen Elsie! Elsie! Sometimes I think you deliberately look for trouble.

Elsa All I 'deliberately look for', Miss Helen, are opportunities to make those young people in my classroom think for themselves.

Helen So what is going to happen?

Elsa Depends on me, I suppose. If I appear before them contrite and apologetic, a stern reprimand. But if I behave the way I really feel, I suppose I could lose my job.

Helen Do you want my advice?

Elsa No.

Helen Well, I'm going to give it to you all the same. Say you're sorry and that you won't do it again.

Elsa Both of those are lies, Miss Helen.

Helen Only little white ones.

Elsa God, I'd give anything to be able to walk in and tell that School Board exactly what I think of them and their educational system. But you're right, there are the pupils as well, and for as long as I'm in the classroom a little subversion is possible. Rebellion starts, Miss Helen, with just one man or woman standing up and saying, 'No. Enough!' Albert Camus. French writer.

Helen You make me nervous when you talk like that.

Elsa And you sound just like one of those parents. You know something? I think you're history's first reactionary-revolutionary. You're a double agent, Helen!

Helen Haven't you got any good news?

Elsa Lots. I still don't smoke. I drink very moderately. I try to jog a few miles every morning.

Helen You're not saying anything about David.

Elsa Turn to the lonely hearts column. There's a sad little paragraph: 'Young lady seeks friendship with young man, etc., etc.'

Helen You're talking in riddles. I was asking you about David.

Elsa And I'm answering you. I've said nothing about him because there's nothing to say. It's over.

Helen You mean . . . you and David . . .?

Elsa Yes, that is exactly what I mean. It's finished. We don't see each other any more.

Helen I knew there was something wrong from the moment you walked in.

Elsa If you think this is me with something wrong, you should have been around two months ago. Your little Elsie was in a bad way. You were in line for an unexpected visit a lot earlier than this, Helen.

Helen You should have come.

Elsa I nearly did. But your letters suggested that you weren't having such a good time either. If we'd got together at that point, we might have come up with a suicide pact.

Helen I don't think so.

Elsa Joke, Miss Helen.

Helen Then don't joke about those things. Weren't you going to tell me?

Elsa I'm trying to forget it, Helen! There's another reason why I didn't come up. It has left me with a profound sense of shame.

Helen Of what?

Elsa Myself. The whole stupid mess.

Helen Mess?

Elsa Yes, mess! Have you got a better word to describe a situation so rotten with lies and deceit that your only sense of yourself is one of disgust?

Helen And you were so happy when you told me about him on your last visit.

Elsa God, that was more than just happiness, Miss Helen. It was like discovering the reason for being the person, the woman, I am for the first time in my life. And a little bit scary . . . realizing that another person could do so much to your life, to your sense of yourself. Even before it all went wrong, there were a couple of times when I wasn't so sure I liked it.

Helen But what happened? Was there a row about something?

Elsa (*bitter little laugh*) Row? Oh, Helen! Yes, there were plenty of those. But they were incidental. There had to be some sort of noise, so we shouted at each other. We also cried. We did everything you're supposed to.

Helen All I know about him is what you told me. He sounded like such a sensitive and good man, well read and intelligent. So right for you.

Elsa He was all of that. (*A moment's hesitation. She is not certain about saying something. She decides to take the chance.*) There's also something about him I didn't tell you. He's married. He has a devoted, loving wife – quite pretty in fact – and a child. A little girl. Shocked you?

Helen Yes. You should have told me, Elsie. I would have warned you.

Elsa That's exactly why I didn't. I knew you would, but I was going to prove you wrong. Anyway, I didn't need

30

any warnings. Anything you could have said to me,
Helen, I'd said to myself from the very beginning . . .
but I was going to prove myself wrong as well. What it
all came down to finally was that there were two very
different ideas about what was happening, and we
discovered it too late. You see, I was in it for keeps,
Helen. I knew that we were all going to get hurt, that
somehow we would all end up being victims of the
situation . . . but I also believed that when the time came
to choose I would be the lucky winner, that he would
leave his wife and child and go with me. Boy, was I
wrong! Ding-dong, wrong-wrong, tolls Elsa's bell at the
close of the day!

Helen Don't do that.

Elsa Defence mechanism. It still hurts. I'm getting
impatient for the time when I'll be able to laugh at it all.
I mustn't make him sound like a complete bastard. He
wasn't without a conscience. Far from it. If anything, it
was too big. The end would have been a lot less messy if
he'd known how to just walk away and close the door
behind him. When finally the time for that did come, he
sat around in pain and torment, crying – God, that was
awful! – waiting for me to tell him to go back to his wife
and child. Should have seen him, Helen. He came up with
postures of despair that would have made Michelangelo
jealous. I know it's all wrong to find another person's
pain disgusting, but that is what eventually happened.
The last time he crucified himself on the sofa in my
lounge I felt like vomiting. He told me just once too
often how much he hated himself for hurting me.

Helen Elsie, my poor darling. Come here.

Elsa (*taut*) I'm all right now. (*Pause.*) Do you know
what the really big word is, Helen? I had it all wrong.

Like most people, I suppose I used to think it was 'love'.
That's the big one all right, and it's quite an event when
it comes along. But there's an even bigger one. Trust.
And more dangerous. Because that's when you drop your
defences, lay yourself wide open, and if you've made a
mistake, you're in big, big trouble. And it hurts like hell.
Ever heard the story about the father giving his son his
first lesson in business?

Miss Helen shakes her head.

I think it's meant to be a joke, so remember to laugh.
He puts his little boy high up on something or other and
says to him, 'Jump. Don't worry, I'll catch you.' The
child is nervous, of course, but Daddy keeps reassuring
him: 'I'll catch you.' Eventually the little boy works up
enough courage and does jump, and Daddy, of course,
doesn't make a move to catch him. When the child has
stopped crying – because he has hurt himself – the father
says: 'Your first lesson in business, my son. Don't trust
anybody.' (*Pause.*) If you tell it with a Jewish accent, it's
even funnier.

Helen I don't think it's funny.

Elsa I think it's ugly. That little boy is going to think
twice about jumping again, and at this moment the same
goes for Elsa Barlow.

Helen Don't speak too soon, Elsie. Life has surprised me
once or twice.

Elsa I'm talking about trust, Miss Helen. I can see
myself loving somebody else again. Not all that
interested in it right at the moment, but there's an even
chance that it will happen again. Doesn't seem as if
we've got much choice in the matter anyway. But
trusting?

Helen You can have the one without the other?

Elsa Oh yes. That much I've learned. I went on loving David long after I realized I couldn't trust him any more. That is why life is just a bit complicated at the moment. A little of that love is still hanging around.

Helen I've never really thought about it.

Elsa Neither had I. It needs a betrayal to get you going.

Helen Then I suppose I've been lucky. I never had any important trusts to betray . . . until I met you. My marriage might have looked like that, but it was habit that kept Stefanus and me together. I was never . . . open? . . . to him. Was that the phrase you used?

Elsa Wide open.

Helen That's it! It's a good one. I was never 'wide open' to anyone. But with you all of that changed. So it's as simple as that. Trust. I've always tried to understand what made you, and being with you, so different from anything else in my life. But, of course, that's it. I trust you. That's why my little girl can come out and play. All the doors are wide open!

Elsa (*breaking the mood*) So there, Miss Helen. You asked for the news . . .

Helen I almost wish I hadn't.

Light has now faded. Miss Helen fetches a box of matches and lights the candles on the table. The room floats up gently out of the gloom, the mirrors and glitter on the walls reflecting the candlelight. Elsa picks up one of the candles and walks around the room with it, and we see something of the magic to come.

Elsa Still works, Miss Helen. In the car driving up I was wondering if the novelty would have worn off a little.

But here it is again. You're a little wizard, you know. You make magic with your mirrors and glitter. 'Never light a candle carelessly, and be sure you know what you're doing when you blow one out!' Remember saying that?

Helen To myself, yes. Many times.

Elsa And to me . . . after you had stopped laughing at the expression on my face when you lit them for the first time. 'Light is a miracle, Miss Barlow, which even the most ordinary human being can make happen.' We had just had our first pot of tea together. Maybe I do take it all just a little for granted now. But that first time . . . I wish I could make you realize what it's like to be walking down a dusty, deserted little street in a God-forsaken village in the middle of the Karoo, bored to death by the heat and flies and silence, and then to be stopped in your tracks – and I mean stopped! – by all of that out there. And then, having barely recovered from that, to come inside and find *this*! Believe me Helen, when I saw your 'Mecca' for the first time, I just stood there and gaped. 'What in God's name am I looking at? Camels and pyramids? Not three, but dozens of Wise Men? Owls with old motorcar headlights for eyes? Peacocks with more colour and glitter than the real birds? Heat stroke? Am I hallucinating?' And then you! Standing next to a mosque made out of beer bottles and staring back at me like one of your owls! (*a good laugh at the memory*) She's mad. No question about it. Everything they've told me about her is true. A genuine Karoo nutcase. (*Walking carefully around Miss Helen in a mock attitude of wary and suspicious examination.*) Doesn't look dangerous, though. Wait . . . she's smiling! Be careful, Barlow! Could be a trick. They didn't say she was violent, though. Just mad. Mad as a hatter. Go on. Take a chance. Say hello and see what happens. 'Hello!'

Both women laugh.

Helen You're exaggerating. It wasn't like that at all.

Elsa Yes, it was.

Helen And I'm saying it wasn't. To start with, it wasn't the mosque. I was repairing a mermaid.

Elsa I forgot the mermaids!

Helen (*serenely certain*) And I was the one who spoke first. I asked you to point out the direction to Mecca. You made a mistake, and so I corrected you. Then I invited you into the yard, showed you around, after which we came into the house for that pot of tea.

Elsa That is precisely what I mean! Who would ever believe it? That you found yourself being asked to point out the direction to Mecca – not London, or New York, or Paris, but Mecca – in the middle of the Karoo by a little lady no bigger than a bird, surrounded by camels and owls . . . and mermaids! . . . made of cement? Who in their right mind is going to believe that? And then this (*the room*), your little miracle of light and colour.

Miss Helen is smiling with suppressed pride and pleasure.

You were proud of yourself, weren't you? Come on, admit it.

Helen (*trying hard to contain her emotion*) Yes, I admit I was a little proud.

Elsa Miss Helen, just a little?

Helen (she can't hold back any longer) All right, then, no! Not just a little. Oh, most definitely not. I was prouder of myself that day than I had ever been in my life. Nobody before you, or since, has done that to me.

I was tingling all over with excitement as we walked around the yard looking at the statues. All those years of working on my Mecca had at last been vindicated. I've got a silly little confession to make about that first meeting. When we came inside and were sitting in here talking and drinking tea and the light started to fade and it became time to light a candle . . . I suddenly realized I was beginning to feel shy, more shy than I had even been with Stefanus on my wedding night. It got so bad I was half-wishing you would stand up and say it was time to go! You see, when I lit the candles you were finally going to see all of me. I don't mean my face, or the clothes I was wearing – you had already seen all of that out in the yard – I mean the real me, because that is what this room is . . . and I desperately, oh so desperately, wanted you to like what you saw. By the time we met I had got used to rude eyes staring at me and my work, dismissing both of them as ugly. I'd lived with those eyes for fifteen years, and they didn't bother me any more. Yours were different. In just the little time we had already been together I had ended up feeling . . . No, more than that: I *knew* I could trust them. There's our big word again, Elsie! I was so nervous I didn't know what we were talking about any more while I sat here trying to find enough courage to get a box of matches and light the candles. But eventually I did and you . . . you looked around the room and laughed with delight! You liked what you saw! This is the best of me, Elsa. This is what I really am. Forget everything else. Nothing, not even my name or my face, is me as much as those Wise Men and their camels travelling to the East, or the light and glitter in this room. The mermaids, the wise old owls, the gorgeous peacocks . . . all of them are me. And I had delighted you!

Dear God. If you only knew what you did for my life that day. How much courage, how much faith in it you gave me. Because all those years of being laughed at and thought a mad old woman had taken their toll, Elsie. When you walked into my life that afternoon I hadn't been able to work or make anything for nearly a year . . . and I was beginning to think I wouldn't ever again, that I had reached the end. The only reason I've got for being alive is my Mecca. Without that I'm . . . nothing . . . a useless old woman getting on everybody's nerves . . . and that is exactly what I had started to feel like. You revived my life.

I didn't sleep that night after you left. My Mecca was a long way from being finished! All the things I still had to do, all the statues I still had to make, came crowding in on me when I went to bed. I thought my head was going to burst! I've never been so impatient with darkness all my life. I sat up in bed all night waiting for the dawn to come so that I could start working again, and then just go on working and working.

Elsa And you certainly did that, Miss Helen. On my next trip you proudly introduced me to a very stern Buddha, remember? The cement was still wet.

Helen That's quite right. That was my next one.

Elsa Then came the Easter Island head, the one with the topknot.

Helen Correct.

Elsa And you still haven't explained to me what it's doing in Mecca – and, for that matter, wise old owls and mermaids as well.

Helen My Mecca has got a logic of its own, Elsa. Even I don't properly understand it.

Elsa And then my favourite! That strange creature, half-cock, half-man, on the point of dropping his trousers. Really Helen!

37

Helen That one is pure imagination. I don't know where it comes from. And I've told you before, he's not dropping his trousers, he's pulling them up.

Elsa And I remain unconvinced. Take another good look at the expression on his face. That's anticipation, not satisfaction. Any surprises this time?

Pause

Helen This time?

Elsa Yes.

Helen No. There aren't any surprises this time.

Elsa Work in progress?

Helen Not at the moment. I haven't managed to get started on anything since you were last here.

Elsa What happened to the moon-mosaic? Remember? Against the back wall! You were going to use those ceramic chips I brought you.

Helen They're safe. There in the corner.

Elsa Yes, I saw them . . . in exactly the same spot where I left them three months ago. It sounded such a wonderful idea, Helen. You were so excited when you told me about it.

Helen And I still am. I've still got it.

Elsa So what are you waiting for? Roll up your sleeves and get on with it.

Helen It's not as simple as that, Elsie. You see . . . that's the trouble. It's still only just an *idea* I'm *thinking* about. I can't see it clearly enough yet to start work on it. I've told you before, Elsie, I have to *see* them very clearly first. They've got to come to me inside like pictures. And

if they don't, well, all I can do is wait . . . and hope that
they will. I wish I knew how to make it happen, but
I don't. I don't know where the pictures come from.
I can't force myself to see something that isn't there.
I've tried to do that once or twice in the past when
I was desperate, but the work always ended up a lifeless, shapeless mess. If they don't come, all I can do is
wait . . . which is what I'm doing. (*Miss Helen is
revealing a lot of inner agitation.*)

Elsa (*carefully*) I'm listening, Miss Helen. Go on.

Helen I try to be patient with myself, but it's hard. There
isn't all that much time left . . . and then my eyes . . .
and my hands . . . they're not what they used to be. But
the worst thing of all is . . . suppose that I'm waiting for
nothing, that there won't be any more pictures inside
ever again, that this time I *have* reached the end? Oh
God, no! Please no. Anything but that. You do
understand, don't you, Elsie?

Elsa I think I do. (*She speaks quietly. It is not going to
be easy.*) Come and sit down here with me, Helen.

   Miss Helen does so, but apprehensively.

It's time to talk about your last letter, Helen.

Helen Do we have to do that now? Can't it wait?

Elsa No.

Helen Please.

Elsa Sorry, Helen, but we've only got tonight.

Helen Then don't spoil it!

Elsa Helen . . . that letter is the reason for me being
here. You do realize that, don't you?

Helen Yes. I guessed that was the reason for your visit. But you must make allowances, little Elsie. I wasn't feeling very well when I wrote it.

Elsa That much is obvious.

Helen But I've cheered up ever so much since then. Truly. And now with your visit . . . I just know everything is going to be all right again. I was very depressed you see. I wrote it in a bad depression. But I regretted posting it the moment after I had dropped it into the letter box. I even thought about asking the Postmaster if I could have it back.

Elsa Why didn't you? (*Pause.*) Or send me a telegram: 'Ignore last letter. Feeling much better.' Six words. That would have done it.

Helen I didn't think of that.

Elsa We're wasting precious time. You wrote it, posted it, and I received it.

Helen So can't we now, please, just forget it?

Elsa (*disbelief*) Miss Helen, do you remember what you said in it?

Helen Vaguely.

Elsa That's not good enough. (*She goes to the bedroom alcove and fetches the letter from her briefcase.*)

Helen What are you going to do?

Elsa Read it.

Helen No! I don't want to hear it.

Elsa You already have, Miss Helen. You wrote it.

Helen But I don't want to talk about it.

Elsa Yes, you must.

40

Helen Don't bully me, Elsa! You know I don't know how to fight back. Please . . . not tonight. Can't we . . .?

Elsa No, we can't. For God's sake, Helen! We've only got tonight and maybe a little of tomorrow to talk.

Helen But you mustn't take it seriously.

Elsa Too late, Helen. I already have. I've driven eight hundred miles without a break because of this. And don't lie to me. You meant every word of it. (*Pause.*) I'm not trying to punish you for writing it. I've come because I want to try and help. (*Elsa sits down at the table, pulls the candle closer and reads. She struggles a little to decipher words. The handwriting is obviously bad.*)

'My very own and dearest little Elsie,
  'Have you finally also deserted me? This is my fourth letter to you and still no reply. Have I done something wrong? This must surely be the darkest night of my soul. I thought I had lived through that fifteen years ago, but I was wrong. This is worse. Infinitely worse. I had nothing to lose that night. Nothing in my life was precious or worth holding on to. Now there is so much and I am losing it all . . . you, the house, my work, my Mecca. I can't fight them alone, little Elsie. I need you. Don't you care about me any more? It is only through your eyes that I now see my Mecca. I need you, Elsie. My eyesight is so bad that I can barely see the words I am writing. And my hands can hardly hold the pen. Help me, little Elsie. Everything is ending and I am alone in the dark. There is no light left. I would rather do away with myself than carry on like this.
  'Your ever-loving and anguished Helen.' (*Elsa carefully folds up the letter and puts it back in the envelope.*)

What's all that about losing your house. Who's trying to get you out?

Helen I exaggerated a little. They're not really being nasty about it.

Elsa Who?

Helen The Church Council. They say it's for my own good. And I do understand what they mean, it's just that . . .

Elsa Slowly, Miss Helen, slowly. I still don't know what you're talking about. Start from the beginning. What has the Church Council got to do with you and the house? I thought it was yours.

Helen It is.

Elsa So?

Helen It's not the house, Elsa. It's me. They discussed me . . . my situation . . . at one of their meetings.

Elsa (*disbelief and anger*) They *what*?

Helen That's how Marius put it. He . . . he said they were worried about me living here alone.

Elsa *They* are worried about *you*?

Helen Yes. It's my health they are worried about.

Elsa (*shaking her head*) When it comes to hypocrisy – and blatant hypocrisy at that – you Afrikaners are in a class by yourselves. So tell me, did they also discuss Getruida's situation? And what about Mrs van Heerden down at the other end of the village? They're about the same age as you and they also live alone.

Helen That's what I said. But Marius said it's different with them.

Elsa In what way?

Helen Well, you see, because of my hands and everything else, they don't believe I can look after myself so well any more.

Elsa Are they right?

Helen No! I'm quite capable of looking after myself.

Elsa And where are you supposed to go if you leave the village? To a niece, four times removed, in Durban, whom you've only seen a couple of times in your life?

Miss Helen goes to a little table at the back and fetches a form which she hands to Elsa.

(*reading*) 'Sunshine Home for the Aged'. I see. So it's like that, is it? That's the lovely old house on the left when you come into Graaff-Reinet, next to the church. In fact, it's run by the church, isn't it?

Helen Yes.

Elsa That figures. It's got a beautiful garden, Miss Helen. Whenever I drive past on my way up here there are always a few old folk in their 'twilight years' sitting around enjoying the sunshine. It's well named. It all looks very restful. So that's what they want to do with you. This is not your handwriting.

Helen No. Marius filled it in for me.

Elsa Very considerate of him.

Helen He's coming to fetch it tonight.

Elsa For an old friend he sounds a little over-eager to have you on your way, Miss Helen.

Helen It's just that they've got a vacancy at the moment. They're usually completely full. There's a long waiting list. But I haven't signed it yet!

Elsa studies Miss Helen in silence for a few moments.

Elsa How bad are your hands? Be honest with me.

Helen They're not *that* bad. I exaggerated a little in my letter.

Elsa You could still work with them if you wanted to?

Helen Yes.

Elsa Is there anything you can't do?

Helen I can do anything I want to, Elsie . . . if I make the effort.

Elsa Let me see them.

Helen Please don't. I'm ashamed of them.

Elsa Come on.

Miss Helen holds out her hands. Elsa examines them.

And these scabs?

Helen They're nothing. A little accident at the stove. I was making prickly-pear syrup for you.

Elsa There seem to have been a lot of little accidents lately. Better be more careful.

Helen I will. I definitely will.

Elsa Pain?

Helen Just a little. (*while Elsa studies her hands*) Just that one letter after your last visit, saying you had arrived back safely and would be writing again soon, and then nothing. Three months.

Elsa I did write, Helen. Two very long letters.

Helen I never got them.

Elsa Because I never posted them.

Helen Elsie! Why? They would have made all the difference in the world.

Elsa (*shaking her head*) No. Muddled, confused, full of self-pity. Knowing now what you were trying to deal with here, they were hardly what you needed in your life.

Helen You're very wrong. Anything would have been better than nothing.

Elsa No, Helen. Believe me nothing was better than those two letters. I've still got them at home. I read them now whenever I need to count my blessings. They remind me of the mess I was in.

Helen That's why I feel so bad now about the letter I wrote you. My problems seem so insignificant compared with yours.

Elsa Don't let's start that, Helen. Sorting our problem priorities isn't going to get us anywhere. In any case, mine are over and done with . . . which leaves us with you. So what are you going to do?

Miss Helen doesn't answer. Elsa is beginning to lose patience.

Come *on*, Helen! If I hadn't turned up tonight, what were you going to say to Dominee Marius Byleveld when he came around?

Helen I was going to ask him to give me a little more time to think about it.

Elsa You were going to *ask* him for it, not *tell* him you *wanted* it? And *do* you need more time to think about it? I thought you knew what you wanted?

Helen Of course I do.

Elsa Then tell me again. And say it simply. I need to hear it.

Helen You know I can't leave here, Elsa!

Elsa For a moment I wasn't so sure. So then what's the problem? When he comes around tonight hand this back to him . . . unsigned . . . and say no. Thank him for his trouble but tell him you are perfectly happy where you are and quite capable of looking after yourself.

Miss Helen hesitates. A sense of increasing emotional confusion and uncertainty.

Helen, you have just said that is what you want.

Helen I know. It's just that Marius is such a persuasive talker.

Elsa Then talk back!

Helen I'm not very good at that. Won't you help me, little Elsie, please, and speak to him as well? You are so much better at arguing than me.

Elsa No, I won't! And for God's sake stop behaving like a naughty child who's been called to the principal's office. I'm sorry, but the more I hear about your Marius, the worse it gets. If you want my advice, you'll keep the two of us well away from each other. I *won't* argue with him on your behalf because there is nothing to argue about. This is not his house, and it most certainly is not his life that is being discussed at Church Council meetings. Who the hell do they think they are? Sitting around a table deciding what is going to happen to you!

Helen Marius did say that they were trying to think of what was best for me.

Elsa No, they're not! God knows what they're thinking about, but it's certainly not that. Dumping you with a lot of old people who've hung on for too long and nobody wants around any more? You're still living your life, Helen, not drooling it away. The only legal way they can get you out of this house is by having you certified. (*Awkward silence.*) We all know you're as mad as a hatter, but it's not quite that bad. (*Another pause.*) One little question though, Miss Helen. You haven't been going around talking about doing away with yourself to anyone have you?

Helen I told you, Katrina is the only person I really see any more.

Elsa And Marius. Don't forget him. Anyway it doesn't matter who it is. All it needs is one person to be able to stand up and testify that they heard you say it.

Helen Well, I haven't.

Elsa Because it would make life a lot easier for them if they ever did try to do something. So no more of that. OK? Did you hear me, Helen?

Helen Yes, I heard you.

Elsa And while you're about it, add me to your list. I don't want to hear or read any more about it either.

Helen I heard you, Elsie! Why do you keep on about it?

Elsa Because talk like that could be grounds for forcibly committing someone to a 'Sunshine Home for the Aged'! I'm sorry, Helen, but what do you expect me to do? Pretend you never said it? Is that what you would have done if our situations had been reversed? If in the middle of my mess I had threatened to do that? God knows, I came near to feeling like it a couple of times. I had a small taste of how bloody pointless everything can seem to be. But if I can hang on, then you most certainly can't throw in the towel – not after all the

rounds you've already won against them. So when the
Dominee comes around, you're going to put on a brave
front. Let's get him and his stupid ideas about an
old-age home right out of your life. Because you're
going to say No, remember? Be as polite and civil as
you like – we'll offer him tea and biscuits and discuss
the weather and the evils of alcohol – but when the time
comes, you're going to thank him for all his trouble and
consideration and then hand this back to him with a
firm 'No, thank you.' (*Another idea.*) And just to make
quite sure he gets the message, you can also mention
your trip into Graaff-Reinet next week to see a doctor
and an optician.

Helen What do you mean?

Elsa Exactly what I said: appointments with a doctor
and an optician.

Helen But I haven't got any.

Elsa You will on Monday. Before I leave tomorrow I'm
going to ask Getruida to take you into Graaff-Reinet
next week. And this time you're going to go. There must
be something they can do about your hands, even if it's
just to ease the pain. And a little 'regmaker' for your
depressions.

Miss Helen wants to say something.

No arguments! And to hell with your vanity as well.
We all know you think you're the prettiest thing in the
village, but if you need glasses, you're going to wear
them. I'll make the appointments myself and phone
through after you've been in to find out what the verdict
is. I'm not trying to be funny, Helen. You've got to prove
to the village that you are quite capable of looking after
yourself. It's the only way to shut them up.

Helen You're going too fast for me, Elsa. You're not allowing me to say anything.

Elsa That's quite right. How many times in the past have we sat down and tried to talk about all of this? And every time the same story: 'I'll think about it, Elsa.' Your thinking has got us nowhere, Helen. This time you're just going to agree . . . and that includes letting Katrina come in a couple of times each week to do the house.

Helen There's nothing for her to do. I can manage by myself.

Elsa No, you can't. (*She runs her finger over a piece of furniture and holds it up for Miss Helen to see the dust.*)

Helen Everything would have been spotless if I had known you were coming.

Elsa It's got to be spotless all the time! To hell with *my* visits and holidays. I don't live here. You do. I'm concerned with *your* life, Helen. And I'm also not blind, you know. I saw you struggling with that large kettle. Yes, let's talk about that. When did you last boil up enough water for a decent bath? Come on, Helen. Can't you remember? Some time ago, right? Is it because of personal neglect that you've stopped caring about yourself or because you aren't able to? Answer me.

Helen I can't listen to you any more, Elsa. (*She makes a move to leave the room.*)

Elsa Don't do that to me Helen! If you leave this room I'm getting into my car and driving back to Cape Town. You wrote that letter. I haven't made it up. All I'm trying to do is deal with it.

Helen No, you're not.

Elsa Then I give up. What in God's name have we been talking about?

Helen A pair of spectacles and medicine for my arthritis and Katrina dusting the house . . .

Elsa Do you want me to read it again?

Helen (*ignoring the interruption*) You're treating that letter like a shopping list. That isn't what I was writing about.

Elsa Then what was it?

Helen Darkness, Elsa! Darkness!

She speaks with an emotional intensity and authority which forces Elsa to listen in silence.

The Darkness that nearly smothered my life in here one night fifteen years ago. The same Darkness that used to come pouring down the chimney and into the room at night when I was a little girl and frighten me. If you still don't know what I'm talking about, blow out the candles!

But those were easy Darknesses to deal with. The one I'm talking about now is much worse. It's inside me, Elsa . . . it's got inside me at last and I can't light candles there. (*Pause.*) I never knew that could happen. I thought I was safe. I had grown up and I had all the candles I wanted. That is all that little girl could think about when she lay there in bed, trying to make her prayers last as long as she could because she was terrified of the moment when her mother would bend down and kiss her and take away the candle. One day she would have her very own! That was the promise: that one day when I was big enough, she would leave one at my bedside for me to light as often as I wanted. That's all that 'getting big' ever meant to me – my very own candle at my bedside.

Such brave little lights! And they taught the little girl how to be that. When she saw one burning in the middle of the night, she knew what courage was. All my life they have helped me to find courage . . . until now.

I'm frightened, Elsie, more frightened than that little girl ever was. There's no 'getting big' left to wait for, no prayers to say until that happens . . . and the candles don't help any more. That is what I was trying to tell you. I'm frightened. And Marius can see it. He's no fool, Elsa. He knows that his moment has finally come.

Elsa What moment?

Helen He's been waiting a long time for me to reach the end of my Mecca. I thought I had cheated him out of it, that that moment would never come.

All those years when I was working away, when it was slowly taking shape, he was there as well . . . standing in the distance, watching and waiting.

I used to peep at him through the curtains. He'd come walking past, then stop, stand there at the gate with his hands behind his back and stare at my Wise Men. And even though he didn't show anything, I know he didn't like what he saw. I used to sing when I was working. He heard me one day and came up and asked: 'Are you really that happy, Helen?'

I laughed. Not at him, believe me not at him, but because I had a secret he would never understand. (*Pause.*) It's his turn to laugh now. But he won't, of course. He's not that sort of man. He'll be very gentle again . . . pull the curtains and close the shutters the way he did that night fifteen years ago . . . because nobody must stare into a house where there's been a death.

If my Mecca is finished, Elsa, then so is my life.

Elsa is overwhelmed by a sense of helplessness and defeat.

Elsa I think I've had it. It's too much for one day. That woman on the road and now you. I honestly don't know how to handle it. In fact, at this moment, I don't think I know anything. I don't know what it means to be walking eighty miles to Cradock with your baby on your back. I don't know whether your Mecca is finished or not. And all I know about Darkness is that that is when you put on the lights. Jesus! I wouldn't mind somebody coming along and telling me what it does all mean.

So where does all of that leave us, Miss Helen? I'm lost. What are you going to do when he comes?

No answer.

Ask him – please – for more time? One thing I can tell you right now is that there's no point to that. If you don't say no tonight, you won't ever, in which case you might as well sign that form and get it over and done with. (*a cruel, relentless tone in her voice*) There's no point in talking about anything until that's settled. So you better think about it, Helen. While you do that, I'll see what I can organize for supper.

She exits into the kitchen. A man's voice off:
'Anybody at home?' Marius appears in the doorway.

Marius Miss Helen! Alone in the dark? I didn't think anybody was home.

Elsa appears from the kitchen.

Ah, Miss Barlow!

Curtain.

Act Two

The same a few minutes later. Marius and Elsa are now at the table with Miss Helen, the centre of attraction being a basket of vegetables which Marius has brought with him. He is about the same age as Miss Helen and is neatly but casually dressed. He speaks with simple sincerity and charm.

Marius (*holding up a potato*) Feast your eyes on this, Miss Barlow! A genuine Sneeuberg potato! A pinch of salt and you've got a meal, and if you want to be extravagant, add a little butter and you have indeed got a feast. We had a farmer from the Gamtoos Valley up here last week, trying to sell potatoes to us! Can you believe it? Did you see him, Helen? He had his lorry parked in front of the Post Office. What's the English expression, Miss Barlow? Coals to – where?

Elsa Coals to Newcastle.

Marius That's it! Well in this case it was very near to being an insult as well. We pride ourselves in these parts on knowing what a potato really is. And here you have it. The 'apple of the earth', as the French would say. But I don't imagine that poor man will come again. Shame! I ended up feeling very sorry for him. 'Don't you people like potatoes?' he asked me. What could I say? I didn't have the heart to tell him he'd wasted his time driving all this distance, that *nobody* comes to the Sneeuberg to sell potatoes! And then, to make me feel really bad, he insisted on giving me a small sack of them before he drove off. I don't think he sold enough to cover the cost of his petrol back home.

I also brought you a few beets and tomatoes. The beets have passed their best now, but if you pickle and bottle them, they'll be more than all right. Have you ever treated our young friend to a taste of that, Miss Helen? (*to Elsa*) It's one of our local specialities. One thing I can assure you ladies is that these vegetables are as fresh as you are ever likely to get. I dug them up myself this afternoon.

Helen It's very kind of you, Marius, but you really shouldn't have bothered.

Marius It wasn't any bother at all. I've got more than enough for myself stored away in the pantry. Would have been a sin to leave them to rot in the ground when somebody else could use them. And at our age we need fresh vegetables, Helen. (*wagging a finger at her*) Marie biscuits and tea are not a balanced diet. (*to Elsa*) In the old days Helen used to have a very fine vegetable garden of her own out there. But as you can see, the humble potato has been crowded out by other things. I don't think there's enough room left out there now to grow a radish. (*He turns back to the basket.*) Yes, the Good Lord was very generous to us this past year. I don't really know that we deserve it, but our rains came just when we needed them. Not too much or too little. Believe me, young lady, we are well experienced in both those possibilities. Not so, Helen?

Elsa The Karoo looked very dry and desolate to me as I drove through it this afternoon.

Marius Dry it certainly is, but not desolate. It might appear that to a townsman's eye – as indeed it did to mine when I first came here! – but that is because we are already deep into our autumn. It will be a good few months before we see rain again.

Elsa I've never thought of this world as having seasons
. . . certainly not the soft ones. To me it has always been
a landscape of extremes, too hot or too cold, too dry or
else Miss Helen is writing to me about floods that have
cut off the village from the outside world. It reminds me
of something I once read where the desert was described
as 'God without mankind'.

Marius What an interesting thought: 'God without
mankind'. I can't decide whether that's Catholic or
Protestant. Would you know?

Elsa (*shaking her head*) No.

Marius Who wrote it?

Elsa A French writer. Balzac. It sums up the way I feel
about the Karoo. The Almighty hasn't exactly made
mankind over-welcome here, has he? In fact, it almost
looks as if he resented our presence. Sorry, Dominee,
I don't mean to be blasphemous or ungenerous to your
world, it's just that I'm used to a gentler one.

Marius You judge it too harshly, Miss Barlow. It has got
its gentle moments and moods as well . . . all the more
precious because there are so few of them. We can't
afford to take them for granted. As you can see, it feeds
us. Can any man or woman ask for more than that from
the little bit of earth he lives on?

Elsa Do you think your Coloured folk feel the same way
about things?

Marius Why should it be any different for them?

Elsa I was just wondering whether they had as many
reasons to be as contented as you?

Marius I was talking about simple gratitude, Miss
Barlow. Wouldn't you say contentment is a more

complicated state of mind? One that can very easily be disturbed. But grateful? Yes! Our Coloured folk also have every reason to be. Ask them. Ask little Katrina, who visits Miss Helen so faithfully, if she or her baby have ever wanted for food . . . even when Koos has spent all his wages on liquor. There are no hungry people, white or coloured, in this village, Miss Barlow. Those of us who are more fortunate than others are well aware of the responsibilities that go with that good fortune. But I don't want to get into an argument. It is my world – and Helen's – and we can't expect an outsider to love or understand it as we do.

Elsa I'll put these (*the vegetables*) away for you, Miss Helen.

Marius Don't bother to unpack them now. I'll collect the basket tomorrow after church. (*Calling after Elsa as she leaves the room.*) And there's no need to wash them. I've already done that. Just put them straight into the pot.

   Exit Elsa.

I've got a feeling that, given half a chance, your young friend and myself *could* very easily find ourselves in an argument. I think Miss Barlow gets a little impatient with our old-fashioned ways and attitudes. But it's too late for us to change now. Right, Helen?

Helen Elsa and I have already had those arguments, Marius.

Marius I hope you put up a good defence on our behalf.

Helen I tried my best.

Marius And yet the two of you still remain good friends.

Helen Oh yes!

Marius And so it should be. A true friendship should be able to accommodate a difference of opinion. You didn't mention anything about her coming up for a visit last time we talked.

Helen Because I didn't know. It's an unexpected visit.

Marius Will she be staying long?

Helen Just tonight. She goes back tomorrow.

Marius Good heavens! All this way for only one night. I hope nothing is wrong.

Helen No. She just decided on the spur of the moment to visit me. But she's got to go back because they're very busy at school. They're right in the middle of exams.

Marius I see. May I sit down for a moment, Helen?

Helen Of course, Marius. Forgive me, I'm forgetting my manners.

Marius I won't stay long. I must put down a few thoughts for tomorrow's sermon. And, thanks to you, I know what I want to say.

Helen Me?

Marius Yes, you. (*teasing her*) You are responsible . . .

Helen Oh dear!

Marius (*a little laugh*) Relax, Helen. I only said 'thanks to you' because it came to me this afternoon while I was digging up your vegetables. I spent a lot of time, while I was out in the garden doing that, just leaning on my spade. My back is giving me a bit of trouble again and, to tell you the truth, I also felt lazy.

I wasn't thinking about anything in particular . . . just looking, you know, the way an old man does, looking around, recognizing once again and saying the names.

Spitskop in the distance! Aasvoelkrans down at the other end of the valley. The poplars with their autumn foliage standing around as yellow and still as that candle flame!

And a lot of remembering.

As you know, Helen, I had deep and very painful wounds in my soul when I first came here. Wounds I thought would never heal. This was going to be where I finally escaped from life, turned my back on it and justified what was left of my existence by ministering to you people's simple needs. I was very wrong. I didn't escape life here, I discovered it, what it really means, the fullness and goodness of it. It's a deep and lasting regret that Aletta wasn't alive to share that discovery with me. Anyway, all of this was going on in my head when I realized I was hearing a small little voice, and the small little voice was saying, 'Thank you.' With every spadeful of earth that I turned when I went down on my knees to lift the potatoes out of the soil, there it was: 'Thank you.' It was mine! I was muttering away to myself the way we old folks are inclined to do when nobody is around. It was me saying, 'Thank you.'

That is what I want to do tomorrow, Helen. Give thanks, but in a way that I've never done before.

I know I've stood there in the pulpit many times telling all of you to do exactly that, but oh dear me, the cleverness and conceit in the soul of Marius Byleveld when he was doing that! I had an actor's vanity up there, Helen. I'm not saying I was a total hypocrite but, believe me, in those thanksgivings I was listening to my Dominee's voice and its hoped-for eloquence every bit as much as to the true little voice inside my heart . . . the voice I heard so clearly this afternoon.

That's the voice that must speak tomorrow! And to do that I must find words as simple as the sky I was standing under this afternoon or the earth I was turning over with my spade. They have got no vanities and conceits. They are just 'there'. If the Almighty takes pity on us, the one gives us rain so that the other can in turn . . . give us this day our daily potato. (*a smile at this gentle little joke*) Am I making sense, Helen? Answer me truthfully.

Helen Yes, you are, Marius. And if all you do tomorrow is say what you have just said to me, it will be very moving and beautiful.

Marius (*sincerely*) Truly, Helen? Do you really mean that?

Helen Every word of it.

Marius Then I will try.

My twentieth anniversary comes up next month. Yes, that is how long I've been here. Twenty-one years ago, on May the sixteenth, the Good Lord called my Aletta to his side, and just over a year later, on June the eleventh, I gave my first sermon in New Bethesda. (*a little laugh at the memory*) What an occasion that was!

I don't know if I showed it, Helen, but let me confess now that I was more than just a little nervous when I went up into the pulpit and looked down at that stern and formidable array of faces. A very different proposition from the town and city congregations I had been preaching to up until then. When Miss de Klerk played the first bars of the hymn at the end of it, I heaved a very deep sigh of relief. None of you had fallen asleep!

Helen is shaking her head.

What's the matter?

Helen Young Miss de Klerk came later. Mrs Niewoudt was still our organist when you gave your first service.

Marius Are you sure?

Helen Yes. Mrs Niewoudt also played at the reception

we gave you afterwards in Mr van Heerden's house. She played the piano and Sterling Retief sang.

Marius You know something, I do believe you're right! Good heavens, Helen, your memory is better than mine.

Helen And you had no cause to be nervous. You were very impressive.

Marius (*a small pause as he remembers something else*) Yes, of course. You were in that congregation. Stefanus was at your side, as he was going to be every Sunday after that for . . . what? Another five years?

Helen Five years.

Marius That was all a long time ago.

Helen More than a long time, Marius. It feels like another life.

Elsa returns with a tray of tea and sandwiches.

Marius Ah, here comes your supper. I must be running along.

Elsa Just a sandwich, Dominee. Neither of us is very hungry.

Marius I'll drop by tomorrow night if that is all right with you, Helen.

Elsa Won't you have a cup of tea with us? It's the least we can offer in return for all those lovely vegetables.

Marius I don't want to intrude. Helen tells me you're here for just the night, Miss Barlow. I'm sure you ladies have got things to talk about in private.

Elsa We've already done quite a lot of that, haven't we, Helen? Please don't go because of me. I have some school work I must see to. I'll take my tea through to the other room.

Helen Don't go, Elsa!

Elsa I told you I had papers to mark, Miss Helen. I'll just get on with that quietly while the two of you have a little chat.

Helen Please!

Elsa All right then, if it will make you happier, I'll bring my work through and do it in here.

Marius No. I've obviously come at an inconvenient time.

Elsa Not at all, Dominee. Miss Helen was expecting you.

Elsa fetches the application form for the old-age home and puts it down on the table. A moment between Elsa and Marius. He turns to Helen for confirmation.

Helen Yes, I was.

Elsa How do you like your tea?

Marius Very well, if you insist. Milk but no sugar, please.

Elsa pours tea, then collects her briefcase from the bedroom alcove and settles down to work at a small table at the back of the room.

You're quite certain you want to discuss this now, Helen?

Helen Yes, Marius.

Marius It can wait until tomorrow.

Helen No, I'm ready.

Marius Right. Just before we start talking, Helen, the good news is that I've spoken to Dominee Gericke in Graaff-Reinet again, and the room is definitely yours –

that is, if you want it, of course. But they obviously can't have it standing empty indefinitely. As it is, he's already broken the rules by putting you at the top of the waiting list, but as a personal favour. He understands the circumstances. So the sooner we decide, one way or the other, the better. But I want you to know that I do realize how big a move it is for you. I want you to be quite certain and happy in your mind that you're doing the right thing. So don't think we've got to rush into it, start packing up immediately or anything like that. A decision must be made, one way or the other, but once you've done that, you can relax and take all the time you need.

> *Marius takes spectacles, a little notebook, pen and pencil from a jacket pocket. The way he handles everything, carefully and precisely, reveals a meticulous and orderly mind. He opens the application form. Miss Helen gives Elsa the first of many desperate and appealing looks. Elsa, engrossed in her work, apparently does not notice it. Marius puts on his spectacles.*

I know we went over this the last time, but there still are just a few questions. Yes . . . we put Stefanus's father's name down as Petrus Johannes Martins, but in the church registry it's down as Petrus *Jacobus*. (*He takes his spectacles off.*) Which one is correct, Helen? Can you remember? You were so certain of Petrus Johannes last time.

Helen I still am. But what did you say the other one was?

Marius Petrus Jacobus.

Helen Jacobus . . . Johannes . . . No, maybe I'm not.

Marius In that case what I think I will do is enter it as Petrus J. Martins. Just as well I checked. (*He puts his spectacles on again and turns back to the form.*) And next . . . yes, the date of your confirmation. Have you been able to find the certificate?

Helen No, I haven't. I'm sorry, Marius. I did look, but I'm afraid my papers are all in a mess.

Marius (*taking his spectacles off*) I've been through the church records, but I can't find anything that sheds any light on it. It's not all that important, of course, but it would have been nice to have had that date as well. (*He replaces his spectacles.*) Let's see . . . what shall we do? You think you were about twelve?

Helen Something like that.

Marius What I'll do is just pencil in 1920 and have one more look. I hate giving up on *that* one. But you surprise me, Helen – of all the dates to have forgotten. That takes care of the form now. (*He consults his notebook.*) Yes. Two little points from Dominee Gericke, after which you can relax and enjoy your supper. He asked me – and do believe me, Helen, he was just trying to be practical and helpful, nothing else – whether you had taken care of everything by way of a last will and testament, and obviously I said I didn't know.

Helen What do you mean, Marius?

Marius That in the event of something happening, your house and possessions will be disposed of in the way that you want them to be. Have you done that?

Helen I've still got a copy of Stefanus's will. He left everything to me.

Marius We're talking about you, Helen. Have you seen a lawyer?

Helen No, I . . . I've never thought of it.

Marius Then it is just as well Gericke asked. Believe me, Helen, in my time as a minister I have seen so many bitterly unhappy situations because somebody neglected to look after that side of things. Families not talking to each other! Lawsuits over a few pieces of furniture! I really do think it is something you should see to. We're at an age now when anything can happen. I had mine revised only a few months ago. (*He glances at the notebook again.*) And finally, he made the obvious suggestion that we arrange for you to visit the home as soon as possible. Just to meet the Matron and other people there and to see your room. He's particularly anxious for you to see it so that you know what you need to bring on your side. He had a dreadful to-do a few months ago with a lady who tried to move a whole houseful of furniture into her little room. Don't get worried, though. There's plenty of space for personal possessions and a few of your . . . ornaments. That covers everything, I think. All that's left now is for you to sign it . . . provided you want to do that, of course. (*He places his fountain pen, in readiness, on the form.*)

Helen Marius . . . please . . . please can I talk for a little bit now?

Marius But of course, Helen.

Helen I've done a lot of thinking since we last spoke . . .

Marius Good! We both agreed that was necessary. This is not a step to be taken lightly.

Helen Yes, I've done a lot of thinking, and I've worked out a plan.

Marius For what, Helen?

Helen A plan to take care of everything.

Marius Excellent!

Helen I'm going into Graaff-Reinet next week, Marius, to see a doctor. I'm going to make the appointment on Monday, and I'll ask Getruida to drive me in.

Marius You make it sound serious, Helen.

Helen No, it's just my arthritis. I'm going to get some medicine for it.

Marius For a moment you had me worried. I thought the burns were possibly more serious than we had realized. But why not save yourself a few pennies and see Dr Lubbe at the home? He looks after everybody there free of charge.

Helen (*hanging on*) And spectacles. I'm also going to make arrangements to see an optician and get a pair of spectacles.

Marius Splendid, Helen! You certainly have been making plans.

Helen And, finally, I've decided to get Katrina to come in two or three times a week to help me with the house.

Marius Katrina?

Helen Little Katrina. Koos Malgas's wife.

Marius I know who you're talking about, Helen. It's just . . . Oh dear! I'm sorry to be the one to tell you this, Helen, but I think you are going to lose your little Katrina.

Helen What do you mean, Marius?

Marius Koos has asked the Divisional Council for a transfer to their Aberdeen depot, and I think he will get it.

Helen So?

Marius I imagine Katrina and the baby will go with him.

Helen Katrina . . .?

Marius Will be leaving the village.

Helen No, it can't be.

Marius It's the truth, Helen.

Helen But she's said nothing to me about it. She was in here just a few days ago and she didn't mention anything about leaving.

Marius She most probably didn't think it important.

Helen How can you say that, Marius? Of course it is! She knows how much I depend on her. If Katrina goes, I'll be completely alone here except for you and the times when Elsa is visiting. (*She is becoming increasingly distressed.*)

Marius Come now, Helen! It's not as bad as that. I know Katrina is a sweet little soul and that you are very fond of her, as we all are, but don't exaggerate things. There are plenty of good women in the location who can come and give you a hand in here and help you pack up . . . if you decide to move. Tell you what I'll do: if you're worried about a stranger being in here with all your personal things, I'll lend you my faithful old Nonna. She's been looking after me for ten years now, and in that time I haven't missed a single thing. You could trust her with your life.

Helen I'm not talking about a servant, Marius.

Marius I thought we were.

Helen Katrina is the only friend I've got left in the village.

Marius That's a hard thing you're saying, Helen. All of us still like to think of ourselves as your friends.

Helen I wasn't including you, Marius. You're different. But as for the others . . . no. They've all become strangers to me. I might just as well not know their names. And they treat me as if I were a stranger to them as well.

Marius You're being very unfair, Helen. They behave towards you in the way you apparently want them to, which is to leave you completely alone. Really, Helen! Strangers? Old Getruida, Sterling, Jerry, Boet, Mrs van Heerden? You grew up in this village with all of them. To be very frank, Helen, it's your manner which now keeps them at a distance. I don't think you realize how much you've changed over the years. You're not easily recognizable to others any more as the person they knew fifteen years ago. And then your hobby, if I can call it that, hasn't really helped matters. This is not exactly the sort of room the village ladies are used to or would feel comfortable in having afternoon tea. As for all of that out there . . . the less said about it, the better.

Helen I don't harm or bother anyone, Marius!

Marius And does anyone harm or bother you?

Helen Yes! Everybody is trying to force me to leave my home.

Marius Nobody is *forcing* you, Helen! In Heaven's name, where do you get that idea from? If you sign this form, it must be of your own free will. You're very agitated tonight, Helen. Has something happened to upset you? You were so reasonable about everything the last time we talked. You seemed to understand that the only motive on our side is to try and do what is best for you. And even then it's only in the way of advice. We can't *tell* you what to do. But if you want us to stop caring about what happens to you, we can try . . . though I don't know how our Christian consciences would allow us to do that.

Helen I don't believe the others care about me, Marius. All they want is to get rid of me. This village has also changed over the past fifteen years. I am not alone in that. I don't recognize it any more as the simple, innocent world I grew up in.

Marius If it's as bad as that, Helen, if you are now really that unhappy and lonely here, then I don't know why you have any doubts about leaving.

Miss Helen's emotional state has deteriorated steadily. Marius's fountain pen has ended up in her hand. She looks down at the application form. A few seconds' pause and then a desperate cry.

Helen Why don't you stop me, Elsa! I'm going to sign it!

Elsa (*abandoning all pretence of being absorbed in her work*) Then go ahead and do it! Sign that fucking form. If that's what you want to do to your life, just get it over and done with, for God's sake!

Marius Miss Barlow!

Elsa (*ignoring him*) What are you waiting for, Helen? You're wasting our time. It's late and we want to go to bed.

Helen But you said I mustn't sign it.

Elsa (*brutally*) I've changed my mind. Do it. Hurry up and dispose of your life so that we can get on with ours.

Helen Stop it, Elsa. Help me. Please help me.

Elsa Sorry, Helen. I've had more woman-battering today than I can cope with. You can at least say no. That woman on the road couldn't. But if you haven't got the guts to do that, then too bad. I'm not going to do it for you.

Helen I tried.

Elsa You call that trying? All it required was one word – no.

Helen Please believe me, Elsa . . . I was trying!

Elsa No good, Helen. If that's your best, then maybe you will be better off in an old-age home.

Marius Gently, Miss Barlow! In Heaven's name, gently! What's got into you?

Elsa Exhaustion, Dominee. Very near total mental and emotional exhaustion, to the point where I want to scream. I've already done that once today, and right now I wouldn't mind doing it a second time. Yes, Helen, I've had it. Why were you 'crying out to me in the dark'? To be an audience when you signed away your life? Is that why I'm here? Twelve hours of driving like a lunatic for that? God. What a farce! I might just as well have stayed in Cape Town.

Marius Maybe it's a pity you didn't. I think I understand now why Helen is so agitated tonight. But unfortunately you are here, and if you've got anything to say to her, in Heaven's name be considerate of the state she is in. She needs help, not to be confused and terrified even more.

Elsa Helen understands the way I feel. We *did* do a lot of talking before you came, Dominee.

Marius I'm concerned with *her* feelings, Miss Barlow, not yours. And if by any chance you are as well, then try

69

to show some respect for her age. Helen is a much older woman than you. You were shouting at her as if she was a child.

Elsa Me, treating her like a child? Oh my God! You can stand there and accuse me of that after what I've just seen and heard from you?

Marius I don't know what you're talking about.

Elsa Then I'll tell you. You were doing everything in your power to bully and blackmail her into signing that. You were taking the grossest advantage of what you call her confusion and helplessness. I've been trying to tell her she's neither confused nor helpless.

Marius So you know what is best for her.

Elsa No, no, no! Wrong again, Dominee. I think *she* does. And if you had given her half a chance, she would have told you that that is not being dumped in an old-age home full of old people who have reached the end of their lives. She hasn't. You forget one thing: I didn't stop her signing that form. She stopped herself.

Marius It was a moment of confusion.

Elsa There you go again! Can't you leave that word alone? She is not confused!

Marius When Helen and I discussed the matter a few days ago . . .

Elsa Don't talk about her as if she were not here. She's right next to you, Dominee. Ask her, for God's sake . . . but this time give her a chance to answer.

Marius Don't try to goad me with blasphemy, Miss Barlow. I'm beginning to think Helen needs as much protection from you as she does from herself.

Elsa You still haven't asked her.

Marius Because I have some sympathy for her condition. Look at her! She is in no condition now, thanks to you, to think clearly about anything.

Elsa She was an emotional mess, thanks to you, before I opened my mouth. Don't expect me to believe you really care about her.

Marius (*trying hard to control himself*) Miss Barlow, for the last time, what you do or don't believe is not of the remotest concern to me. Helen is, and my concern is that she gets a chance to live out what is left of her life as safely and happily as is humanly possible. I don't think that should include the danger of her being trapped in here when this house goes up in flames.

Elsa What are you talking about?

Marius Her accident. The night she knocked over the candle.

Elsa is obviously at a loss.

You don't know about that? When was it, Helen? Four weeks ago?

Pause. Miss Helen doesn't respond.

I see. You didn't tell your friend about your narrow escape. I think I owe you an apology, Miss Barlow. I assumed you knew all about it.

Elsa You owe me nothing. Just tell me what happened.

Marius Yes, it was about four weeks ago. Helen knocked over a candle one night and set fire to the curtains. I try not to think about what would have happened if Sterling hadn't been looking out of his window at that moment and seen the flames. He rushed

71

over, and just in time. She had stopped trying to put out the flames herself and was just standing staring at them. Even so she picked up a few bad burns on her hands. We had to get Sister Lategan out of bed to treat them. But it could have been a lot worse.

Elsa is staring at Miss Helen.

We don't want that on our consciences. So you see, Miss Barlow, our actions are not quite as pointless or as uncaring as they must have seemed to you.

Elsa One of the lamps started smoking badly, and there was a little accident at the stove while you were making prickly-pear syrup for me! Oh boy! You certainly can do it, Helen. Don't let us ever again talk about trust between the two of us. Anyway, that settles it. I leave the two of you to fight it out . . . and may the best man win! I'm going to bed.

Helen Give me a chance to explain.

Elsa (*ignoring the plea*) Good night. See you in the morning. I'll be making an early start, Helen.

Helen Don't abandon me, Elsa!

Elsa You've abandoned yourself, Helen! Don't accuse me of that! You were the first to jump overboard. You haven't got enough faith in your life and your work to defend them against him. You lied to me . . . and such stupid bloody lies! What was the point? For that matter, what is the point of anything? Why *did* you make me come up? And then all our talk about trust! God, what a joke. You've certainly made me make a fool of myself again, but this time I don't think it's funny. In fact, I fucking well resent it.

Helen I didn't tell you because I was frightened you would agree with them.

Elsa Don't say anything, Helen. You're making it worse. (*She studies Miss Helen with cruel detachment.*) But you might have a point there. Now that I've heard about your 'little accident', I'm beginning to think they might be right. (*She indicates the room.*) Corrugated iron and wooden walls? Give it half a chance and this would go up like a bonfire. (*She is hating herself, hurting herself every bit as much as she is hurting Miss Helen, but is unable to stop.*) And he says you were just standing and staring at it. What was that all about? Couldn't you make a run for it? They say that about terror – it makes you either run like hell or stand quite still. Sort of paralysis. Because it was just an accident, wasn't it, Helen? I mean, you weren't trying anything else, were you? Spite everybody by taking the house with you in a final blaze of glory! Dramatic! But it's a hell of a way to go. There are easier methods.

Miss Helen goes up to Elsa and stares at her.

Helen Who are you?

The question devastates Elsa.

Marius Ladies, ladies, enough! Stop now! I don't know what's going on between the two of you, but in Heaven's name stop it. I think Helen is aware of the dangers involved, Miss Barlow. And now that you do as well, can't we appeal to you to add your weight to ours and help persuade her to do the right thing? As I am sure you now realize, our only concern has been her well-being.

Elsa You want my help.

Marius Yes. If now at last you understand why we were trying to persuade Helen to move to the home, then on her behalf I am indeed appealing to you. We don't per-secute harmless old ladies, Miss Barlow.

Elsa And one that isn't so harmless?

Marius Now what are you trying to say?

Elsa That Helen isn't harmless, Dominee. Anything but that. That's why you people can't leave her alone.

Marius For fifteen years we have done exactly that.

Elsa Stoning her house and statues at night is not leaving her alone. That is not the way you treat a harmless old lady.

Marius In Heaven's name! Are you going to drag that up? Those were children, Miss Barlow, and it was a long, long time ago. It has not happened again. Do you really mean to be that unfair? Can't you bring as much understanding as you claim to have of Helen's situation to a few other things as well? You've seen what is out there . . . (*He gestures at the window and Miss Helen's 'Mecca'.*) How else do you expect the simple children of the village to react to all that? It frightens them, Miss Barlow. I'm not joking! Think back to your impression-able years as a little girl. I know for a fact that all the children in the village believe this house is haunted and that ghosts walk around out there at night. Don't scoff at them. I'm sure there were monsters and evil spirits in your childhood as well. But as I said, that was all a long, long time ago. The moment we discovered what they were doing, we in turn did everything we could to put a stop to it. Mr Lategan, the school principal, and I both lectured them in the sternest possible manner. Come now, Miss Barlow, have you learned nothing about us in the course of the few years that you've been visiting the village?

Elsa A lot more than I would have liked to. Those children didn't arrive at their attitude to Helen on their own. I've also heard about the parents who frighten

74

naughty children with stories about Miss Helen's 'monsters'. They got the courage to start throwing stones because of what they had heard their mothers and fathers saying. And as far as *they* are concerned, Helen is anything but a harmless old lady. God, what an irony. We spend our time talking about 'poor, frightened Miss Helen', whereas it's all of you who are really frightened.

Marius I can only repeat what I've already said to Helen: the people you are talking about grew up with her and have known her a lot longer than you.

Elsa Not any more. You also said that, remember? That stopped fifteen years ago when she didn't resign herself to being the meek, churchgoing little widow you all expected her to be. Instead she did something which small minds and small souls can never forgive . . . she dared to be different! Which does make you right about one thing, Dominee. Those statues out there are monsters. And they are that for the simple reason that they express Helen's freedom. Yes, I never thought it was a word you would like. I'm sure it ranks as a cardinal sin in these parts. A free woman! God forgive us!

Have you ever wondered why I come up here? It's a hell of a long drive, you know, if the only reason is sympathy for a lonely old lady whom nobody is talking to any more. And it's also not for the scenery.

She challenges me, Dominee. She challenges me into an awareness of myself and my life, of my responsibilities to both that I never had until I met her. There's a hell of a lot of talk about freedom, and all sorts of it, in the world where I come from. But it's mostly talk, Dominee, easy talk and nothing else. Not with Helen. She's lived it. One dusty afternoon five years ago, when I came walking down that road hoping for nothing more than to get away from the flies that were driving me mad, I met the first truly free spirit I have ever known. (*She looks at*

Miss Helen.) It is her betrayal of all of that tonight that has made me behave the way I have.

A pause. Marius has been confronted with something he has never had to deal with before.

Marius You call that . . . that nightmare out there an expression of freedom?

Elsa Yes. Scary, isn't it? What did you call it earlier? Her hobby? (*She laughs.*) Oh no, Dominee. It's much more dangerous than that . . . and I think you know it.

Marius In another age and time it might have been called idolatry.

Elsa Did you hear that, Helen? (*to Marius*) You know what you've just said, don't you?

Marius (*total conviction*) Oh yes . . . yes, indeed I do. I am also choosing my words very carefully, Miss Barlow.

When I first realized that it was my duty as a friend and a Christian to raise the question with Helen of a move to an old-age home, I decided I would do so on the basis of her physical well-being and safety and nothing else. Helen will tell you that that is all we have ever talked about. I came here tonight meaning once again to do only that. But you have raised other issues, chosen to talk about more than that . . . which forces me now to do so as well. Because there is a lot more than Helen's physical well-being that has worried me, Miss Barlow – and gravely so! Those 'expressions of freedom' have crowded out more than just a few fresh vegetables. I do not take them lightly any more.

I remember the first one very clearly, Helen. I made the mistake of smiling at it, dismissing it as an idle whim coming out of your loneliness. In fact, I think that is how you yourself described it to me, as something to pass away the time. I was very wrong, wasn't I? And very slow in realizing what was really happening. I only began to feel uneasy about it all that first Sunday you weren't in church.

The moment I stood up there in front of the congregation, I knew your place was empty. But even then, you see, I thought you were sick. After the service I hurried around here, but instead of being in bed there you were outside in the yard making yet another . . . (*at a loss for words*) . . . I don't really know what to call them.

Helen (*a small but calm voice. She is very still*) It was an owl, Marius. My first owl.

Marius It couldn't have waited until after the service, Helen?

Helen Oh no! (*quietly emphatic*) The picture had come to me in here the night before. I just had to go to work immediately while it was still fresh in my mind. They don't last long, Marius. After a little while it becomes very hard to remember clearly what you saw. I tried explaining to Elsa how it all works . . . but I don't suppose any of you will ever understand.

But don't ever think that missing church that Sunday was something I did lightly, Marius. You don't break the habit of a lifetime without realizing that that life will never quite be the same again. I was already dressed and ready! I had my Bible and hymn book, I was on the point of leaving this room as I had done every Sunday for as long as I could remember . . . but I knew that if I did, I would never make that owl . . . I think I also knew that if I didn't, that if I put aside my Bible and hymn book, took off my hat and changed my dress and went to work . . . Yes! That was my very first owl!

Marius Helen, Helen! I grieve for you! You turned your back on your Church, on your faith and then on us for that? Do you realize that that is why you are now in trouble and so helplessly alone? Those statues out there can't give you love or take care of you the way we wanted to. And, God knows, we were ready to do that. But you spurned us, Helen. You turned your back on our love and left us for the company of those cement monstrosities.

Elsa, who has been listening and watching quietly, begins to understand.

Elsa Helen, listen to me. Listen to me carefully because if you understand what I'm going to say, I think everything will be all right. They're not only frightened of you, Helen; they're also jealous. It's not just the statues that have frightened them. They were throwing stones at something much bigger than that – you. Your life, your beautiful, light-filled, glittering life. And they can't leave it alone, Helen, because they are so, so jealous of it.

Helen (*calmly*) Is that true, Marius?

Marius Helen, has your trust in me been eroded away to the extent that you can ask me that? Does she have so much power over you that you will now believe anything she says?

Helen Then . . . it isn't true?

Marius Dear God, what is there left for me to say or do that will make you listen to me the way you do to her?

Helen But I have been listening to you, Marius.

Marius No, you haven't! If that were so, you wouldn't be asking me to defend myself against the accusations of someone who knows nothing, nothing, about my true feelings for you. I feel as if I were on trial, Helen. For what? For caring about you? (*He confronts Miss Helen.*) That I am frightened of what you have done to yourself and your life, yes, that is true! When I find that the twenty years we have known each other, all that we have shared in that time, are outweighed by a handful of visits from her, then yes again. That leaves me bewildered and jealous. Don't you realize that you are being used, Helen – she as much as admitted to that – to prove some lunatic notion about freedom? And since we're talking about it, yes yet again, I *do* hate that word. You aren't free, Helen. If anything, exactly the opposite. Don't let her deceive you. If there is one last thing you will let me do for you, then let it be this: see yourself as I do and tell me if that is what you call being 'free'. A life I care about as deeply as any I have known, trapped now finally in the nightmare this house has become . . . with an illiterate little Coloured girl and a stranger from a different world as your only visitors and friends! I know I'm not welcome in here any more. I can feel it the moment I walk in. It's unnatural, Helen. Your life has become as grotesque as those creations of yours out there.

Why, Helen? Why? I will take that question with me to my grave. What possessed you to abandon the life you had, your faith?

Helen What life, Marius? What faith? The one that brought me to church every Sunday? (*shaking her head*) No. You were much too late if you only started worrying about that on the first Sunday I wasn't there in my place. The worst had happened long, long before that. Yes. All those years when, as Elsa said, I sat there so obediently next to Stefanus, it was all a terrible, terrible lie. I tried hard, Marius, but your sermons, the prayers, the hymns, they had all become just words. And there came a time when even they lost their meaning.

Do you know what the word 'God' looks like when you've lost your faith? It looks like a little stone, a cold, round, little stone. 'Heaven' is another one, but it's got an awkward, useless shape, while 'Hell' is flat and smooth. All of them – damnation, grace, salvation – a handful of stones.

Marius Why didn't you come to me, Helen? If only you had trusted me enough to tell me, and we had faced it together, I would have broken my soul to help you win back that faith.

Helen It felt too late. I'd accepted it. Nothing more was going to happen to me except time and the emptiness inside and I had got used to that . . . until the night in here after Stefanus's funeral. (*Pause. Miss Helen makes a decision.*) I've never told you about that night, Marius. I've told no one, not even Elsa, because it was a secret, you see, a very special one, and it had to stay that way while I was working on my Mecca. But so much has happened here tonight, it feels right to do so now. (*Pause.*) You brought me home from the cemetery, remember, and when we had got inside the house and you had helped me off with my coat, you put on the kettle for a pot of tea and then . . . ever so thoughtfully . . . pulled the curtains and closed the shutters. Such a small little thing, and I know that you meant well by it, that you didn't want people to stare in at me and my grief . . . but in doing that it felt as if you were putting away my life as surely as the undertaker had done to Stefanus a little earlier when he closed the coffin lid. There was even an odour of death in here with us, wasn't there, sitting in the gloom and talking, both of us in black, our Bibles in our laps? Your words of comfort didn't help. But that wasn't your fault. You didn't know I wasn't mourning Stefanus's death. He was a good man, and it was very sad that he had died so young, but I never loved him. My black widowhood was really for my own life, Marius. While Stefanus was alive there had at least been some pretence at it . . . of a life I hadn't lived. But with him gone . . .! You had a little girl in here with you, Marius, who had used up all the prayers she knew and was dreading the moment when her mother would bend down, blow out the candle and leave her in the dark. You lit one for me before you left – there was a lot of darkness in this room – and after you had gone I sat here with it. Such a sad little light, with its little tears of wax running down the side! I had none. Neither for Stefanus nor for myself. You see, nothing hurt any more. That little candle did all the crying in here that night, and it burned down very low while doing that. I don't know how much time had passed, but I was just sitting here staring into its flame. I had surrendered myself to what was going to happen when it went out . . . but then instead of doing the same, allowing the darkness to defeat it, that small, uncertain little light seemed to find its courage again. It started to get brighter and brighter. I didn't know whether I was awake any longer or dreaming because a strange feeling came over me . . . that it was leading me . . . leading me far away to a place I had never been to before. (*She looks around the room and speaks with authority.*) Light the candles, Elsa. That one first.

> *She indicates a candelabra that has been set up very prominently on a little table. Elsa lights it.*

And you know why, Marius? That is the East. Go out there into the yard and you'll see that all my Wise Men and their camels are travelling in that direction. Follow that candle on and one day you'll come to Mecca. Oh yes, Marius, it's true! I've done it. That is where I went that night and it was the candle you lit that led me there. (*She is radiantly alive with her vision.*) A city, Marius! A city of light and colour more splendid than anything I had ever imagined. There were palaces and beautiful buildings everywhere, with dazzling white walls and glittering minarets. Strange statues filled the courtyards. The streets were crowded with camels and turbaned men speaking a language I didn't understand, but that didn't matter because I knew, oh I just knew, it was Mecca! And I was on my way to the grand temple.

In the centre of Mecca there is a temple, Marius, and in the centre of the temple is a vast room with hundreds of mirrors on the walls and hanging lamps, and that is where the Wise Men of the East study the celestial geometry of light and colour. I became an apprentice that night.

Light them all, Elsa, so that I can show Marius what I've learned!

> *Elsa moves around the room lighting all the candles, and as she does so its full magic and splendour is revealed. Miss Helen laughs ecstatically.*

Look, Marius! Look! Light. Don't be nervous. It's harmless. It only wants to play. That is what I do in here. We play with it like children with a magical toy that never ceases to delight and amuse. Light just one little candle in here, let in the light from just one little star, and the dancing starts. I've even taught it how to skip around corners. Yes, I have! When I lie in bed and look in *that* mirror I can see *that* mirror, and in *that* one the full moon when it rises over the Sneeuberg *behind* my back! This is my world and I have banished Darkness from it.

It is not madness, Marius. They say mad people can't tell the difference between what is real and what is not. I can. I know my little Mecca out there, and this room, for what they really are. I had to learn how to bend rusty wire into the right shape and mix sand cement to make my Wise Men and their camels, how to grind down beer bottles in a coffee mill to put glitter on my walls. My hands will never let me forget. They'll keep me sane. It's the best I could do, as near as I could get to the real Mecca. The journey is over now. This is as far as I can go.

I won't be using this. (*the application form*) I can't reduce my world to a few ornaments in a small room in an old-age home.

Marius takes the form. When he speaks again we sense a defeated man, an acceptance of the inevitable behind the quiet attempt to maintain his dignity.

Marius Mecca! So that's where you went. I'll look for it on my atlas of the world when I get home tonight. That's a long way away, Helen! I didn't realize you had travelled that far from me. So to find you I must light a candle and follow it to the East! (*He makes a helpless gesture.*) No. I think I'm too old now for that journey . . . and I have a feeling that you will never come back.

Helen I'm also too old for another journey, Marius. It's taken me my whole life to get here.

I know I've disappointed you – most probably, bitterly so – but, whatever you do, please believe me that it wasn't intentional. I had as little choice over all that has happened as I did over the day I was born.

Marius No, I think I do believe you, Helen . . . which only makes it all the harder to accept. All these years it has always felt as if I could reach you. It seemed so inevitable that I would, so right that we should find each other again and be together for what time was left to us in the same world. It seems wrong . . . terribly wrong . . . that we won't. Aletta's death was wrong in the same way.

Pause.

Helen What's the matter, Marius?

83

Marius I am trying to go. It's not easy . . . trying to find the first moment of a life that must be lived out in the shadow of something that is terribly wrong.

Helen We're trying to say goodbye to each other, aren't we, Marius?

Marius Yes, I suppose it had come to that. I never thought that was going to happen tonight, but I suppose there *is* nothing else left to say. (*He starts to go. He sees Elsa, hesitates for a few seconds, but there is nothing to say to her either.*) Be sure all the candles are out when you go to bed, Helen. (*He pauses at the door.*) I've never seen you as happy as this! There is more light in you than in all your candles put together.

> *He leaves. A silence follows his departure. Elsa eventually makes a move to start blowing out the candles.*

Helen No, don't. I must do that. (*From this point on Miss Helen goes around the room putting out the candles, a quiet but deliberate and grave punctuation to what follows.*)

Elsa Tell me about his wife.

Helen Her name was Aletta. Aletta Byleveld. I've only seen pictures of her. She must have been a very beautiful woman.

Elsa What happened?

Helen Her death?

Elsa Yes.

Helen All I know is that there was a long illness. And a very painful one. They never had any children. Marius was a bitter and lonely man when he first came to the valley. Why do you ask?

Elsa Because he was, and most probably still is, in love with you.

Helen Elsa . . .

Elsa Yes. I don't suppose I would have ever guessed it if it hadn't been for tonight. Like all good Afrikaners, he does a good job of hiding his feelings. But it is very obvious now.

Helen (*agitated*) No, Elsie. When he used the word 'love' he meant it in the way . . .

Elsa No, Helen. I'm not talking about the good shepherd's feelings for one of his flock. Marius Byleveld, the man, loves you Helen, the woman.

Helen What are you talking about? Look at me, Elsa. Look at my hands . . .

Elsa You fool! Do you think that is what we see when we look at you? You heard him: 'There is more light in you than in all your candles put together.' And he's right. You are radiant. You can't be that naive and innocent, Helen!

Miss Helen wants to deny it, but the validity, the possible truth, of what Elsa has said is very strong.

It's a very moving story. Twenty years of loving you in the disguise of friendship and professional concern for your soul. (*There is an unnatural and forced tone to her voice.*) Anyway, that's his problem, right, Helen? You did what you had to. In fact, you deserve a few bravos for your performance tonight. I'm proud of you. I told you that you never needed me. And you did more than just say no to him. You affirmed your right, as a woman . . . (*Pause.*) Do you love him? The way he loves you?

Miss Helen thinks before speaking. When she does so there is no doubt about her answer.

85

Helen No, I don't.

Elsa Just asking. You're also an Afrikaner. You could also be hiding your real feelings the way he did. That would make it an even better story! The two of you in this Godforsaken little village, each loving the other in secret!

Helen Are you all right, Elsa?

Elsa No.

Helen What's wrong?

Elsa It's my turn to be jealous.

Helen Of what?

Elsa (*with a helpless gesture*) Everything. You and him . . . and, stupid as it may sound, I feel fucking lonely as well.

Helen You are jealous? Of us . . . Marius and me? With your whole life still ahead of you?

Elsa Even that woman on the road has at least got a baby in her arms at this moment. She's got something, for Christ's sake! Mind you, it's cold out there now. It could be on her back again. She might have crawled out of her stormwater drain and started walking to keep warm.

Helen Leave that poor woman alone now, Elsa!

Elsa She won't leave me alone, Helen!

Helen For all you know, she might have got a lift.

Elsa (*another unexpected flash of cruelty*) I hope not.

Helen (*appalled*) Elsa! That is not you talking. You don't mean that.

86

Elsa Yes, I do! A lift to where, for God's sake? There's no Mecca waiting for her at the end of that road, Helen. Just the rest of her life, and there won't be any glitter on that. The sooner she knows what the score really is, the better.

Helen Then think about the baby, Elsa.

Elsa What the hell do you think I've been doing? Do you think I don't care? That baby could have been mine, Helen! (*Pause. Then a decision.*) I may as well vomit it all out tonight. Two weeks after David left me I discovered I was pregnant. I had an abortion. (*Pause.*) Do you understand what I'm saying, Helen?

Helen I understand you, Elsa.

Elsa I put an abrupt and violent end to the first real consequence my life has ever had.

Helen I understand, Elsa.

Pause.

Elsa There is a little sequel to my story about giving that woman a lift. When I stopped at the turn-off and she got out of the car, after I had given her what was left of my food and the money in my purse, after she had stopped thanking me and telling me over and over again that God would bless me, after all of that I asked her who she was. She said: 'My English name is Patience.' She hitched up the baby, tightened her *doek,* picked up her little plastic shopping bag and started walking. As I watched her walk away, measuring out the next eighty miles of her life in small steps, I wanted to scream. And about a mile further on, in the *kloof,* I did exactly that. I stopped the car, switched off the engine, closed my eyes and started to scream.

I think I lost control of myself. I screamed louder and longer than I have ever done in my life. I can't describe it, Helen. I hated her, I hated the baby, I hated you for dragging me all the way up here . . . and most of all I hated myself. That baby is mine, Helen. Patience is my sister, you are our mother . . . and I still feel fucking lonely.

Helen Then don't be so cruel to us. There were times tonight when I hardly recognized you. Why were you doing it?

Elsa I wanted to punish us.

Helen For what? What have we done to deserve that?

Elsa I've already told you. For being old, for being black, for being born . . . for being twenty-eight years old and trusting enough to jump. For our stupid helplessness.

Helen You don't punish people for that, Elsa. I only felt helpless tonight when I thought I had lost you.

Elsa So what do you want me to do, Helen?

Helen Stop screaming.

Elsa And cry instead?

Helen What is wrong with that? Is it something to be ashamed of? I wish I still could . . . not for myself . . . for you, Patience, her little baby. Was it a boy or a girl?

Elsa I don't know. I'll never know.

Her moment of emotional release has finally come. She cries. Miss Helen comforts her.

I'll be all right.

Helen I never doubted that for a moment.

Elsa (*total exhaustion*) God Almighty, what a day! I'm dead, Helen, dead, dead, dead . . .

Helen No, you're not. You're tired . . . and you've got every right and reason to be.

She fetches a blanket and puts it over Elsa's shoulders.

Elsa I wasn't much of a help tonight, was I?

Helen You were more than that. You were a 'challenge'. I like that word.

Elsa But we didn't solve very much.

Helen Nonsense! Of course we did. Certainly as much as *we* could. I *am* going to see a doctor and an optician, and Katrina . . . (*She remembers.*) . . . or somebody else, will come in here a few times a week and help me with the house.

Elsa My shopping list!

Helen It is as much as 'we' could do, Elsa. The rest is up to myself and, who knows, maybe it will be a little easier after tonight. I won't lie to you. I can't say that I'm not frightened any more. But at the same time I think I can say that I understand something now.

The road to my Mecca *was* one I had to travel alone. It was a journey on which no one could keep me company, and because of that, now that it is over, there is only me there at the end of it. It couldn't have been any other way.

You see, I meant what I said to Marius. This is as far as I can go. My Mecca is finished and with it – (*Pause.*) I must try to say it, mustn't I? – the only real purpose my life has ever had. (*She blows out a candle.*) I was wrong to think I could banish darkness, Elsa. Just as I taught myself how to light candles, and what that means, I must teach myself now how to blow them out . . . and what that means. (*She attempts a brave smile.*) The last phase of my apprenticeship . . . and if I can get through it, I'll be a master!

Elsa I'm cold.

Helen Cup of tea to warm you up and then bed. I'll put on the kettle.

Elsa And I've got just the thing to go with it. (*She goes into the bedroom alcove and returns with her toilet bag, from which she takes a small bottle of pills.*) Valiums. They're delicious. I think you should also have one.

Helen (*all innocence*) So tiny! What are they? Artificial sweeteners?

The unintended and gentle irony of her question is not lost on Elsa. A little chuckle becomes a good laugh.

Elsa That is perfect, Helen. Yes, they're artificial sweeteners.

Helen I don't know how I did it, but that laugh makes me as proud of myself as of any one of those statues out there.

She exits to put on the kettle. Elsa goes to the window and looks out at Mecca. Miss Helen returns.

Elsa Helen, I've just thought of something. You know what the real cause of all your trouble is? You've never made an angel.

Helen Good Heavens, no. Why should I?

Elsa Because I think they would leave you alone if you did.

Helen The village doesn't need more of those. The cemetery is full of them . . . all wings and halos, but no

glitter. (*tongue-in-cheek humour*) But if I did make ⟨
it wouldn't be pointing up to Heaven like the rest.

Elsa No? What would it be doing?

Helen Come on, Elsa, you know! I'd have it pointing to
the East. Where else? I'd misdirect all the good Christian
souls around here and put them on the road to Mecca.

Both have a good laugh.

Elsa God, I love you! I love you so much it hurts.

Helen What about trust?

Pause. The two women look at each other.

Elsa Open your arms and catch me! I'm going to jump!

Curtain.

A PLACE WITH THE PIGS

Characters

Pavel
Praskovya

A Place with the Pigs was first performed at the Yale Repertory Theatre, USA. The cast was as follows:

Pavel Athol Fugard
Praskovya Suzanne Shepherd

Directed by Athol Fugard

The play was subsequently performed at the Market Theatre, Johannesburg, South Africa, with the following cast:

Pavel Athol Fugard
Praskovya Lida Meiring

Directed by Athol Fugard

The first United Kingdom production was at the Cottesloe Theatre, South Bank, London, on 16 February 1988. The cast was as follows:

Pavel Jim Broadbent
Praskovya Linda Basset

Directed by Athol Fugard
Designed by Douglas Heap

Note

The writing of this play was provoked by
the true story of Pavel Navrotsky, a deserter
from the Soviet army in the Second World War,
who spent forty-one years in hiding in a pigsty.

Scene One

THE ANNIVERSARY OF THE GREAT VICTORY

A pigsy, in a small village, somewhere in the author's imagination. A dank, unwholesome world. One of the pens has been converted into a primitive living area . . . only bare essentials but all of them obviously already in use for quite a few years. Walls are covered with an attempt to keep track of the passing of time . . . bundles of six strokes with another one across for the seven days of the week, the weeks and necessary odd days circled into months, the months blocked off into years . . . 1944 to 1954. It is a noisy, restless period in the sty – the pigs are waiting to be fed – a cacophony of grunts, squeals and other swinish sounds. Pavel Ivanovich Navrotsky is in the living area. He is in his mid-thirties, a desperate, haunted-looking individual. He is busy with pencil and paper trying to rehearse a speech.

Pavel 'Comrades, Pavel Ivanovich Navrotsky is not dead. He is alive. It is he who stands before you. I beg you, listen to his story and then deal with him as you see fit. Comrades, I also beg you to believe that it is a deeply repentant man who speaks . . .' (*He can hardly hear himself above the noise from the pigs. He speaks louder.*) '. . . that it is a deeply repentant man who speaks these words to you . . .' SHUT UP! (*He grabs a stick and rushes around the sty, lashing out at the pigs.*) Silence, you filthy bastards! I want silence! Silence! Silence! (*Squeals and then a slight abatement of noise. Pavel returns to his speech.*) 'Comrades, I also beg you to believe that it is a deeply repentant man who speaks these words to you and who acknowledges the error of

99

his ways . . . (*making a correction*) acknowledges in full his guilt. I, Pavel Ivanovich Navrotsky, ask only that in your judgment of me . . . (*another correction*) ask only that in deciding on my punishment, for I have already judged myself and found myself guilty, I ask only that you temper that punishment with mercy.'

The pigs are starting up again. Pavel goes to a door.

Praskovya! Praskovya! (*no reply*) Praskovya!

Praskovya (*a distant voice*) I'm coming . . . I'm coming!

Pavel Well, hurry up.

Praskovya appears, burdened with buckets of pigswill.

Praskovya I'm coming as fast as I can.

Pavel You're late.

Praskovya I'm not, Pavel.

Pavel Don't argue with me, woman! Listen to them. They're going berserk. I can't hear myself think in here.

Praskovya All right then, I'm late.

Pavel Well then, get on with it, Praskovya . . . feed them! You appear to have forgotten that in just a few hours' time I face the severest, the single most decisive test of my entire life.

Praskovya I know that, Pavel.

Pavel I find that hard to believe.

Praskovya God only gave me two arms and two legs, and I've been working them since I woke up this morning as if I'd been sentenced to hard labour. If you're interested in the truth, Pavel, I'm feeding the pigs an hour earlier than usual so that I will be free to give you all the attention and help I can.

Pavel (*back with his speech*) 'Comrades! Standing before you is a miserable wretch of a man, a despicable, weak creature worthy of nothing but your contempt. In his defence, I say only that if you had witnessed the years of mental anguish, of spiritual torment, which he has inflicted on himself in judgment of himself, then I know, Comrades, that the impulse in your noble and merciful hearts would be: "He has suffered enough. Let him go." For ten years he has been imprisoned by his own conscience in circumstances which would make the most hardened among you wince. Yes, for ten years . . .' (*His voice trails off into silence. Wandering around the sty.*) Ten years! Has it really been ten years?

Praskovya Yes.

Pavel Not nine?

Praskovya No.

Pavel Or eleven?

Praskovya No.

> *Pavel is counting the years as blocked out on the walls.*

You've checked it and double-checked it a dozen times already, Pavel.

Pavel Yes . . . ten years, two months and six days to be precise. There it is! (*stepping back with pride as an artist would from his canvas*) Nobody can argue with that, can they? 'There, Comrades, count it for yourselves . . . every day of my self-imposed banishment from the human race!'

Praskovya Sometimes, coming in here to feed you and them, it feels as if we've been at it for twenty.

Pavel Only twenty? Is that your worst? I've had days when it felt as if I'd been in here a hundred years. Two hundred! I've already lived through centuries of it. You must understand, Praskovya, life in here has involved dealing with two realities, two profound philosophic realities which have dominated my entire existence, permeated every corner of my being . . . Pig shit and Time. Just as my body and every one of its senses has had to deal with pig shit . . . smelling it, feeling it, tasting it . . . just so my soul has had to reckon with Time . . . leaden-footed little seconds, sluggish minutes, reluctant hours, tedious days, monotonous months and then, only then, the years crawling past like old tortoises.

Praskovya You must tell that to the comrades, Pavel.

Pavel I intend to.

Praskovya It sounds very impressive.

Pavel (*his speech*) Oh yes, don't worry . . . I intend to draw a very vivid picture of what I have had to endure in here right from that very first night.

Praskovya It was a Sunday night. Your first night in here.

Pavel I don't think the actual day is all that important.

Praskovya Just mentioning it, in case you're interested in the truth. I know it for certain because the storm had kept me from church and I was trying to make up for it before going to bed by saying my prayers a second time, and then a third . . . when I heard the scratching at the door.

Pavel's attention is riveted by her memories of that most decisive night in his life. Encouraged by his attention she continues.

At first I thought it was just a poor dog trying to find shelter from the blizzard. But then came the tapping at the window! Oh dear me, I thought, no dog can reach up there, not even on its hind legs! Suppose it's a big black bear! And when I peeped through the curtains . . . Mother of God! . . . that is what I thought I saw, what you looked like . . . all hair and beard and muffled up in your big coat with the snow swirling behind you. But when you tapped again I saw your hand, so I unbolted the door and let you in. But even then it took me some minutes to realize that the pathetic creature I was looking at was you, Pavel. You should have seen yourself.

Pavel (*greedy for still more*) Yes yes yes . . .

Praskovya Your lips were blue, your fingers frozen stiff. You could hardly hold the mug of soup I tried to get you to drink. I had to feed you like a baby. And then, when your tongue had thawed out enough for your first words . . . (*She shakes her head in disbelief.*)

Pavel Yes yes . . .

Praskovya You asked for your slippers!

Pavel Go on.

Praskovya And then when I brought them to you, when you saw them, you broke down and started crying. Clutching them to your breast and sobbing . . . Oh, Pavel! Sobbing in a way that nearly broke my heart! . . . You got up, staggered out of the house and collapsed in here.

> *Pavel fetches a small bundle which has been carefully hidden away somewhere in the living area. He sits down at the table and, after wiping his hands clean on his shirt, reverently unwraps it. He produces a pair of slippers.*

Pavel Oh, dear God! Every time I touch them, or just look at them . . . sometimes when I even just think about them . . . a flood of grief and guilt wrecks my soul as it did that night ten years ago. Look, Praskovya, look . . . do you see? . . . Little flowers and birds.

Praskovya The needlework is very fine.

Pavel My mother's hands!

Praskovya And what a clever pair of hands they were. (*still admiring the slippers*) And just look at the colours, still so bright and fresh! You should wear them, Pavel. One day the rats are going to find them.

Pavel Wear them? In here? How can you suggest such a thing! That would be sacrilege. No, my conscience will not allow me to wear these until the day when I am once again a free man. That is my most solemn vow! (*a little flutter of hope*) And who knows, Praskovya, this could be that day. Listen . . .

In the distance we hear the sound of a brass band . . . the discordancies of individual instruments being warmed up.

The band has arrived! They're getting ready. (*Pause. Then quietly*) During the war, at the front, deserters weren't even given a trial. Just forced to their knees and then a bullet in the back of the head. I saw it . . . blood, bright red blood on the snow. (*putting his papers in order*) Pray for me, Praskovya.

Praskovya I already have.

Pavel Then pray again . . . pray harder! Bully God with your prayers. I don't just deserve mercy, I've earned it!

Praskovya I will be down on my knees, Pavel, praying harder than I have ever prayed in my life from that moment you walk out that door and leave me. But, for the last time, Pavel, are you quite sure you are doing the right thing?

Pavel Yes yes YES! Let's go over the ceremony once more.

Praskovya Again?

Pavel Yes, a hundred times again, if necessary. For God's sake, Praskovya, my life is at stake.

Praskovya Everybody has been told to gather in the village square at ten o'clock. The ceremony will start with the arrival of the Ex-Soldiers' Brigade, the Young Pioneers and the Collective Fire Brigade. They are going to march through the village along the route taken by our troops on the glorious day of the liberation ten years ago. When everybody has settled down, we will all join in singing the Hymn of the Revolution. This will be followed by words of welcome from the Village Chairman and the reading of a message from the Central Committee in Moscow. Then the singing of the Victory Anthem, which brings us to the grand climax . . . Comrade Secretary Chomski's speech and the unveiling of the monument. After the unveiling, the School Principal will read out the names of the gallant dead, and with each name, the widow, mother or daughter of the departed will step forward and lay her wreath at the foot of the monument . . .

Pavel Which is when I will make my move! I will stay hidden at the back of the crowd until the reading of the names, but when they reach mine . . . I will step forward and declare myself. 'Comrades, Pavel Ivanovich Navrotsky is not dead. He is alive. It is he who stands here before you. I beg you, listen to his story and then deal with him as you see fit.'

Praskovya I'm frightened, Pavel.

Pavel You're frightened! How do you think I feel? I'm the one who is going to be standing up there with a thousand pairs of eyes staring at me, judging me.

Praskovya Suppose something goes wrong?

Pavel (*hanging on*) Nothing is going to go wrong.

Praskovya I think you may have forgotten what this village is like, Pavel. There are going to be some mean and uncharitable souls out there.

Pavel We've already had this discussion, Praskovya . . . and we agreed that the ceremony and the music and the speeches will have an elevating influence on their thoughts and feelings . . . They will have been lifted up to a higher plane . . . They will be forgiving . . .

Praskovya (*who has her doubts*) Boris Ratnitski forgiving? Or old Arkadina Petrovna? She packed off a husband, two brothers and three sons to the war and not one of them came back. They say she's got a picture of Hitler somewhere in her house which she spits on every morning when she wakes up.

Pavel (*a cry of despair*) Praskovya! Praskovya! I am trying to hold on to what little courage I have left in my bruised and battered soul. Don't destroy it! Give me support, woman! (*He calms down.*) There is no other way. This is my only chance. The alternative is madness . . . or suicide! I mean it, Praskovya. One more day in here, and I'll cut my throat! (*steadying himself*) But that is not going to be necessary, because I have prepared a very moving and eloquent plea to the comrades. I promise you, Praskovya, there will not be many dry eyes out there by the time I am finished. (*the papers for his speech*) Where is it? . . . Where is it? . . . Yes . . . Listen: '. . . dark nights of despair from which the next day's dawn brought no release . . .' And what about this: 'Remorse was the

bitter bread of my soul in its cold, grey and foul-smelling
entombment . . .' Many was the time you yourself said
I could have made a career of the stage if I had wanted
to. Well, Fate has done it. Today I must give the
performance of and for my life. And I am ready for it,
Praskovya. (*his speech*) When I stand there in front of
them in my uniform, the truth and sincerity of these
words will strike home.

Praskovya Stand there in your what?

Pavel My uniform . . . as Comrade Private Pavel
Ivanovich Navrotsky, first class, of the Sarazhentsy
Brigade . . .

Praskovya Pavel . . .

Pavel They won't see me as an enemy . . .

Praskovya Pavel . . .

Pavel . . . to be punished for his desertion and betrayal
of the Cause. Oh no . . .

Praskovya Pavel!! (*She finally manages to silence him.*)
I have got your suit, your fine black suit shaken out and
aired and all ready for you.

Pavel My suit?

Praskovya Yes. Don't you remember? You got married
in it.

Pavel Of course I remember it. But I'm going to wear
my uniform.

Praskovya Pavel, please . . .

Pavel We haven't got time for pointless arguments,
Praskovya. Don't you understand anything! I'm
surrendering. A soldier does not surrender in the fine
black suit he got married in.

Praskovya Please listen to me, Pavel . . .

Pavel No! Why are you making it so hard for me, Praskovya! Do I have to argue with you and fight about everything? I've had enough of it now. Just do as I say. Go and fetch my uniform. Praskovya! Move!

A leaden-footed Praskovya leaves the sty.

(*washing himself*) Courage, Pavel. Courage! It's nearly over. One way or the other this purgatory is nearly at an end. (*a farewell circuit of the pens*) Did you hear that my darlings? I'll be leaving you soon. Yes, my little shit-eaters, you'll have to find another victim to torment with your bestiality. So, in memory of the years we have shared in here, Pavel Ivanovich will leave you with one last gesture of his deep, oh so deep and abiding loathing and disgust.

He grabs his stick and brutalizes the pigs, striking and prodding them viciously. The exercise affords him considerable satisfaction. An exhausted and happy Pavel retires to his living area. Praskovya returns. In terrified silence she hands over to the still manic and panting Pavel a miserable little bundle. He unwraps it. It produces a few moth-eaten remnants of his uniform . . . cap, torn old tunic, one legging, etc.

What's this?

Praskovya I tried to tell you.

Pavel Praskovya . . .?

Praskovya That's it. And you're lucky there is that much left of it. When you gave it to me you said I must burn it, but I thought that was a wasteful thing to do with such a good bundle of rags, because that is all it was . . . so I just stuffed it away in a corner and whenever I needed one . . . (*Her voice trails off.*) I never dreamt you would ever need it again.

Pavel (*stunned disbelief*) Are you telling me that this . . .
No! It can't be. You are not telling me that, are you?

Praskovya Yes.

Pavel Yes, what?

Praskovya Yes, that is what I'm telling you.

Pavel That this . . .

Praskovya . . . is your uniform . . . what is left of it.

Pavel But the buttons . . . shiny brass buttons . . . six of
them, all the way down here in the front.

Praskovya There were no buttons left when you came
home that night.

Pavel Are you sure?

Praskovya Yes.

Stunned silence from Pavel as he examines the rags.

I'm afraid the mice have had a little nibble as well.

*Pavel slips on what is left of his tunic. Praskovya
shakes her head. He puts on the cap and salutes.
Praskovya shakes her head again.*

Somebody might laugh.

Pavel is devastated.

Take my advice and wear your suit. It's all ready for you.
A clean white shirt. And I've given your black shoes a
really good polish . . . shining like mirrors they are. It
won't make all that much difference surely. So instead
of Private Navrotsky the soldier, they'll see responsible,
sober, law-abiding Comrade Pavel Ivanovich they all
remember so well. It might even work to your advantage.

Pavel For God's sake, Praskovya! Didn't you hear me?

This is a military occasion. A deserter does not appear before his court martial in his wedding suit. 'Why aren't you in uniform, Private Navrotsky?' 'Comrade Sergeant, my wife used it to mop the floor, and then the mice and the moths made a meal of what was left.' That is sure to save me from the firing squad! (*doubts begin*) No . . . no . . . wait . . . let me think . . . let me think. (*agitated pacing*) This calls for very careful thought . . . a reappraisal of the situation in the light of new and unexpected developments. There has got to be a simple solution . . . which we will find, provided we stay calm and don't panic. (*Pause. His nerve is beginning to fail.*) Suppose I'm wrong, Praskovya.

Praskovya About what?

Pavel Them . . . (a *gesture to the world outside*) Suppose my innocent faith in human nature, my trusting belief in the essential goodness of our comrades' hearts . . . (*Swallows.*) . . . is a big, big mistake. That instead of forgiveness and understanding, when they hear my story . . . maybe . . . just maybe . . . they will hate and despise me. See in me and my moment of weakness ten years ago, a reminder of their *own* weaknesses . . . weaknesses they do not wish to confess to or be reminded of. Because you are certainly right about one thing, Praskovya Alexandrovna . . . that is not an assembly of saints out there clearing their throats for the singing of the anthem. Oh, most certainly not. If the truth were known about some of our respectable comrades out there, I wouldn't be the only one pleading for mercy today. My theory about the elevation of their thoughts and feelings on to a higher plane is dependent on there being enough basic humanity left in them to allow that to happen. But as you so perceptively pointed out, Praskovya, knowing some of them, that amounts to asking for a small miracle. (*hitting his head*) Stupid! Stupid! Stupid! I've been in here so long, I've forgotten what human nature is really like. Compassion and forgiveness? I stand as much chance of getting that from the mob out there as I do from these pigs.

The brass band is now in full swing.

Praskovya So what is it going to be, Pavel? They sound just about ready. It's now or never. (*Pause.*) Did you hear me, Pavel? It's time to go. Are you still going out there?

Pavel (*very small and very frightened*) I can't. It's no good, Praskovya . . . I just can't. I won't get a fair trial. They won't even give me a hearing. The moment I appear they'll throw themselves on me and tear me apart like a pack of Siberian wolves. (*He throws away the papers for his speech.*)

Praskovya So this is the end of it, then.

Pavel For me it is. You are the one who must give the performance now.

Praskovya Me?

Pavel Yes. So prepare yourself.

Praskovya What do you mean?

Pavel Your black dress . . . and didn't you say something about flowers? . . . A funeral wreath! When you hear my name . . . weep, Praskovya . . . weep! Because your Pavel is now as good as in his grave.

Praskovya (*nervous*) You want me to go out there . . . in front of all those people . . . and pretend you're dead.

Pavel Isn't that what you've been doing for the past ten years?

Praskovya Yes, that's true . . . but not on such a grand scale, Pavel. Widow's weeds and flowers, with a brass band playing!

Pavel Are you trying to get out of it?

Praskovya Yes! No! If you want me to go out there, Pavel, I'll do it. But I want you to know that I'm as frightened of going out there as you are. You don't seem to realize that I hardly see anybody any more. The only dealings I have with the outside world now is when I take one of the pigs down to the butcher. For the rest, I'm as much a prisoner in the house as you are in here.

Pavel You're wasting time, Praskovya. If you're not out there ready to step forward when my name is called, people will get suspicious and start asking questions.

She is very reluctant to move.

I'm warning you, at this rate you will end up mourning my real death before the day is over.

Praskovya All right, all right . . . I'm going. But I'm telling you, Pavel, this feels like a big, bad sin. Hiding you was one thing, but what you're asking me to do now . . .!

She exits, shaking her head with misgivings. The brass band is now playing away vigorously in the distance.

Pavel (*with the slippers*) Oh, Mama! These did it. It's all wrong, I know, because you made them with such love for your little Pavel, but if you could see what they have done to him, you would rise from your grave and curse the day you stitched them together. (a *helpless gesture*) It all seemed so simple at first! They gave me a uniform and a gun, taught me how to salute and then on a fine spring day, I kissed Praskovya goodbye and marched off with the others to win the war. And the thought of these, (*the slippers*) waiting for me at home, kept me going . . . kept me smiling and whistling away even when the marches were forced and long. At first the others teased me about them. But as the weeks passed and we tramped

further and further away from home, they eventually
stopped laughing. The time came, when sitting around at
night with no songs left to sing or jokes to tell, sooner or
later one of them would say in a small voice: 'Hey, Pavel,
tell us about your slippers.' The men would stare into the
fire with sad, homesick eyes while I talked about them,
about slipping my feet into their cosy padded comfort
and settling down next to the stove with Praskovya, to
talk about the weather or the pigs or the latest village
gossip . . . the silly unimportant little things that break
a big man's heart when he is far away from home.

That first winter wasn't too bad. 'Next spring,' we
said, trying to cheer each other up, 'we'll be back home
next spring.' We even managed somehow to get through
the second one with our spirits still intact. But a year
later, there we were, once again, watching the first snow
fall, and our victorious march back home seemed even
further away than ever. And what a winter that one
turned out to be, Mama! The oldest among us could not
remember snow that deep or temperatures that low . . .
winds so sharp and cold the skin blistered and cracked
open to the bone. Our hands could barely hold the
pitiful crusts of bread we were given as rations. And for
what? Why were we all dying of hunger and cold when
we had warm homes and young wives waiting for us?
The stupidity of it all made me want to vomit up food
I didn't have in my belly. That is when they (*the slippers*)
lost their innocence and began to torment me. Sitting
there huddled in the trench, an image of them would
come floating into my deranged mind . . . and with them,
smells and sounds . . . of pine logs cracking and hissing
away in the stove . . . crusty warm bread and freshly
churned butter . . . Weak as I was, I might still have been
able to cope with that, but then the little voice started
whispering. 'Go home, Pavel Ivanovich, go home.' I tried
to shut my ears to it with prayers and patriotic songs,

but nothing helped. It just carried on . . . laughing at me and my faltering loyalty, mocking all that was sacred . . . 'There are no flags in either heaven or hell, no causes beyond the grave.' And always the same refrain. 'Go home, Pavel Ivanovich, your slippers are waiting for you. Go home!'

In the distance the brass band and voices singing.

Am I such a terrible sinner, Mama, for having yielded to temptation under those circumstances . . . half crazed as I was with hunger and cold? One night . . . all I wanted was one more night beside the stove in these slippers, and then I would have happily laid down my life defending our Motherland. But when I came to my senses in here, Praskovya told me that a month had already passed. One day, one week, one month . . .! It would have all come to the same thing in the end . . . one bullet in the back of the head.

An excited and happy Praskovya bursts into the sty. She is now dressed in black and carries her Bible and a small Russian flag.

Praskovya Pasha . . . Pasha . . . It's all right, Pasha. It's all over and it's all right. Do you want to hear about it, Pavel?

He stares at her in silence. She produces a little black box.

To start with, you've been awarded a medal . . . for making the Supreme Sacrifice . . . (*the inscription on the medal*) 'Pavel Ivanovich Navrotsky. A Hero of the People.' Your mother would have been so proud. Your name is also inscribed on the monument. As for Comrade Secretary Chomski's speech . . . You did the right thing after all, Pavel, in not going out there. You would have had a hard time making an appearance after

what he had to say. He started off by urging all of us . . .
'sons and daughters of our Glorious Revolution' . . . to
take a lesson in self-sacrifice and dedication to the Cause
from the noble comrades whose names have been
chiselled in granite for all future generations to read.
The world we live in is safe, Pavel, thanks to the likes
of you . . . 'the Russian bears who mauled the fascist
mongrels' . . . our children, and their children, and their
children's children, will grow up in a world of plenty for
all, thanks to the likes of you . . . the brave fifty of
Sarazhentsy who sacrificed their lives defending the
Revolution in the Winter Campaign of '43. And finally,
the fact that you lie somewhere in an unmarked grave
doesn't really matter, because your memory is enshrined
for ever in the hearts of the People. (*She pins the medal to
Pavel's chest.*) As for our comrades out there . . . a sight
to behold! They wept for you, Pavel, as if you were their
very own flesh and blood. When I returned to my place
after laying my flowers, I thought I was going to end up
bruised all over from the embraces I got for 'our beloved
Pavel Ivanovich'. I'm not exaggerating. That old skinflint
Smetalov . . . he buried his bald head in those money-
grabbing paws of his and wept! All of them . . . Tamara,
Galina, Nastasia . . . every single one of them had the
chance for a really good cry thanks to you. There would
have been a lot of disappointed people out there if you
had cut short that grief with an unexpected appearance.
But do you want to know what is strangest of all, Pavel?
There was a time out there when I myself was so overcome with emotion at the thought of your lonely and
bitter death so far away from home, that I also started
to cry! Yes! Under the power of Comrade Secretary
Chomski's words, for some minutes I myself believed
that you were dead. Look! I'm ready to start again.
(*wiping away her tears*) But that still isn't the end of it.
I don't mean to upset you, but it will be on my conscience

unless I tell you. When it was all over, Smetalov insisted on walking back with me, and on the way . . . he proposed to me. At least that is what I think he was doing. 'The joyful vision of my pigs and his cows under the same roof' . . . is how he put it. He said it would be a happy ending to the sad story of the Widow Navrotsky. I couldn't get rid of him! He's coming back next week for an answer. (*She makes the sign of the cross.*) Lord have mercy on us . . . Our souls will surely roast in hell for what we have done today. And if our comrades ever find out, we'll be in for a double dose of it. We have lied to them, Pavel . . . publicly! We have made fools of them and a mockery of the anniversary celebrations. Now they will never forgive us.

Pavel How is it possible! Like the pigs, all I do in here is eat, sleep and defecate, yet my burden of guilt grows heavier, and heavier. Instead of being diminished by my suffering, it seems to draw nourishment from it . . . like those mushrooms that flourish and get fat on the filth in here. Has it finally come to that, Praskovya? Is my soul now nothing more than a pigsty?

Praskovya That sounds like a theological question, Pavel. I don't think I know enough to take it on.

Pavel Does ten years of human misery count for nothing in the Divine Scales of Justice?

Praskovya I think it would be wiser if I left that one alone as well. These are all matters beyond my simple woman's head. I will leave you to deal with them. (*She gets up to go.*)

Pavel Where are you going?

Praskovya Get changed and then back to work. Celebrations are over. There are chores waiting for me in the house.

Pavel (*staring at her, dumbfounded*) Just like that?

Praskovya Just like what?

Pavel You are going to walk away from me, leave me in here . . . just like that.

Praskovya Life goes on, Pavel.

Pavel Whose life?

Praskovya Everybody's, I suppose.

Pavel Mine as well?

Praskovya Yes. I pray to God that it goes on as well.

Pavel (*crude sarcasm*) Thank you very much for that information, Praskovya. So, my life is going to go on! How wonderful! Just think of all the challenging possibilities that lie ahead of me in here. The fact that the pigs will be my only company makes the prospect even more exciting, doesn't it? (*rubbing his hands together in mock relish.*) So what should it be? Something in the line of religion? I'm being serious! Maybe there are souls worth saving inside those little mountains of lard. I'll coax them out. Give them all good Christian names and preach the Gospel. St Pavel of the Pigs! You don't like that? Then what about politics? Yes, that's a possibility as well. This pigsty is a very political situation. In those poor, dumb creatures we might have the last truly under-privileged and exploited working class of the world. I could embrace their cause, become a subversive element and breed rebellion. So that when next you try to lead some poor helpless comrade off to the butcher, you find a small revolution on your hands. Have I overlooked any possibilities? Please say something before you go off to peel potatoes or scrub the floors . . .

Praskovya The potatoes are already peeled . . . I did that first thing this morning . . . and none of the floors need scrubbing. If you're interested in the truth, Pavel, there is a pile of dirty clothes waiting for me. This is washday. So get ready for it . . . I am going to walk away from you.

Pavel Just like that.

Praskovya Just like that.

Exit Praskovya. Pavel alone. The pigs grunting away contentedly.

Scene Two

BEAUTY AND THE BEAST

*The pigsty. A lot of time has passed. Once again a
chorus of pig noises initiates the scene. Pavel is slumped
in mindless apathy. He is swatting flies with what looks
suspiciously like the last remnant of one of his cherished
slippers. The other is on one of his feet. After a few
minutes of this he sweeps together all the dead flies and
counts them. That done, he gets up and goes over to a
wall where we now see that his calendar of days has
been defaced by a tally of dead flies. The score at the
moment: 9,762. He adds 23 to this, bringing the total up
to 9,785. A few vacant seconds as he stands scratching
himself. His next move is to take up his stick and go
around the sty tormenting the pigs . . . a pastime he
pursues without either enthusiasm or joy. In the middle
of this he stops suddenly and stares in disbelief . . . a
butterfly has somehow managed to get into the sty. His
mood slowly undergoes a total transformation as he
watches it flutter around. He is ravished by its beauty,
reminding him as it does of an almost forgotten world
of sunlight and flowers, a world he now hasn't seen for
many, many years. Suppressed calls for Praskovya.
He decides to catch the butterfly. A hurried search for
something to use as a net . . . he decides on his slipper.
He hurries back in search of the butterfly . . . a few
seconds of panic when he can't find it . . . ecstatic relief
and laughter when he does. He stalks it like a hunter,
clambering in and out of pens, but it keeps eluding him.
His laughter grows and grows. He stops suddenly.*

Pavel (*addressing himself with disbelief*) What is this?

Can it be true? Are you laughing, Pavel Ivanovich? (*answering himself with conviction*) Yes, good comrade. That is perfectly true. I'm trying to catch a butterfly . . . and I'm laughing. (*which he does with renewed abandon*) Praskovya! I'm laughing!

(*back to the butterfly, his slipper ready*) We must get you out of here, my dainty darling. This is no place for a little beauty like you. Where are you? Little fluttering friend, where are you? Please . . . oh, dear God! . . . *please* don't die in here. Let me give you back to the day outside, to the flowers and the summer breeze . . . and then in return take, oh, I beg you! . . . take just one little whisper of my soul with you into the sunlight. Be my redemption! Ha!

> *He sees it and freezes . . . it has settled in one of the pens. Pavel approaches cautiously, ready to pounce. Once again a sudden stop, his eyes widening with horror at the prospect of impending disaster.*

No . . . don't . . . no . . . No!

> *He is too late. A pig eats the butterfly. He goes berserk with rage.*

Murderer! Murderer!!

> *Grabbing a knife, he jumps into the pen and after a furious struggle kills the pig. Terrible gurgles and death squeals from the unfortunate animal. Praskovya bursts in to find a bloodstained, sobbing Pavel.*

Praskovya Pavel . . . Pavel . . .!

Pavel Too late . . . too late . . .

Praskovya (*sees him*) Oh, my God! What happened? Have you tried to kill yourself? (*She examines him frantically.*)

Pavel (*still sobbing*) No . . . no . . .

Praskovya This isn't your blood?

Pavel My soul, Praskovya . . . it's my soul that bleeds.

Praskovya Well then, there is something else in here bleeding in the old-fashioned way. (*She follows a trail of blood back to the pen and sees the dead pig.*) Oh, dear me, just look at her! Did you do that, Pavel? (*She is very impressed.*) And all by yourself!

> *Praskovya fetches a bucket of water and a rag and helps the still distraught Pavel to clean himself.*

What happened? Come now . . . tell me all about it and then you'll feel better.

Pavel (*collecting himself*) A butterfly, Praskovya . . . a happy, harmless little beauty with rusty-red wings . . . remember them? From our childhood? . . . Skipping among the blue cornflowers . . .

Praskovya Oh yes, I remember those!

Pavel Well, one of them found its way in here somehow . . . I was busy chastising the pigs when I suddenly saw it fluttering around. I thought to myself, 'Oh dear, this is no place for a little butterfly to be. Let me catch it so that Praskovya can set it free outside.' Which is what I then tried to do. But . . . the strangest thing, Praskovya! While I was chasing it . . . (*a little laugh at the memory*) . . . and once I nearly had it! . . while I was chasing it, it was as if something inside me, something that had been dead for a long, long time, slowly came back to life again. All sorts of strange feelings began to stir inside me . . . and the next thing I knew I was laughing! Can you believe that, Praskovya? Me laughing! In here!

Praskovya I wish I'd been here for that.

Pavel I called you.

Praskovya I remember that laugh very well. Such a good one it was! But how do we end up with a dead pig?

Pavel I'm coming to that. Don't interrupt me.

Praskovya I'm sorry.

Pavel The little butterfly . . .

Praskovya Yes.

Pavel I was chasing it and laughing . . . the way I used to when I was a little boy. A moment of magic, Praskovya! . . . as if it had found . . . in here! . . . a mysterious path back to my childhood . . . back to the meadows where I used to romp and play, with flowers and birdsong all around me, a blue wind-swept sky overhead . . .

Praskovya That is very beautiful, Pavel.

Pavel Oh, yes. So there we were: the butterfly and the little boy . . . Beauty and Innocence! (*Pause.*) It settled in that pen.

Praskovya (*at last she understands*) Oh dear dear dear . . .

Pavel (*nodding*) Beauty and Innocence were joined by the Beast. (*For a few seconds his emotions again leave him at a loss for words.*) It was horrible, Praskovya. I saw it coming but there was nothing I could do to stop it. First the mean black little eyes focused, the bristles on its snout started quivering in anticipation . . . but before I could move a muscle it had opened its loathsome mouth and that was the end of it.

Praskovya Don't take it too much to heart, Pavel. You tried your best, and God will bless you for your efforts.

Pavel God will do nothing of the sort. God doesn't give a damn about what goes on in here.

Praskovya (*not sure she has heard correctly*) Pavel?

Pavel And if he does, there is nothing he can do about it.

Praskovya (*deeply shocked*) What are you saying, Pavel Ivanovich!

Pavel I'm saying that God has no jurisdiction in here. And do you know why? Because this is hell! Yes! I know where I am now. I at last know this place for what it really is. Hell! The realm of the damned. *This* is my punishment, Praskovya . . . to watch brutes devour Beauty and then fart . . . to watch them gobble down Innocence and turn it into shit . . . (*breaking down once again*) And it is more than I can endure. I'm reaching the end, Praskovya. Those few seconds of innocent laughter might well have been the death rattle of my soul.

Praskovya Come now, Pavel, I know you are very upset but don't exaggerate. You can't have it both ways.

Pavel What do you mean?

Praskovya You can't be both dying *and* in hell.

Pavel Why not?

Praskovya Because any little child will tell you that hell is where you will go *after* you're dead.

Pavel (*nearly speechless with outrage*) You are going to split hairs with me at a time like this?

Praskovya Just thought you might be interested in the truth, Pavel.

Pavel Well, I'm not! Because what you call 'The Truth' invariably involves the reduction of profound philosophic and moral issues to the level of your domestic triviality.

123

Praskovya All right, all right, have it your own way. But at the risk of making you even more angry, Pavel, I think I should also point out that only last week I had to let out your trouser seams because you're putting on a little weight around the waist . . . and now you've just killed a full-grown pig with your bare hands. That doesn't sound like a dying man to me.

Pavel I meant it *spiritually*! *Inside*! Didn't you hear me? I was talking about my *soul*.

Praskovya Oh, I see . . .

Pavel No, you don't! You see nothing. The full tragic significance of what is happening in here is beyond your comprehension. (*to the wall, with its tally of dead flies*) Look! Look at what I've become! Look at what my life has been reduced to. Nine thousand seven hundred and eighty-five dead flies! The days of my one and only life on this earth are passing, while I sit in mindless imbecility at that table swatting flies. And when I get bored with that, what is my other soul-uplifting diversion? Tormenting the pigs. *They* are now a higher form of life than me. That's the truth! They have at least got a purpose. Crude as it may be, pork sausages and bacon does give their lives a meaning . . . which is more than can be said of mine. I'm not deluding myself, am I, Praskovya? I wasn't always like this. The man you married . . . he was like other men, wasn't he? . . . decent and hard-working with dreams and plans for a good and useful life. Remember our last night together before I went off to the war . . . how we sat up in bed and talked about the future and what we were going to do when I came back . . . the plans we had for a family, for more pigs and a bigger and better sty. That was *Me* . . . the same man whose greatest pleasure now is to flatten another fly on the table top. Do you know what his ambition is? A hundred

thousand squashed flies. (*wandering around the sty*) And
to think that my greatest fear was that I would lose my
mind. (*hollow laughter*) That would have been a happy
ending compared to what is really in store for me in
here. The punishment reserved for me, Praskovya, is to
live on in total sobriety and sanity knowing that I am
losing my soul, that a day will come when I'll be no
better than that brute I killed. And when that has happened, should Beauty chance to cross my path again . . .
(*He swats the imaginary butterfly as he did the flies.*)
And look at what I'll be using! (*the tattered slipper*)
Do you recognize this? Can you detect any trace of its
former delicacy and beauty under the crust of filth that
now covers it? My mother's slippers! These were my
most cherished possessions. Look at them now. (*Hurls
his slippers into one of the pens.*) There . . . let's make a
thorough job of it . . . turn them into shit as well. A life
with nothing sacred left in it is a soulless existence,
Praskovya. It is not a life worth living.

> *Praskovya does not know how to respond. She
> alternately nods and then shakes her head and in this
> fashion gets through a respectful silence before again
> venturing to speak.*

Praskovya (*timidly*) Pavel . . . I don't mean to interrupt
but . . . can I ask a question?

> *No response from Pavel.*

What immediate effect does all of that have on things . . .
and the situation in here . . . What I mean is . . . I don't
want to interfere but it is getting on for supper time and
well . . . must I go on with it . . . or what?

> *No response from Pavel.*

I was making cabbage soup and dumplings.

No response.

Pavel?

Pavel *(violently)* I heard you!

Another pause.

Praskovya Well?

Pavel *(it is not easy for him)* Have we got a little aniseed for the dumplings?

Praskovya Yes.

Pavel Soup and dumplings.

Scene Three

THE MIDNIGHT WALK

The pigsty. A lot more time has passed. There is yet another layer of graffiti on the walls, consisting this time of obscenities and rude drawings of the pigs. The animals are in a subdued mood as the scene starts. It is night. A lit candle on the table. Pavel is on his bunk, propped up against pillows. He appears to be a very sick man. Laboured, desperate breathing. Praskovya is in attendance. Laid out in readiness is a woman's outfit . . . dress, shawl, hat and shoes.

Pavel (*struggling to speak*) Is it time yet?

Praskovya Just a little longer.

Pavel You said that at least an hour ago.

Praskovya There are still a few lights on in the street. It won't be safe until they are all out. Be patient.

Pavel 'Be patient'! I'm dying . . . of suffocation . . . and she says, 'Be patient'!

Praskovya Shall I keep fanning you?

Pavel Useless! All that does . . . is circulate . . . the stench . . . and foul air in here. I need fresh air . . . fresh air . . . fresh air . . .

Praskovya And you are going to get it. Just hang on a few minutes more. It won't be long now before the village will be in bed and fast asleep and then we can take our chance . . . (*Makes the sign of the cross.*) And may God help us. Let me say once again, Pavel, that I'm feeling more than just a little nervous. You've had some strange ideas in here, but this one . . . If it wasn't for your condition I would never have agreed to it. So remember your promise . . . no arguments when we get out there. You don't know your way around any more so *I'm* leading the way, and we're going as far as the big poplar and then coming back. If you are up to it and it looks safe, we can maybe think about a more round-about route for our return. But that's all. Agreed? (*She sees that Pavel is crying.*) Now what's the matter? Really, Pavel, you spend half your time in tears these days.

Pavel Give me your hand . . . feel my heart.

Praskovya Oh my word yes! What's that all about, Pavel?

Pavel Fear. I'm frightened.

Praskovya Then shouldn't we abandon this crazy idea?

Pavel No . . . no . . . it's not just *that*. Everything! My whole life. For all of his fifty-one years, Pavel Ivanovich Navrotsky has been a frightened man . . . and I'm so tired of it now, Praskovya . . . tired . . . tired . . .

Praskovya Don't aggravate your condition with morbid thoughts. Try to look on the bright side of things.

Pavel No, I *must* speak. There are things about me that I've kept hidden, unconfessed truths, that choke me tonight as much as the fetid air in here.

Praskovya All right, Pavel. *I'm* listening.

Pavel (*sitting up*) I'm a coward, Praskovya! Please, no denials . . . I've got to say it. Pavel Ivanovich Navrotsky is a coward. It's true, Praskovya. Where other men are motivated by patriotism, or ambition . . . I have been driven by fear. The other night, knowing that my end is now near, I tried to remember my childhood, tried to recall for the last time just a few images of those carefree, happy years of innocence . . . but do you know what were the only memories that came to me? Frightened little Pavel hiding away from trouble! From big bullies looking for a fight, or my angry father with his belt in his hand . . . hiding away under my bed, in the cupboard under the stairs, in the cellar, in the shed at the bottom of the garden. I had a secret little book in which I kept a list of all the places I had found to hide. I believed that if I could find a hundred small, dark little places into which I could crawl and lie very still and where no one would find me, then I would be safe all my life. I only got as far as sixty-seven. And it didn't end in my childhood, Praskovya. As I grew up I refined the art of hiding away. I ended up being able to do it even when I was in the middle of a crowd of people! Like our wedding. I've got a terrible confession to make, Praskovya, you married my black suit. I was hiding away inside it at the time. Or that 'brave' soldier who waved goodbye to you when he marched off to the war. The only brave thing about him was his uniform. I was hiding away inside that one as well. My courage lasted for as long as those buttons were bright. And how does it all end? In a pigsty! And guess what Pavel Navrotsky is doing in the pigsty? This is number sixty-eight. (*He collapses back on his pillows.*)

Praskovya There, you've got it off your chest. Do you feel better now?

Pavel No . . . if anything I feel worse. If I don't breathe fresh air within the next few minutes, you'll be hiding me away in my grave before the night is out.

Praskovya Come now, Pavel . . . none of that! I'll go and check again. (*She exits and returns after a few seconds.*) Yes, we can chance it now. All the lights are out.

Pavel, helped by Praskovya, gets to his feet and then struggles into the woman's outfit. A difficult operation because of his condition. At the end of it he is very exhausted and has to support himself by leaning on the table.

Pavel Mirror.

Praskovya What?

Pavel Mirror!

Praskovya fetches a mirror and holds it up so that Pavel can see himself. He straightens up and studies his reflection.

(*tapping a spot on his chest*) Have you . . . have you got . . . a little brooch or something . . .?

Praskovya exits. Pavel adjusts his outfit while she is gone. She returns with a pretty little box covered with seashells in which she keeps her precious things. Pavel rummages through its contents and chooses a brooch. Praskovya pins it on the dress.

Praskovya Very good!

Pavel Not too loose around the waist?

Praskovya No. In fact, I think that dress looks better on you than it ever did on me.

Pavel Really?

Praskovya Oh, yes. If it wasn't for your whiskers, I'd believe that you were the mother or wife of some good family. Just keep your face covered and say nothing and nobody will be any the wiser. But don't get carried away. If we do meet somebody out there or get stopped or whatever, *I'll* do the talking. The story is that you are my cousin, Dunyasha, from Yakutsk, and she's as deaf as a doornail, 'so don't waste your breath talking to her. She can't hear a thing.' Ready? (*Makes the sign of the cross.*) Say a quiet prayer that there are no hooligans prowling around ready to take advantage of two helpless women.

They sneak out into the night. The assault on Pavel's senses is total . . . a gentle breeze, the smell of the earth, stars in the sky, crickets and the distant barking of a dog. It is more than he can cope with. After a few deep breaths of freedom, he reels giddily.

Mother of God, what's happening? Pavel? Is this a stroke? Please don't die on me out here!

Pavel The air, Praskovya . . . the fresh air . . . it's making me drunk . . . hold me . . . hold me up, I think I'm going to faint . . .

Praskovya That settles it! Back into the sty! Come, Pavel, while you're still on your legs. The whole idea is madness. I should never have agreed to it.

Pavel No no no . . . it's passing . . . I'll be all right. (*A low soft moan of ecstasy escapes from his lips.*)

Praskovya Not so loud!

Pavel Stars, Praskovya . . . stars . . . Look!

Praskovya Yes, I can see them! But for God's sake keep your voice down. At this rate we'll have the whole village awake before we've even started.

Pavel And the little crickets! Listen! This is not a dream, is it, Praskovya?

Praskovya No, it isn't, but God knows I wish it was.

Pavel Just another dream to torment me when I wake up and find myself back in that shithouse. Pinch me, Praskovya. Come on, pinch me.

She does so.

Ouch! Oh yes, I felt that! So then it's true. I'm awake and all of this beauty, this soul-ravishing beauty is real! Mother Earth . . . I give myself to you.

Opening his arms as if to embrace all of creation, he lurches off into the night. Praskovya follows frantically.

Praskovya You're going the wrong way! Left . . . Pavel . . . Dunyasha . . . turn left . . .

Pavel arrives at the big poplar. A few seconds later he is joined by Praskovya, exhausted and breathless from trying to keep up with him.

In heaven's name stop, Pavel! What's the matter with you? Do you want us to be caught? We're supposed to look like two sober and sensible women out for a stroll and a breath of fresh air before bed. You've been tearing through the night as if a man was after you. We're lucky nobody came dashing out to defend our virtue. (*looking around*) Well, anyway, here we are. Let's rest a few minutes and get our breath, and enjoy ourselves, then we can make our way back. But for the sake of my poor old legs, let's take it easy this time.

Pavel is sniffing the air like a hungry dog.

Yes, wild roses! They've put on quite a show this year. Masses of them everywhere!

Pavel (*still delirious with freedom*) This is wicked.

Praskovya What have you done now?

Pavel This star-studded, rose-scented magnificence! I have no moral right to it, Praskovya. My sins have made me an outcast on this earth, like Adam thrown out of Eden . . . but here I am trying to sneak back past the

Guardian Angel for one last little taste of Paradise.

Praskovya Don't worry about it too much. It looks as if the Almighty had decided to turn a blind eye on what we're up to otherwise we would have been struck down long ago. And it's not as if we're going to make a habit of it . . . I hope.

Pavel You know, Praskovya, I thought that in that sty I had become some sort of moral degenerate, that my soul had rotted away in the ocean of pigshit and piss I've been swimming in since God alone knows when. But that is not true! I still have it!

Praskovya Moderate your language, Pavel. That is not the way a good woman talks.

Pavel Oh, most definitely . . . I feel it tonight . . . I feel it stirring!

Praskovya All right, I believe you. But now that you know you've still got it, don't let it stir you up too much. You're making me nervous, Pasha.

Pavel I can't help myself. That little breeze wafting the scent of roses this way is at work on my emotions as if it were a hurricane. I am aroused! I have urges!

Praskovya God help us. I saw it coming.

Pavel Strange and powerful urges!

Praskovya Urges to do what, Pavel?

Pavel That road! That road stretching before us, Praskovya . . . it beckons!

Praskovya (*firmly*) No.

Pavel Yes! Let's keep walking.

Praskovya (*even more firmly*) And I say no! This is as

far as we go. We haven't got enough time left, Pavel, 'specially if we're going to take it easy going back. These summer nights are very short. It won't be long now before the sparrows start chirping and we see a little light in the east.

Pavel No no no no . . . you don't understand. I'm not talking about adding just a few miserable minutes to this stolen little outing. I'm saying: Let's follow that road into the Future!

Praskovya To where? It leads to Barabinsk, Pavel.

Pavel All right! So it's to Barabinsk we go . . . and then beyond! The Future, Praskovya. A New Life.

Praskovya What are you suggesting, Pavel?

Pavel Escape.

Praskovya You mean . . .?

Pavel Yes, that's right . . . the unmentionable . . . the unthinkable . . . Escape! What's the matter with you, Praskovya! Have you been so brainwashed that you've forgotten what the word means?

Praskovya But what about the house, Pavel . . . all our things . . . the pigs . . .?

Pavel Turn our back on the lot and walk away. Yes! Abandon everything. There must be no going back. If we go back, we'll never do it.

Praskovya So we must set off, just as we are?

Pavel Yes. Here and now!

Praskovya You dressed as a woman, not a rouble in our pockets . . .!

Pavel We'll live like gypsies.

Praskovya You don't know anything about gypsies, Pavel! You've gone mad tonight. I'm not listening to you any more.

Pavel If I have, it's a divine madness because it has given me a vision of my Freedom. Yes, Praskovya! I'd rather die in a ditch beside that road, under the stars with a clean wind in my hair, than return to that sty and die of suffocation from pig fart.

Praskovya Pavel, please calm down and listen to me. If you take to that road and go on walking, you won't die in a ditch with the stars and the wind and all the rest of it. You'll end up in gaol or in front of a firing squad. Come to your senses, Pavel! Look at you. You'll never get away with it in broad daylight. Your splendid 'future' will last as long as it takes to walk to the next village where the police will nab you. Come now, Pasha . . . we're too old for all these grand ideas. Let's just turn around quietly and go home.

Pavel Home? Don't use that word! I don't know what it means any more. Waiting for me back there is a foul dungeon which I share with a dozen other uncouth inmates. No . . . no . . . no . . . I've got this far . . . I'm not going back.

Praskovya (*giving up*) OK, Pavel, I've tried my best. If that's the way you want it, go ahead, take to the road and walk. Believe me I will pray very hard that you find your 'freedom' and enjoy a long and happy 'future'.

Pavel What do you mean? Aren't you coming?

Praskovya No, you walk alone. I've had enough. This is as far as I go.

Pavel You can't just abandon me, Praskovya.

Praskovya You've got it the wrong way around, Pavel. *You* are abandoning *me*. *You're* the one who is leaving. What are you waiting for?

Pavel You seem to be in a hurry to get rid of me, Praskovya.

Praskovya It's just that I want to get home while it's still dark, but I also feel I should at least wave goodbye to you when you set off.

Pavel All right, all right . . . I'm going. (*adjusting his dress*) So then, this is it. Goodbye, Praskovya.

Praskovya Goodbye, Pavel.

> *Pavel takes a few uncertain steps along the road. Praskovya waves. Pavel stops and then returns to her side.*

Pavel Tell you what . . . I'll strike a bargain. If you wait here with me for the sunrise, I'll go back with you. Please, Praskovya! Do you realize how long it has been since I last felt the golden light of a new day . . . saw my shadow on the earth! That's all I ask. It can't be long now surely. Look . . . isn't the sky already turning grey over there?

Praskovya If it is, then it also won't be long before we find ourselves in very serious trouble. By the time the sun rises half the village is already up and about the day's business. No, Pavel. This is the end of it. It's not that I don't love you, but my nerves can't take any more. After they've arrested you, tell them they'll find me at home. (*She abandons Pavel at the big poplar and scuttles off back home.*)

Pavel Are you leaving me?

Praskovya (*a voice in the night*) Yes.

Pavel You can't!

Praskovya I have!

Pavel, irresolutely, tries to stand his ground.

As the first light of day waxes, his courage wanes. Eventually . . .

Pavel Praskovya!

He hurries after Praskovya.

The sty. Praskovya is waiting. Pavel bursts in . . . a dishevelled, desperate figure. He has been running and it takes him a few seconds to get his breath back.

Your pious soul will rejoice to hear that an Avenging Angel of the Lord did appear to chase Adam out of Eden. It took the form of a big, vicious brute with a black muzzle and long white fangs who came snarling at me out of the darkness. I've got his teeth marks on my ankle to prove it. (*looking around with disbelief*) I don't believe it! I'm back in here. I was actually out in the world . . . the world of men and women, trees and flowers, of sunsets and sunrises . . . it was there in front of me, a road leading to a new life, but of my own free will, I turned around and came *running* . . . yes, *running*! . . . back to this. Oh, God. I was so near escaping. One small burst of courage! That was all it needed. And if you had given me a little support and encouragement, Praskovya, I would have found that courage. A few words would have done it. 'Here's my hand, Pavel. Let's walk.' So what if it had only lasted a few golden hours? Wouldn't that have been better than the next eternity of this? But no, here I am again . . . And why? Because you have finally come to believe that this is where I belong. My Home! Yes, that wasn't just an insensitive slip of the tongue out there, was it!! That is what you believe!

Praskovya tries to say something.

So what does that make me? A pig?

Another attempt from Praskovya to speak.

Some sort of superior pig that God has endowed with language and rational thought? Your favourite, your pet pig who you favour with bowls of cabbage soup and dumplings while the others get hogwash. Is that how you see me now? (*Pavel leaves Praskovya, wanders around the sty and then steadies himself for a final declaration.*) For thirty years I have tried to hang on to my manhood in here, tried to defend my dignity against assaults on every front . . . body, mind and soul. Your betrayal is the last straw. I am broken. These are the last words that you will ever hear from me. I abandon my humanity! From now on, Praskovya, feed me at the trough with the others.

He tears off his clothes and throws himself naked into one of the pens with the pigs. A few seconds of silence while Praskovya considers this development. She then gets up and goes over to the pen where Pavel has joined the pigs.

Praskovya I hope you're not being serious, Pavel.

No response.

Because if you are . . . well . . . I think you might have gone too far this time. This is very insulting, I'll have you know, both to me and to God. I married a man, not a pig, and as far as the Almighty is concerned, I'm sure he'd like me to remind you that you're supposed to be made in His image. So for the sake of everybody concerned, please get out of there.

No response.

You are provoking me, Pavel. I warn you I might do something we are both going to regret. So for the last

time, I beg you. Get out of there. (*She kneels and prays.*)
Dear Lord Jesus Christ, I know it's all wrong to be down
on my knees praying to you in a pigsty, but I need your
understanding and forgiveness at this moment as never
before in my life. Dear Lord Jesus, I am being tempted to
sin very badly. Feelings I never knew I had have got hold
of my soul and are trying to make me do wicked, wicked
things. The reason for this urgent prayer, Lord Jesus, is
to beg you, to beseech you . . . please *don't* give me the
strength to resist temptation. Amen. (*Praskovya gets up
and fetches Pavel's stick. She rolls up her sleeves, kicks
off her shoes, tucks her skirt into her bloomers and then
climbs into the pen.*) This is going to hurt me every bit as
much as I intend hurting you.

    Pavel gets his first whack. A cry of pain.

Out you get! Come on. Move!

    *Another whack, another cry. Pavel crawls frantically
    out of the sty. Praskovya keeps after him.*

If you want me to stop . . . *ask* me.

    Another blow . . . another cry.

You better speak to me, Pavel, because I hate to say it,
but this isn't hurting me at all.

Pavel (*can't take any more*) Stop! Stop! You're killing me!

Praskovya Don't worry, I won't go that far. But I would
like to hear a few more words.

    Another whack.

Pavel Stop it, Praskovya! Have you gone mad?

Praskovya Now on to your legs.

Pavel No. Leave me alone.

Praskovya puts all she's got into one final blow.

All right! All right! (*He crawls to his feet.*)

Praskovya We've done it!

Pavel Help me, Praskovya . . . help me!

Praskovya fetches a bucket of water and empties it over him.

Praskovya You're on your two legs again, Pavel, and talking. That's as much as I can do for you. Now help yourself . . .

She exits. Pavel alone . . . naked, covered in mud and hurting . . . a picture of abject misery.

Scene Four

ORDERS FROM THE COMMISSAR

Night. Pavel, still naked and dirty, but now wrapped in one of his blankets. He sits, a lonely, desolate figure in the Stygian gloom of the sty. He is totally exhausted and talking to himself in a desperate effort to stay awake. Pig noises as usual from the darkness.

Pavel Right step, march, left step, march. Comrade Private, head up . . . come on . . . Up! Up! Open your eyes. (*responding*) There. Wide open!

They are. No, they're not. You're falling asleep again.

Because I am tired for God's sake! I am utterly and totally exhausted.

No no no no, Pavel. If you close your eyes and sleep through another night in here, that will be the end of it.

Then do something. Help me! I'll tell you a story, Pavel. Are you listening? Once upon a time, in a small village, there was a very very stupid man who woke up one morning and decided that he wanted to be a pig.

Oh shut up! Don't you want to hear the rest of it?

It's got a very funny ending, Pavel. His feet turn into trotters, his nose becomes a snout . . .

I said shut up!

(*looking around*) I'm awake. Thank God. That was close! OK . . . Back to work. Where were we? Yes . . . we were dealing with the extremely critical situation which has developed in here, and we were . . . going to . . . we were going . . . to . . . we . . . were . . . going . . . to . . . (*His head falls forward. A few seconds of sleep.*) PAVEL!!! (*He snaps awake with terror and guilt.*) I didn't do it! I didn't do it! I swear I didn't do it!

(*an oily, evil voice*) Naughty . . . naughty! You got away with a few seconds there, didn't you? Very naughty, little Pavel. I think Daddy should take off his belt and drag you out from under the bed and give you a bloody good thrashing!!

(*abject terror*) I'm sorry, I'm sorry. I won't do it again.

Don't waste our time with promises. We've had them from you before and they've all come to nothing. You know something, Navrotsky . . . you're a total failure . . . and a pathetic one at that! Praskovya was right . . . all you've learnt in here is how to whine and wallow in with self-pity.

(*nodding encouragement*) Good, good . . . keep it up keep it up . . . Oh, you're finally interested in the truth, are you? Right! You are also a cowardly deserter . . . a traitor to your Motherland . . . And for what? Can you even remember why you betrayed your country and its people? A pair of slippers. (*heavily sarcastic tone of voice*) A pair of pretty red slippers which dear old Mama made for her darling little Pavel.

DON'T drag my mother into this! Say anything you like about me but *leave my mother alone*!

What do you mean 'leave her alone'! Giving birth to you makes the old bitch an accomplice in all your treachery.

STOP NOW! (*Pause.*)

WELL done, Pavel. Well done. Brutal and ugly . . . but it worked. Head clear? Oh yes. Crystal clear. Then back to work. No sleep in here until we have found a solution to my now very desperate dilemma. To do that we first need to get to the Root of the Matter, the Root of the Problem. And while we're digging around looking for it, let's keep an eye open at the same time for The Last Straw so that at long last we can get on with it and break the bloody Camel's Back. But hang on now, not so fast! Why waste a perfectly good last straw on imaginary camels when we've got so many fucking real pigs that need to have their backs broken? Now we're getting somewhere. We are going to take that Last Straw and break the back of every fucking pig in here. (wild laughter). Crack crack crack crack crack crack crack. Bravo! You've done it, Pavel . . . Pavel . . . Pavel . . . Pavel . . . (*His lunacy spirals away into a voice of quiet and final despair.*) Pavel . . . Pavel . . . stop now. Leave the pigs alone. And if you can't do that . . . why don't you then just let them go? (*Pause. Pavel floats back slowly out of his delirium.*) Who said that? Where did that thought come from? Me.

(*to his mirror*) *You* said that?

Yes.

Say it again. Those animals have endured enough abuse from you, Pavel. Why don't you just let them go now?

Just like that? Just . . .

That's right. Just open the doors, then open the pens and let them go. (*Pavel is left almost speechless by the unexpectedness of the idea.*)

Unbelievable! So simple . . . so obvious! . . . just let them go. Yes yes yes . . . of course! It makes total sense. Just . . . open the doors, open the pens and let them go!

(*back to his mirror*) Then do it, Pavel.

Now?

Yes. Now! What are you waiting for?

All right, all right. Hold your horses while I think about my pigs. Your suggestion might be simple, but that doesn't mean it's easy. It involves me ending a relationship that has survived decades of filth and nonsense and mutual abuse. I can't just turn my back on it and walk away as if it all meant nothing.

(*laughing at himself in disbelief*) My God, Pavel, you're amazing! You're up to your old tricks, aren't you? You're stalling for time. Yes, we've caught you at it again . . .

backing away from the moment of decision and action. Well, it has got to stop! You are going to do it and you are going to do it now. Open the doors, open the pens and let them go. That's an order.

All right. All right. (*A terrified Pavel obeys orders. His first move is to throw open the doors to the outside world. He then goes around the pens, waking up the pigs.*) Wake up! Wake up! (*kicking and rattling boards*) Come on! It's all over. Your hour of liberation has come. The Commissar has ordered your immediate and unconditional release.

Pig noises increase in volume and agitation as the animals stir into life.

All of you . . . onto your trotters . . . Can't you smell it? Freedom! Now out . . . out . . . out . . .

Pavel opens the pens. The pandemonium rises to a powerful climax as the animals stampede out of the sty. Praskovya appears. Nightgown and lamp. She sees the open door, the empty pens and realizes what Pavel has done. The sound of liberated, squealing pigs recedes in the distance. A few stunned seconds as the two of them listen to the virginal silence in the sty. Praskovya sits down next to Pavel.

Praskovya (*whisper*) It's like being in church, isn't it? You feel you've got to say everything in a whisper . . . and think only good thoughts. And so . . . suddenly so calm. And peaceful. My word, Pavel, this is very hard to believe, you know. I never thought it could ever feel like this in here. All the years and years of shouting and violence . . . just gone! (*shaking her head*) No. This has got to be a dream.

Pavel You're awake, Praskovya.

Praskovya It's really all over?

144

Pavel Yes.

Praskovya How did you do it?

Pavel I obeyed orders.

Praskovya What do you mean? Orders from who?

Pavel (*pointing to the mirror*) Him. 'The Commissar'! Don't ask me where he came from or what he was doing in here. A good soldier, which I never was, doesn't ask questions. He just obeys orders. They were very simple. 'Open the doors, open the pens and let them go.'

Praskovya Just like that?

Pavel Just like that.

Praskovya (*suppressed laugh but still whispering*) I think there's something wrong with me. You've just chased our livelihood out into the night . . . our only source of income . . . our one and only security . . . we sit here on the brink of ruin and all I want to do is laugh. What about you?

Pavel I feel nothing.

Praskovya Well, I'm sorry, but I can't help it . . . I want to laugh.

Pavel Go ahead.

Praskovya You don't laugh in church, Pavel!

But she does so all the same. Praskovya has a long, side-splitting silent laugh at themselves and their ruination . . . gestures to the open doors, the empty pens, themselves . . . 'All is kaput' . . . etc. etc. Her laugh is infectious. Exhausted as he is, Pavel manages a faint flicker of a response.

And now I want to cry.

Pavel Go ahead. You're allowed to do that in church, aren't you?

Praskovya Oh, yes . . . and as loud as you like. (*wiping her eyes*) Oh, Pavel, I'm so proud of you! I would never have had the imagination or the courage to do it.

Pavel Imagination? Courage? Who are you talking about, Praskovya?

Praskovya You.

Pavel (*shaking his head*) It wasn't like that at all. It was exhaustion that did it. Total and final mental, physical and spiritual exhaustion. I *had* to do something, and that was all I could think of.

Praskovya This is no time for modesty, Pavel. With that one bold move you have freed us. Let me confess to you now that I had finally given up all hope of us ever escaping from it. I had come to believe that only death would end our misery . . . and I was more than ready for mine. In fact, if you're interested in the truth, Pavel, I was down on my knees telling the Good Lord as much when I heard the commotion down here. But instead, here we sit like two ordinary people with nothing better to do. I don't know about you, but I feel a little light-headed and silly . . . silly enough in fact to want to sing a little song . . .

Pavel A song! That's right! People . . . sing, don't they?

Praskovya When they're happy, but sometimes also when they're sad. Mine would have been a happy song.

Pavel Do you still know one?

Praskovya I think so. (*She sings a little happy song.*) So what is the next bold move, Pavel?

Pavel (*the open doors*) Isn't it obvious?

Praskovya You're going out there again?

Pavel (*nods*) But I won't hide away in your dress this time. I'm going out there as myself. (*a helpless gesture*) I didn't know it was coming. I thought I was just getting rid of the pigs so that I could have a little peace and quiet in here. I wanted to close my eyes and sleep more than I've wanted anything in my whole life. But when they started stampeding through those doors to their freedom . . .!!! God, Praskovya, it was epic! The stuff of history. I wanted to join them. If I'd had any clothes on I would have led that charge of liberation out into the world.

Praskovya You are going to surrender to the authorities?

Pavel Yes. It's a crooked fate that ties up a man's freedom and his surrender in the same bundle, but I've got no choice. (*the weak and desperate little smile of the faint-hearted*) I think it's another order . . . to go out there and face judgment and take my punishment. It's been a long loneliness in here. I've forgotten what it means, what it feels like to look into another man's eyes . . . or to be looked at by them. I'm still frightened . . . but there is something else now as well and it's bigger than my fear . . . I'm homesick, Praskovya, for other men and women. I don't belong in here. Even if my punishment turns out to be a firing squad . . . those men, looking at me down the barrels of their guns, will be 'home' in a way this sty could never have been.

Praskovya So then let's do it. I'll get you something to wear. (*Starts to leave and then stops.*) It's a pity we can't take on that walk to Barabinsk. I'm ready for it now.

She exits. First faint light of the new day through the open doors. Pavel gets a bucket of water and starts to wash himself. The graffiti on the walls catches his attention. He takes a rag and tries to clean it off. Too exhausted to do a thorough job. Praskovya comes back with Pavel's black wedding suit. She has changed out of her nightgown.

Pavel What do you have there?

Praskovya Don't you recognize it? Your wedding suit.

Pavel My God. That goes back a few years. Is it still wearable?

Praskovya Oh, yes. After all that drama we had about your uniform, I've made a point of looking after this very carefully. I had a feeling you might need it again one day.

Pavel starts to change into the suit.

How are we going to do it, Pavel? There aren't any anniversary celebrations on the go this time. I don't think it will work to just stand on a street corner and announce to the world who you are and what you've done. I'm not sure anybody will bother to listen to you. There are all sorts of loonies around these days and nobody pays them any attention except the police. Maybe that's your best idea, the police station.

Pavel (*offended*) I'm not just a common criminal, Praskovya. As I remember it, the *Military Manual* listed desertion as one of the most serious offences a soldier could commit. I'll hand myself over at the military barracks. (*He is now dressed.*) Come . . . let's go.

Praskovya If it's any consolation, I think we're in time for the sunrise you missed yesterday.

They leave the sty.

MY CHILDREN! MY AFRICA!

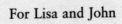

For Lisa and John

Characters

Mr M
Thami
Isabel

My Children! My Africa! was first performed at the
Market Theatre, Johannesburg, on 27 June 1989.
The cast was as follows:

Mr M John Kani
Thami Rapulana Seiphemo
Isabel Kathy-Jo Ross

Director Athol Fugard
Designer Susan Hilferty
Lighting Mannie Manim

Act One

SCENE ONE

Classroom of the Zolile High School.

Mr M is at a table with Thami and Isabel on either side of him. A lively inter-school debate is in progress. Everybody is speaking at the same time.

Mr M Order please!

Isabel I never said anything of the kind.

Thami Yes you did. You said that women were more –

Mr M I call you both to order!

Isabel What I said was that women –

Thami . . . were more emotional than men –

Isabel Correction! That women were more intuitive than men –

Mr M Miss Dyson and Mr Mbikwana! Will you both please –

Isabel You are twisting my words and misquoting me.

Thami I am not. I am simply asking you –

Mr M Come to order!

Grabs the school bell and rings it violently. It works. Silence.

I think it is necessary for me to remind all of you exactly what a debate is supposed to be. (*Opens and reads from a little black dictionary that is at hand on the table.*) My dictionary defines it as follows: 'The orderly and

regulated discussion of an issue with opposing
viewpoints receiving equal time and consideration.'
Shouting down the opposition so that they cannot be
heard does not comply with that definition. Enthusiasm
for your cause is most commendable but without
personal discipline it is as useless as having a good
donkey and a good cart but no harness. We are now
running out of time. I am therefore closing the open
section of our debate. No more interruptions from
the floor please. We'll bring our proceedings to a close
with a brief, I repeat *brief,* three minutes at the most,
summing up of our arguments. Starting with the
proposers of the motion: Mr Thami Mbikwana of
the Zolile High School, will you please make your
concluding statement.

*Thami stands up. Wild round of applause from the
audience. He is secure and at ease: he is speaking to
an audience of schoolmates. His 'concluding statement' is outrageous; and he knows it and enjoys it.*

Thami I don't stand here now and speak to you as your
friend and schoolmate. That would lessen the seriousness
of my final words to you. No! Close your eyes, forget
that you know my face and voice, forget that you know
anything about Thami Mbikwana. Think of me rather as
an oracle, of my words as those of the great ancestors of
our traditional African culture, which we turn our back
on and desert to our great peril!

The opposition has spoken about sexual exploitation
and the need for women's liberation. Brothers and
sisters, these are foreign ideas. Do not listen to them.
They come from a culture, the so-called Western
Civilization, that has meant only misery to Africa and
its people. It is the same culture that shipped away
thousands of our ancestors as slaves, the same culture
that has exploited Africa with the greed of a vulture

during the period of colonialism, and the same culture which continues to exploit us in the twentieth century, under the disguise of concern for our future. The opposition has not been able to refute my claim that women cannot do the same jobs as men because they are not the equals of us physically and that a woman's role in the family, in society, is totally different to that of a man's. These facts taken together reinforce what our fathers, and our grandfathers and our great-grandfathers knew; namely that happiness and prosperity for the tribe and the nation is achieved when education of the little ladies takes these facts into consideration. Would it be right for a woman to go to war while man sits at the sewing machine? I do not have milk in my breasts to feed the baby while my wife is out digging up roads for the Divisional Council.

Wild laughter.

Brothers and sisters, it is obvious that you feel the same as I do about this most serious matter. I hope that at the end of this debate, your vote will reflect your agreement with me.

Wild applause and whistles.

Mr M Thank you, Mr Mbikwana.

Thami sits.

And now finally, a last statement from the captain of the visiting team, Miss Isabel Dyson of Camdeboo Girls' High.

Polite applause. Isabel stands. She takes on the audience with direct, unflinching eye contact. She is determined not to be intimidated.

Isabel You have had to listen to a lot of talk this after- noon about traditional values, traditional society, your great ancestors, your glorious past. In spite of what has been implied I want to start off by telling you that I have as much respect and admiration for your history and tradition as anybody else. I believe most strongly that there are values and principles in traditional African society which could be studied with great profit by the Western Civilization so scornfully rejected by the previous speaker. But at the same time, I know, and you know, that Africa no longer lives in that past. For better or for worse it is part now of the twentieth century and all the nations on this continent are struggling very hard to come to terms with that reality. Arguments about sacred traditional values, the traditional way of life, etcetera and etcetera, are used by those who would like to hold back Africa's progress and keep it locked up in the past. Maybe there was a time in the past when a woman's life consisted of bearing children and hoeing the fields while men sharpened their spears and sat around waiting for another war to start. But it is a silly argument that relies on that old image of primitive Africa for its strength. It is an argument that insults your intelligence. Times have changed. Sheer brute strength is not the determining factor any more. You do not need the muscles of a prize fighter when you sit down to operate the computers that control today's world. The American space programme now has women astronauts on board the space shuttles doing the same jobs as men. As for the difference in the emotional and intellectual qualities of men and women, remember that it is a question of difference and not inferiority and that with those differences go strengths which compensate for weaknesses in the opposite sex.

And lastly, a word of warning. The argument against equality for women, in education or any other field, based on alleged 'differences' between the two sexes, is an argument that can very easily be used against any other 'different' group. It is an argument based on prejudice, not fact. I ask you not to give it your support. Thank you.

She sits. Polite applause.

Mr M Thank you, Miss Dyson. We come now to the vote. But before we do that, a word of caution. We have had a wonderful experience this afternoon. Don't let it end on a frivolous and irresponsible note. Serious issues have been debated. Vote accordingly. To borrow a phrase from Mr Mbikwana, forget the faces, remember the words. If you believe that we have the right to vote out there in the big world, then show here, in the classroom, that you know how to use it. We'll take it on a count of hands, and for the benefit of any over-enthusiastic supporters, only one hand per person please. Let me read the proposal once again: 'That in view of the essential physical and psychological differences between men and women, there should be correspondingly different educational syllabuses for the two sexes.' All those in favour raise a hand.

Mr M, Thami and Isabel count hands.

Seventeen?

Thami and Isabel nod agreement.

All those against.

They all count again.

Twenty-four?

Reactions from Thami and Isabel.

The proposal is defeated by twenty-four votes to seventeen. Before we break just a reminder about the special choir practice this afternoon. Members of the choir must please join Mrs Magada in Number Two Classroom after school.

(*to Isabel and Thami*) Allow me to offer you my congratulations, Miss Dyson, on a most well-deserved victory. What do you say, Mbikwana?

Thami (*to Isabel*) Your concluding statement was a knockout.

Mr M You didn't do too badly yourself.

Isabel You made me so angry!

Thami (*all innocence*) I did?

Isabel Ja, you did.

Thami laughs.

I was beginning to think you actually believed what you were saying.

Thami But I do!

Isabel Oh, come on . . .!

Mr M (*rubbing his hands with pleasure*) All I can say is . . . Splendid! Splendid! Splendid! The intellect in action. Challenge and response. That is what a good debate is all about. And whatever you do, young lady, don't underestimate your achievement in winning the popular vote. It wasn't easy for that audience to vote against Mbikwana. He's one of them, and a very popular 'one of them' I might add. (*waving a finger at Thami*) You were quite shameless in the way you tried to exploit that loyalty.

Thami (*another laugh*) Was that wrong?

Mr M No. As the saying goes, all is fair in love, war and debating. But the fact that you didn't succeed is what makes me really happy. I am very proud of our audience. In my humble opinion they are the real winners this afternoon. You two just had to talk and argue. Anybody

160

can do that. They had to listen . . . intelligently!

Isabel They certainly gave me a good time.

Mr M That was very apparent, if I may say so, Miss Dyson. I can't thank you enough for coming to us today. I sincerely hope there'll be another occasion.

Isabel Same here.

Mr M Good! (*Consults his watch.*) Now you must excuse me. There is a staff meeting waiting for me. Will you look after Miss Dyson, please, Mbikwana?

Thami Yes, teacher.

Mr M leaves. Isabel and Thami pack away into their school cases the papers and books they used in the debate. Without the mediating presence of Mr M they are both a little self-conscious. First moves in the ensuing conversation are awkward.

Isabel I wish we had a teacher like . . . Mr . . . (*pronouncing the name carefully*) M ya lat ya. Did I say it right?

Thami Yes you did, but nobody calls him that. He's just plain Mr M to everybody.

Isabel Mr M.

Thami That's right.

Isabel Well, I think he's wonderful.

Thami He's OK.

Isabel I had a geography teacher in Standard Seven who was a little bit like him. Full of fun and lots of energy.

Thami Ja, that's Mr M all right.

Pause.

Isabel I meant what I said to him. I really did have a good time.

Thami Same here.

Isabel You did? Because to be honest with you, I wasn't expecting it.

Thami Me neither.

Isabel No?

Thami Nope.

Isabel Why not?

Thami (*embarrassed*) Well . . . you know . . .

Isabel Let me guess. You've never debated with girls before.

He nods, smiling sheepishly.

And white girls at that! I don't believe it. You boys are all the same.

Thami But you were good!

Isabel Because I happen to feel very strongly about what we were debating. But it was also the whole atmosphere you know. It was so . . . so free and easy. The debates at my school are such stuffy affairs. And so boring most of the time. Everything is done according to the rules with everybody being polite and nobody getting excited . . . lots of discipline but very little enthusiasm. This one was a riot!

Thami (*finger to his lips*) Be careful.

Isabel Of what?

Thami That word.

162

Isabel Which one?

Thami Riot! Don't say it in a black township. Police start shooting as soon as they hear it.

Isabel Oh . . . I'm sorry . . .

Thami (*having a good laugh*) It's a joke, Isabel.

Isabel Oh . . . you caught me off guard. I didn't think you would joke about those things.

Thami Riots and police? Oh yes, we joke about them. We joke about everything.

Isabel OK, then I'll say it again; this afternoon was a riot.

Thami Good! Try that one on your folks when you get home tonight. Say the newspapers have got it all wrong. You had a wonderful time taking part in a little township riot.

This time Isabel does get the joke. They have a good laugh.

Isabel Oh ja, I can just see my mom and dad cracking up at that one.

Thami They wouldn't think it was funny? (*The subject of white reaction to location humour amuses him enormously.*)

Isabel Are you kidding? They even take the Marx Brothers seriously. I can just hear my mom: 'I think it is very wrong to joke about these things, Isabel!'

Thami Dyson! That's an English name.

Isabel Sober, sensible, English-speaking South African. I'm the third generation.

Thami What does your dad do?

Isabel He's a chemist. The chemist shop in town. Karoo Pharmacy. That's ours. My mother and sister work in it as well, and on Saturdays, provided there isn't a hockey match, so do I.

Thami Any brothers?

Isabel No. Just the four of us.

Thami A happy family.

Isabel Ja, I suppose you could call us that. Mind you, Lucille would say it would be a lot happier if only her little sister would be, as she puts it, 'more accommodating of others'.

Thami What does she mean?

Isabel She means she doesn't like the fact that I've got opinions of my own. I'm the rebel in the family.

Thami That sounds interesting.

Isabel I can't help it. Whenever it's time for a family *indaba* . . . you know, when we sit down in the lounge to discuss family business and things . . . I just always seem to end up disagreeing with everybody and wanting to do things differently. But other than that, ja, an average sort of happy family. What else do you want to know? Go ahead, anything . . . provided I also get a turn to ask questions.

Thami studies her.

Eighteen years old. I think I want to be a writer. My favourite subject is English and my favourite sport, as you might have guessed, is hockey. Anything else?

Thami Yes. What did you have for breakfast this morning?

164

Isabel Auntie, our maid, put down in front of me a plate of steaming, delicious jungle oats over which I sprinkled a crust of golden brown sugar, and while that was melting on top I added a little moat of chilled milk all around the side. That was followed by brown-bread toast, quince jam and lots and lots of tea.

Thami Yes, you're a writer.

Isabel You think so?

Thami You made me hungry.

Isabel My turn now?

Thami Yep.

Isabel Let's start with your family.

Thami Mbikwana! (*He clears his throat.*) Mbikwana is an old Bantu name and my mother and my father are good, reliable, ordinary, hard-working Bantu-speaking black South African natives. I am the one-hundred-thousandth generation.

Isabel You really like teasing, don't you.

Thami Amos and Lilian Mbikwana. They're in Cape Town. My mother is a domestic and my father works for the railways. I stay here with my grandmother and married sister. I was sent to school in the peaceful platteland because it is so much safer, you see, than the big city with all its temptations and troubles. (*Laughs.*) Another Bantu joke.

Isabel You're impossible!

*They are now beginning to relax with each other.
Isabel finds the class register on the desk.*

'Zolile High School. Standard Ten.' (*Opens it and reads.*) Awu.

Thami (*pointing to the appropriate desk in the classroom*) There. Johnny. Centre-forward in our soccer team.

Isabel Bandla.

Thami There.

Isabel Cwati.

Thami There.

Isabel Who was the chap sitting there who laughed at *all* your jokes and applauded *everything* you said?

Thami Stephen Gaika. He's mad!

Isabel Your best friend?

Thami They are all my friends.

Isabel And where does . . . (*Finds his name in the register.*) Thami Mbikwana sit?

Thami points. Isabel goes to the desk and sits.

Thami Yes, that's the one. For nearly two years I've sat there . . . being educated!

Isabel (*reading names carved into the wood of the desk*) John, Bobby, Zola, Bo . . . Boni . . .

Thami Bonisile.

Isabel Where's your name?

Thami You won't find it there. I don't want to leave any part of me in this classroom.

Isabel That sounds heavy.

Thami It's been heavy. You've got no problems with it, hey?

Isabel With school? No, not really. Couple of teachers have tried their best to spoil it for me, but they haven't succeeded. I've had a pretty good time in fact. I think I might even end up with the old cliché . . . you know, school years, best years, happiest years . . . Whatever it is they say.

Thami No. I won't be saying that.

Isabel That surprises me.

Thami Why?

Isabel Ja, come on, wouldn't you be if I said it? You're obviously clever. I'll bet you sail through your exams.

Thami It's not as simple as just passing exams, Isabel. School doesn't mean the same to us that it does to you.

Isabel Go on.

Thami I used to like it. Junior school? You should have seen me. I wanted to have school on Saturdays and Sundays as well. Yes, I did. Other boys wanted to kill me. I hated the holidays.

Isabel So what happened?

Thami I changed.

Isabel Ja, I'm listening.

Thami (*a shrug*) That's all. I changed. Things changed. Everything changed.

Isabel (*realizing she is not going to get any more out of him*) Only five months to go.

Thami I'm counting.

Isabel What then?

Thami After school? (*another shrug*) I don't know yet. Do you?

Isabel Ja. Rhodes University. I want to study journalism.

167

Thami Newspaper reporter.

Isabel And radio, TV. It's a very wide field now. You can specialize in all sorts of things. (*perplexed*) Don't you want to study further, Thami?

Thami I told you, I'm not sure about anything yet.

Isabel What does Mr M say?

Thami It's got nothing to do with him.

Isabel But you're his favourite, aren't you?

   Non-committal shrug from Thami.

I bet you are. And I also bet you anything you like that he's got a career planned out for you.

Thami (*sharply*) What I do with my life has got nothing to do with him.

Isabel Sorry.

Thami I don't listen to what he says and I don't do what he says.

Isabel I said I'm sorry, I didn't mean to interfere.

Thami That's all right. It's just that he makes me so mad sometimes. He always thinks *he* knows what is best for me. He never asks me how I feel about things. I know he means well, but I'm not a child any more. I've got ideas of my own now.

Isabel (*placating*) Ja, I know what you mean. I've had them in my life as well. They always know what is best for you, don't they? So anyway, listen . . . I'm going to write up the debate for our school newspaper. I'll send you a copy if you like.

Thami You got a school newspaper! How about that!

Isabel It's a bit unethical reporting on a contest in which
I took part, and won, but I promise to be objective.
I made notes of most of your main points.

Thami You can have my speech if you want it.

Isabel Hell, thanks. That will make it much easier . . .
and guarantee there won't be any misquotes!

*Thami hands over the speech. It is obvious that
they both want to prolong the conversation, but this
is prevented by the sound of Mr M's bell being rung
vigorously in the distance. They check their
wristwatches.*

Isabel Oh my God, look at the time!

They grab their schoolcases and run.

SCENE TWO

Isabel alone. She speaks directly to the audience.

Isabel It's on the edge of town, on the right-hand side
when you drive out to join the National Road going
north to Middelberg. Unfortunately, as most of
Camdeboo would say, you can't miss it. I discovered the
other day that it has actually got a name – Brakwater –
from the old farm that used to be there. Now everybody
just calls it 'the location'. There's been a lot of talk lately
about moving it to where it can't be seen. Our mayor,
Mr Pienaar, was in our shop the other day and I heard
him say to my dad that it was 'very much to be
regretted' that the first thing that greeted any visitor to
the town was the 'terrible mess of the location'. To be
fair to old Pienaar he has got a point, you know. Our
town is very pretty. We've got a lot of nicely restored
National Monument houses and buildings. 'Specially in

the main street. Our shop is one of them. The location is quite an eyesore by comparison. Most of the houses – if you can call them that! – are made of bits of old corrugated iron or anything else they could find to make four walls and a roof. There are no gardens or anything like that. You've got to drive in first gear all the time because of the potholes and stones, and when the wind is blowing and all the dust and rubbish flying around . . .! I think you'd be inclined to agree with our mayor. I've actually been into it quite a few times. With my mom to visit Auntie, our maid, when she was sick. And with my dad when he had to take emergency medicines to the clinic. I can remember one visit, just sitting in the car and staring out of the window trying to imagine what it would be like to live my whole life in one of those little pondoks. No electricity, no running water. No privacy! Auntie's little house has only got two small rooms and nine of them sleep there. I ended up being damn glad I was born with a white skin.

But don't get the wrong idea. I'm not saying I've spent a lot of time thinking about it seriously or anything like that. It's just been there, you know, on the edge of my life, the way it is out there on the edge of town. So when Miss Brockway, our principal, called me in and told me that the black school has started a debating society and had invited us over for a debate, I didn't have any objections. She said it was a chance for a 'pioneering intellectual exchange' between the two schools. She also said she had checked with the police and they had said it would be all right provided we were driven straight to the school and then straight out afterwards. There's been a bit of trouble in the location again and people are starting to get nervous about it. So off we went – myself, Renée Vermaas and Cathy Bullard, the CGH Debating Team – feeling very virtuous about our 'pioneering' mission into the location. As Renée tactfully put it:

'Shame! We must remember that English isn't their home language. So don't use too many big words and speak slowly and carefully.'

They were waiting for us in what they called Number One Classroom. (*shaking her head*) Honestly, I would rate it as the most bleak, depressing, dingy classroom I have ever been in. Everything about it was grey – the cement floor, the walls, the ceiling. When I first saw it I thought to myself, how in God's name does anybody study or learn anything in here. But there they were, about forty of them, my age, mostly boys, not one welcoming smile among the lot of them. And they *were* studying something and very intently . . . three privileged and uncomfortable white girls, in smart uniforms, from a posh school, who had come to give them a lesson in debating. I know I'm a good debater and one of the reasons for that is that I always talk very directly to the audience and the opposition. I am not shy about making eye contact. Well, when I did it this time, when it was my turn to speak and I stood up and looked at those forty unsmiling faces, I suddenly realized that I hadn't prepared myself for one simple but all important fact: they had no intention of being grateful to me. They were sitting there waiting to judge me, what I said and how I said it, on the basis of total equality. Maybe it doesn't sound like such a big thing to you, but you must understand I had never really confronted that before, and I don't just mean in debates. I mean in my life!

I'm not saying I've had no contact across the colour line. Good heavens no! I get as much of that as any average young white South African. I have a great time every morning with Auntie in the kitchen when she's cooking breakfast and we gossip about everything and everybody in town. And then there's Samuel with his crash helmet and scooter . . . he delivers medicines for my dad . . . I have wonderful long conversations with

him about religion and the meaning of life generally.
He's a very staunch Zionist. Church every Sunday. But
it's always 'Miss Isabel', the *baas*' daughter, that he's
talking to. When I stood up in front of those black
matric. pupils in Number One Classroom it was a very
different story. I wasn't at home or in my dad's shop or
in my school or any of the other safe places in my life.
I was in Brakwater! It was *their* school. It was *their*
world. I was the outsider and I was being asked to prove
myself. Standing there in front of them like that I felt . . .
exposed! . . . in a way that has never happened to me
before. Cathy told me afterwards that she's never heard
me start a debate so badly and finish it so strongly.

God, it was good! I don't know when exactly it happened, but about halfway through my opening address,
I realized that everything about that moment . . . the
miserable little classroom, myself, my voice, what I was
saying and them hearing and understanding me, because
I knew they understood me . . . they were staring and
listening so hard I could feel it on my skin! . . . all of it
had become one of the most real experiences I have ever
had. I have never before had so . . . so exciting! . . . a
sense of myself. Because that is what we all want, isn't
it? For things to be real, our lives, our thoughts, what we
say and do? That's what I want, now. I didn't really
know it before that debate, but I do now. You see
I finally worked out what happened to me in the classroom. I discovered a new world! I've always thought
about the location as just a sort of embarrassing back
yard to our neat and proper little white world, where
our maids and our gardeners and our delivery boys went
at the end of the day. But it's not. It's a whole world of
its own with its own life that has nothing to do with us.
If you put together all the Brakwaters in the country,
then it's a pretty big one – and if you'll excuse my language, there's a hell of a lot of people living in it! That's

quite a discovery you know. But it's also a little . . .
what's the word? . . . disconcerting! You see, it means
that what I thought was out there for me . . . No, it's
worse than that! It's what I was made to believe was out
there for me . . . the ideas, the chances, the people . . .
'specially the people! . . . all of that is only a small
fraction of what it could be. (*shaking her head*) No.
Or as Auntie says in the kitchen when she's not happy
about something . . . *Aikona!* Not good enough. I'm
greedy. I want more. I want as much as I can get.

SCENE THREE

Isabel alone.
  *Mr M enters, hat in hand, mopping his brow with a
handkerchief.*

Mr M Miss Dyson! There you are.

Isabel (*surprised*) Hello!

Mr M My apologies for descending on you out of the
blue like this but I've been looking for you high and low.
One of your schoolmates said I would find you here.

Isabel Don't apologize. It's a pleasure to see you again,
Mr M.

Mr M (*delighted*) Mr M! How wonderful to hear you
call me that.

Isabel You must blame Thami for my familiarity.

Mr M Blame him? On the contrary, I will thank him
most gratefully. Hearing you call me Mr M like all the
others at the school gives me a happy feeling that you
are also a member of my very extended family.

Isabel I'd like to be.

Mr M Then welcome to my family, Miss –

Isabel (*before he can say it*) 'Isabel' if you please, Mr M, just plain 'Isabel'.

Mr M (*bowing*) Then doubly welcome, young Isabel.

Isabel (*curtsey*) I thank you, kind sir.

Mr M You have great charm, young lady. I can understand now how you managed to leave so many friends behind you after only one visit to the school. Hardly a day passes without someone stopping me and asking: 'When is Isabel Dyson and her team coming back?'

Isabel Well? When are we?

Mr M You would still welcome a return visit?

Isabel But of course.

Mr M Why so emphatically 'of course'?

Isabel Because I enjoyed the first one so emphatically very much.

Mr M The unruly behaviour of my young family wasn't too much for you?

Isabel Didn't I also get a little unruly once or twice, Mr M?

Mr M Yes, now that you mention it. You certainly gave as good as you got.

Isabel (*with relish*) And that is precisely why I enjoyed myself . . .

Mr M You like a good fight.

Isabel Ja. 'Specially the ones I win!

Mr M Splendid! Splendid! Splendid! Because that is precisely what I have come to offer you.

Isabel Your Thami wants a return bout, does he?

Mr M He will certainly welcome the opportunity to salvage his pride when it comes along . . . his friends are teasing him mercilessly . . . but what I have come to talk to you about is a prospect even more exciting than that. I have just seen Miss Brockway and she has given it her official blessing. It was her suggestion that I approach you directly. So here I am. Can you spare a few minutes?

Isabel As many as you like.

Mr M It came to me as I sat there in Number One trying to be an impartial referee while you and Thami went for each other hammer and tongs, no holds barred and no quarter given or asked. I don't blame our audience for being so unruly. Once or twice I felt like doing some shouting myself. What a contest! But at the same time, what a waste, I thought! Yes, you heard me correctly. A waste! They shouldn't be fighting each other. They should be fighting together! If the sight of them as opponents is so exciting, imagine what it would be like if they were allies. If those two stood side by side and joined forces, they could take on anybody . . . and win! For the next few days that is all I could think of. It tormented me. When I wrote my report about the debate in the school diary, that was the last sentence. 'But oh! What a waste!'
  The truth is, I've seen too much of it, Isabel. Wasted people! Wasted chances! It's become a phobia with me now. It's not easy, you know, to be a teacher, to put your heart and soul into educating an eager young mind which you know will never get a chance to develop further and realize its full potential. The thought that you and Thami would be another two victims of this

175

country's lunacy was almost too much for me. The time for lamentations is past. (*Takes an envelope from his pocket.*) Two days ago I received this in the mail. It's the programme for this year's Grahamstown Schools' Festival. It has given me what I was looking for . . . an opportunity to fight the lunacy. The Standard Bank is sponsoring a new event: an inter-school English Literature quiz. Each team to consist of two members. I'll come straight to the point. I have suggested to Miss Brockway that Zolile High and Camdeboo High join forces and enter a combined team. As I have already told you, she has agreed and so has the Festival director, who I spoke to on the telephone this morning. There you have it, Isabel Dyson. I anxiously await your response.

Isabel I'm in the team?

Mr M Yes.

Isabel And . . .? (*Her eyes brighten with anticipation.*)

Mr M That's right.

Isabel Thami!

Mr M Correct!

Isabel Mr M, you're a genius!

Mr M (*holding up a hand to stop what was obviously going to be a very enthusiastic response*) Wait! Wait! Before you get carried away and say yes, let me warn you about a few things. It's going to mean a lot of very hard work. I am appointing myself team coach and as Thami will tell you, I can be a very hard taskmaster. You'll have to give up a lot of free time, young lady.

Isabel Anything else?

Mr M Not for the moment.

Isabel Then I'll say it again. Mr M, you're a genius!
(*Her joy is enormous, and she shows it.*) How's that for
unruly behaviour?

Mr M The very worst! They couldn't do it better on the
location streets. What a heartwarming response, Isabel.

Isabel What were you expecting? That I would say no?

Mr M I didn't know what to expect. I knew that you
would give me a sympathetic hearing, but that I would
be swept off my feet, literally and figuratively . . . no.
I was most certainly not prepared for that. Does my silly
little idea really mean that much to you?

Isabel None of that, Mr M! It's not silly and it's not
little, and you know it.

Mr M All right. But does it really mean that much
to you?

Isabel Yes it does.

Mr M (*persistent*) But why?

Isabel That visit to Zolile was one of the best things that
has happened to me. I don't want it to just end there,
one visit and that's it.

> *Mr M listens quietly, attentively, an invitation to
> Isabel to say more.*

It feels like it could be the beginning of something. I've
met you and Thami and all the others and I would like
to get to know you all better. But how do I do that?
I can't just go after you chaps like . . . well, you know
what I mean. Roll up and knock on your doors like you
were neighbours or just living down the street. It's not as
easy as that with us, is it? You're in the location, I'm in
the town . . . and all the rest of it. So there I was, feeling
more and more frustrated about it all when along you

come with your 'silly little' idea. It's perfect! Do I make sense?

Mr M Most definitely. Make some more.

Isabel I've been thinking about it you see. When I told my mom and dad about the debate and what a good time I'd had, I could see that they didn't really under- stand what I was talking about. 'Specially my mom. I ended up getting very impatient with her, which wasn't very smart of me because the harder I tried to make her understand the more nervous she got. Anyway, I've cooled off now and I realize why she was like that. Being with black people on an equal footing, you know . . . as equals, because that is how I ended up feeling with Thami and his friends . . . that was something that had never happened to her. She didn't know what I was talking about. And because she knows nothing about it, she's frightened of it.

Mr M You are not.

Isabel No. Not any more.

Mr M So you were.

Isabel Well, not so much frightened, as sort of uncertain. You see, I walked into that classroom thinking I knew what to expect, but after a few minutes in Number One Classroom I realized I was wrong by a mile.

Mr M What had you expected, Isabel?

Isabel You know, that everybody would be nice and polite and very, very grateful.

Mr M And we weren't?

Isabel You were, but not them. Thami and his friends. (*She laughs at the memory.*) Ja, to be honest, Mr M, that family of yours *was* a bit scary at first. But not any

178

more! I feel I've made friends with Thami . . . and the others, so now it's different.

Mr M Simple as that?

Isabel Simple as that.

Mr M Knowledge has banished fear.

Isabel That's right.

Mr M Bravo. Bravo, and yet again bravo! If you knew what it meant to me to hear you speak like that. I wasn't wrong. From the moment I first shook hands with you I knew you were a kindred spirit.

Isabel Tell me more about the competition.

Mr M First prize is five thousand rand which the bank has stipulated must be spent on books for the school library. We will obviously divide it equally between Camdeboo and Zolile when you and Thami win.

Isabel Yes, what about my team-mate. What does he say? Have you asked him yet?

Mr M No, I haven't *asked* him Isabel, and I won't. I will *tell* him, and when I do I trust he will express as much enthusiasm for the idea as you have. I am an old-fashioned traditionalist in most things, young lady, and my classroom is certainly no exception. I teach, Thami learns. He understands and accepts that that is the way it should be. You don't like the sound of that, do you?

Isabel Does sound a bit dictatorial, you know.

Mr M It might sound that way but I assure you it isn't. We do not blur the difference between the generations in the way that you white people do. Respect for authority, right authority, is deeply ingrained in the African soul. It's all I've got when I stand there in Number One.

179

Respect for my authority is my only teaching aid.
If I ever lost it those young people will abandon their
desks and take to the streets. I expect Thami to trust
my judgment of what is best for him, and he does.
That trust is the most sacred responsibility in my life.

Isabel He's your favourite, isn't he?

Mr M Good Heavens! A good teacher doesn't have
favourites! Are you suggesting that I might be a bad one?
Because if you are, (*looking around*) you would be right,
young lady. Measured by that yardstick I am a very bad
teacher indeed. He is my favourite. Thami Mbikwana!
Yes, I have waited a long time for him. To tell you the
truth I had given up all hope of him ever coming along.
Any teacher who takes his calling seriously dreams about
that one special pupil, that one eager and gifted young
head into which he can pour all that he knows and loves
and who will justify all the years of frustration in the
classroom. There have been pupils that I'm proud of, but
I've always had to bully them into doing their schoolwork. Not with Thami. *He* wants to learn the way other
boys want to run out of the classroom and make mischief.
If he looks after himself he'll go far and do big things.
He's a born leader, Isabel, and that is what your
generation needs. Powerful forces are fighting for the
souls of you young people. You need *real* leaders. Not
rabble-rousers. I know Thami is meant to be one. I know
it with such certainty it makes me frightened. Because it
is a responsibility. Mine and mine alone.

    I've got a small confession to make. In addition to
everything I've already said, there's another reason for
this idea of mine. When you and Thami shine at the
Festival, as I know you will, and win first prize and we've
pocketed a nice little cheque for five thousand rand, I am
going to point to Thami and say: 'And now ladies and
gentlemen, a full university scholarship if you please.'

Isabel And you'll get it. We'll shine, we'll win, we'll pocket that cheque and Thami will get a scholarship.

Mr M's turn for an enthusiastic response.

Mr M (*embarrassment and laughter*) Your unruly behaviour is very infectious!

Isabel My unruly behaviour? I like that! I caught that disease in the location, I'll have you know.

Mr M The future is ours, Isabel. We'll show this stupid country how it is done.

Isabel When do we start?

Mr M Next week. We need to plan our campaign very carefully.

Isabel I'll be ready.

SCENE FOUR

Mr M alone. He talks directly to the audience.

Mr M 'I am a man who in the eager pursuit of knowledge forgets his food and in the joy of its attainment forgets his sorrows, and who does not perceive that old age is coming on.' (*He shakes his head.*) No. As I'm sure you have already guessed, that is not me. My pursuit of knowledge is eager, but I do perceive, and only too clearly, that old age is coming on, and at the best of times I do a bad job of forgetting my sorrows. Those wonderful words come from the finest teacher I have ever had, that most wise of all the ancient philosophers . . . Confucius! Yes. I am a Confucian. A black Confucian! There are not many of us. In fact I think there's a good chance that the only one in the country is talking to you at this moment. I claim him as my teacher because I have read very carefully, and many times, and I will read it many times more, a little book I have about him, his life, his thoughts and utterances. Truly, they *are* wonderful words, my friends, wonderful, wonderful words! My classroom motto comes from its pages: 'Learning undigested by thought is labour lost, thought unassisted by learning is perilous!' But the words that challenge me most these days are something he said towards the end of his life. At the age of seventy he turned to his pupils one day and said that he could do whatever his heart prompted, without transgressing what was right.

What do you say to that?

Think about it. *Anything* his heart prompted, *anything* that rose up as a spontaneous urge in his soul, *without* transgressing what was right!

What a heart, my friends! Aren't you envious of old Confucius? Wouldn't it be marvellous to have a heart you could trust like that? Imagine being able to wake up in the morning in your little room, yawn and stretch, scratch a few flea bites and then jump out of your bed and eat your bowl of mealie-pap and sour milk with a happy heart because you know that when you walk out into the world you will be free to obey and act out, with a clear conscience, all the promptings of your heart. No matter what you see out there on the battlegrounds of location streets, and believe me, there are days now when my eyesight feels more like a curse than a blessing, no matter what stories of hardship and suffering you hear, or how bad the news you read in the newspaper, knowing that the whole truth, which can't be printed, is even worse . . . in spite of all that, you need have no fear of your spontaneous urges, because in obeying them you will not transgress what is right. (*Another shake of his head, another rueful smile.*) No, yet again. Not in this life, and most certainly not in this world where I find myself, will those wonderful words of Confucius ever be mine. Not even if I lived to be one hundred and seventy, will I end up with a calm, gentle Chinese heart like his. I wish I could. Believe me, I really wish I could. Because I am frightened of the one I've got. I don't get gentle promptings from it, my friends. I get heart attacks. When I walk out into those streets, and I see what is happening to my people, it jumps out and savages me like a wild beast. (*thumping his chest with a clenched fist*) I've got a whole zoo in here, a mad zoo of hungry animals . . . and the keeper is frightened! All of them. Mad and savage!

Look at me! I'm sweating today. I've been sweating for a week. Why? Because one of those animals, the one called Hope, has broken loose and is looking for food. Don't be fooled by its gentle name. It is as dangerous as Hate and Despair would be if they ever managed to break out. You think I'm exaggerating? Pushing my metaphor a little too far? Then I'd like to put you inside a black skin and ask you to keep Hope alive, find food for it on these streets where our children, our loved and precious children go hungry and die of malnutrition. No, believe me, it is a dangerous animal for a black man to have prowling around in his heart. So how do I manage to keep mine alive, you ask. Friends, I am going to let you in on a terrible secret. That is why I am a teacher.

It is all part of a secret plan to keep alive this savage Hope of mine. The truth is that I am worse than Nero feeding Christians to the lions. I feed young people to my Hope. Every young body behind a school desk keeps it alive. So you've been warned! If you see a hungry gleam in my eyes when I look at your children . . . you know what it means. That is the monster that stands here before you.

Full name: Anela Myalatya. Age: fifty-seven. Marital status: bachelor. Occupation: teacher. Address: the back room of the Reverend Mbopa's house next to the Anglican church of St Mark. It's a little on the small side.

183

You know those big kitchen-size boxes of matches they sell these days . . . well, if you imagine one of those as Number One Classroom at Zolile High, then the little matchbox you put in your pocket is my room at the Reverend Mbopa's. But I'm not complaining. It has got all I need – a table and chair where I correct homework and prepare lessons, a comfortable bed for a good night's insomnia and a reserved space for my chair in front of the television set in the Reverend Mbopa's lounge.

So there you have it. What I call my life rattles around in these two matchboxes . . . the classroom and the backroom. If you see me hurrying along the streets you can be reasonably certain that one of those two is my urgent destination. The people tease me. 'Faster, Mr M,' they shout to me from their front doors. 'You'll be late.' They think it's a funny joke. They don't know how close they are to a terrible truth . . . Yes! The clocks are ticking, my friends. History has got a strict timetable. If we're not careful we might be remembered as the country where everybody arrived too late.

SCENE FIVE

Mr M waiting.
Isabel hurries on, carrying hockey stick, togs and her school case. She is hot and exhausted.

Isabel Sorry, Mr M, sorry. The game started late.

Mr M I haven't been waiting long.

Isabel unburdens herself and collapses with a groan.

Did you win?

Isabel No. We played a team of friendly Afrikaans-speaking young Amazons from Jansenville and they licked us hollow. Four–one! It was brutal! God, they were fit. And fast. They ran circles around us on that hockey field. I felt so stupid. I kept saying to myself, 'It's only a game, Isabel. Relax! Enjoy it! Have a good time!' But no, there I was swearing under my breath at poor little Hilary Castle for being slow and not getting into position for my passes. (*laughing at herself*) You want to know something really terrible? A couple of times I actually wanted to go over and hit her with my hockey stick. Isn't that awful? It's no good, Mr M, I've got to face it: I'm a bad loser. Got any advice for me?

Mr M On how to be a good one?

Isabel Ja. How to lose graciously. With dignity. I mean it. I really wish I could.

Mr M If I did have advice for you, Isabel, I think I would be well advised to try it out on myself first . . .

Isabel Why? You one as well?

Mr M nods.

I don't believe it.

Mr M It's true, Isabel. I'm ashamed to say it, but when I lose I also want to grab my hockey stick and hit somebody.

A good laugh from Isabel.

Believe me, I can get very petty and mean if I'm not on the winning side. I suppose most bachelors end up like that. We get so used to having everything our own way that when something goes wrong . . .! So there's my advice to you. Get married! If what I've heard is true, holy matrimony is the best school of all for learning how to lose.

Isabel I don't think it's something you can learn. You've either got it or you haven't. Like Thami. Without even thinking about it I know *he's* a good loser.

Mr M Maybe.

Isabel No. No maybes about it. He'd never grab his hockey stick and take it out on somebody else if he didn't win.

Mr M You're right. I can't see him doing that. You've become good friends, haven't you?

Isabel The best. These past few weeks have been quite an education. I owe you a lot, you know. I think Thami would say the same . . . if you would only give him the chance to do so.

Mr M What do you mean by that remark, young lady?

Isabel You know what I mean by that remark, *Mr Teacher*! It's called Freedom of Speech.

Mr M I've given him plenty of freedom, within reasonable limits, but he never uses it.

Isabel Because you're *always* the teacher and he's *always* the pupil. Stop teaching him all the time, Mr M. Try just talking to him for a change . . . you know, like a friend. I bet you in some ways I already know more about Thami than you.

Mr M I don't deny that. In which case tell me, is he happy?

Isabel What do you mean? Happy with what? Us? The competition?

Mr M Yes, and also his schoolwork and . . . everything else.

Isabel Why don't you ask him?

Mr M Because all I'll get is another polite 'Yes teacher'. I thought maybe he had said something to you about the way he really felt.

Isabel (*shaking her head*) The two of you! It's crazy! But ja, he's happy. At least I think he is. He's not a blabber-mouth like me, Mr M. He doesn't give much away . . . even when we talk about ourselves. I don't know what it was like in your time, but being eighteen years old today is a pretty complicated business as far as we're concerned. If you asked me if I was happy, I'd say yes, but that doesn't mean I haven't got any problems. I've got plenty and I'm sure it's the same with Thami.

Mr M Thami has told you he's got problems?

Isabel Come on, Mr M! We've all got problems. I've got problems, you've got problems, Thami's got problems.

Mr M But did he say what they were?

Isabel You're fishing for something, Mr M. What is it?

Mr M Trouble, Isabel. I'm sorry to say it, but I'm fishing for trouble and I'm trying to catch it before it gets too big.

Isabel Thami is in trouble?

Mr M Not yet, but he will be if he's not careful. And all his friends as well. It's swimming around everywhere trying to stir up things. In the classroom, out on the streets.

Isabel Oh, you mean that sort of trouble. Is it really as bad as people are saying?

Mr M There's a dangerous, reckless mood in the location. 'Specially among the young people. Very silly things are being said, Isabel, and I've got a suspicion that even sillier things are being whispered among themselves.

I know Thami trusts you. I was wondering if he had told you what they were whispering about.

Isabel (*shocked by what Mr M was asking of her*) Wow! That's a hard one you're asking for, Mr M. Just suppose he had, do you think it would be right for me to tell you? *We* call that splitting, you know, and you're not very popular if you're caught doing it.

Mr M It would be for his own good, Isabel.

Isabel Well, he hasn't . . . thank God! So I don't have to deal with that one. (*Pause.*) If I ever did that to him, and he found out, that would be the end of our friendship, you know. I wish you hadn't asked me.

Mr M (*realizing his mistake*) Forgive me, Isabel. I'm just overanxious on his behalf. One silly mistake now could ruin everything. Forget that I asked you and . . . please . . . don't mention anything about our little chat to Thami. I'll find time to have a word with him myself.

Thami appears, also direct from the sports field.

Thami Hi folks. Sorry I'm late.

Isabel I've just got here myself. Mr M is the one who's been waiting.

Thami Sorry, teacher. The game went into extra time.

Isabel Did you win?

Thami No. We lost one–nil. But it was a good game. We're trying out some new combinations and they nearly worked. The chaps are really starting to come together as a team. A little more practice, that's all we need.

Isabel Hear that, Mr M? What did I tell you. And look at him. Smiling! Happy! Even in defeat, a generous word for his team-mates.

Thami What's going on?

Isabel Don't try to look innocent, Mbikwana. Your secret is out. Your true identity has been revealed. You are a good loser, and don't try to deny it.

Thami Me? You're wrong. I don't like losing.

Isabel It's not a question of liking or not liking, but of being able to do so without a crooked smile on your face, a knot in your stomach and murder in your heart.

Thami You lost your game this afternoon?

Isabel Whatever made you guess! We were trounced. So be careful. I'm looking for revenge.

Mr M Good! Then let's see if you can get it in the arena of English Literature. What do we deal with today?

Thami Nineteenth-century poetry.

Mr M (*with relish*) Beautiful! Beautiful! Beautiful! (*making himself comfortable*) Whose service?

> *Thami picks up a stone, hands behind his back, then clenched fists for Isabel to guess. She does. She wins. Their relationship is now obviously very relaxed and easy.*

Isabel Gird your loins, Mbikwana. I want blood.

Thami I wish you the very best of luck.

Isabel God, I hate you.

Mr M First service, please.

Isabel Right. I'll give you an easy one to start with. The Lake Poets. Name them.

Thami Wordsworth . . .

Isabel Yes, he was one. Who else?

Thami Wordsworth and . . .

Isabel There was only one Wordsworth.

Thami I pass.

Isabel Wordsworth, Southey and Coleridge.

Thami I should have guessed Coleridge!

Mr M One–love.

Isabel First line of a poem by each of them, please.

Thami Query, Mr Umpire! How many questions is that?

Mr M One at a time please, Isabel.

Isabel Coleridge.

Thami
> 'In Xanadu did Kubla Khan
> A stately pleasure-dome decree . . .'

And if you don't like that one what about:

> 'Tis the middle of the night by the castle clock
> And the owls have awakened the crowing cock
> Tu-whit Tu-whoo.'

And if you're still not satisfied . . .

Isabel Stop showing off, young man.

Mr M One–all.

Isabel Wordsworth.

Thami
> 'Earth has not anything to show more fair:
> Dull would he be of soul who could pass by
> A sight so touching in its majesty . . .'

Mr M One–two.

Isabel Southey.

Thami Pass.

Isabel
'From his brimstone bed, at break of day
A-walking the Devil is gone,
His coat was red and his breeches were blue,
And there was a hole where his tail came through.'

Thami Hey, I like that one!

Isabel A Poet Laureate to boot.

Mr M Two–all.

Isabel One of them was expelled from school. Who was it and why?

Thami Wordsworth. For smoking in the lavatory.

Isabel (*after a good laugh*) You're terrible, Thami. He should be penalized, Mr Umpire, for irreverence! It was Southey and the reason he was expelled – you're going to like this – was for writing a 'precocious' essay against flogging.

Thami How about that!

Mr M Three–two. Change service.

Thami I am not going to show you any mercy. What poet was born with deformed feet, accused of incest and died of fever while helping the Greeks fight for freedom? 'A love of liberty characterizes his poems and the desire to see the fettered nations of Europe set free.'

Isabel Byron.

Thami Lord Byron, if you please.

Mr M Two–four.

Isabel One of your favourites.

Thami You bet.
'Yet, Freedom! yet, thy banner, torn, but flying,
Streams like the thunder-storm against the wind.'

Do you know the Christian names of Lord Byron?

Isabel Oh dammit! . . . it's on the tip of my tongue.
Henry?

Thami shakes his head.

Herbert?

Thami How many guesses does she get, Mr Umpire?

Isabel All right, give him the point. I pass.

Thami George Gordon.

Mr M Three–four.

Thami To whom was he unhappily married for one long
year?

Isabel Pass.

Thami Anne Isabella Milbanke.

Mr M Four–all.

Thami Father's occupation?

Isabel Pass.

Thami John Byron was a captain in the army.

Mr M Five–four.

Thami What other great poet was so overcome with
grief when he heard news of Lord Byron's death, that
he went out and carved into a rock: 'Byron is dead.'

Isabel Matthew Arnold?

Thami No. Another aristocrat . . . Alfred Lord Tennyson.

Mr M Six–four. Change service.

Isabel Right. Whose body did your Lord Byron burn on a beach in Italy?

Thami Shelley.

Mr M Four–seven.

Isabel And what happened to Mr Shelley's ashes?

Thami In a grave beside John Keats in Rome.

Mr M Four–eight.

Isabel Shelley's wife. What is she famous for?

Thami Which one? There were two. Harriet Westbrook, sixteen years old, who he abandoned after three years and who drowned herself? Or number two wife – who I think is the one you're interested in – Mary Wollstonecraft, the author of *Frankenstein*.

Mr M Four–nine.

Isabel How much?

Mr M Four–nine.

Isabel I don't believe this! (*She grabs her hockey stick.*)

Thami (*enjoying himself immensely*) I crammed in two poets last night, Isabel. Guess who they were?

Isabel Byron and Shelley. In that case we will deal with Mr John Keats. What profession did he abandon in order to devote himself to poetry?

Thami Law.

Isabel You're guessing and you're wrong. He qualified as a surgeon.

Mr M Five–nine.

Isabel What epitaph, composed by himself, is engraved on his tombstone in Rome?

Thami Pass.

Isabel 'Here lies one whose name was writ in water.'

Mr M Six—nine. Let's leave the Births, Marriages and Deaths column, please. I want to hear some more poetry.

Thami Whose service?

Mr M Yours.

Thami
'I must go down to the seas again, to the lonely sea
    and the sky,
And all I ask is a tall ship and a star to steer her by . . .'

Isabel
'And the wheel's kick and the wind's song and the
    white sails shaking,
And a grey mist on the sea's face and a grey dawn
    breaking . . .
I must go down to the seas again, to the vagrant
    gypsy life,
To the gull's way and the whale's way where the
    wind's like a whetted knife . . .'

Thami
'And all I ask is a merry yarn from a laughing
    fellow-rover,
And quiet sleep and a sweet dream when the long
    trick's over.'

Mr M Bravo! Bravo! Bravo! But who gets the point?

Isabel Give it to John Masefield, Mr Umpire. (*to Thami*) Nineteenth century?

Thami He was born in 1878. To tell you the truth I couldn't resist it. You choose one.

Isabel
   'I met a traveller from an antique land
   Who said: "Two vast and trunkless legs of stone
   Stand in the desert . . . near them, on the sand,
   Half sunk, a shattered visage lies, whose frown
   And wrinkled lip, and sneer of cold command
   Tell that its sculptor well those passions read
   Which yet survive, stamped on these lifeless things
   The hand that mocked them, and the heart that fed:
   And on the pedestal these words appear:'

Thami
   ' "My name is Ozymandias, king of kings.
   Look on my works, ye Mighty, and despair!'

Isabel
   ' "Nothing beside remains. Round the decay
   Of that colossal wreck, boundless and bare,
   The lone and level sands stretch far away." '

Thami And that point goes to Mr Shelley.

Isabel (*takes a notebook from her school case*) You'll be interested to know, gentlemen, that Ozymandias is not a fiction of Mr Shelley's very fertile imagination. He was a real, live Egyptian king. Rameses the Second! According to *Everyman's Encyclopaedia* . . . 'One of the most famous of the Egyptian kings . . . erected many monuments . . . but his oppressive rule left Egypt impoverished and suffering from an incurable decline.'

Thami What happened to the statue?

Isabel You mean how was it toppled?

Thami Yes.

Isabel Didn't say. Weather, I suppose. And time. Two thousand four hundred BC . . . that's over four thousand years ago. Why? What were you thinking?

Thami I had a book of Bible stories when I was small, and there was a picture in it showing the building of the pyramids by the slaves. Thousands of them, like ants, pulling the big blocks of stone with ropes, being guarded by soldiers with whips and spears. According to that picture the slaves must have easily outnumbered the soldiers one hundred to one. I actually tried to count them all one day but the drawing wasn't good enough for that.

Isabel What are you up to, Mbikwana? Trying to stir up a little social unrest in the time of the Pharaohs, are you?

Thami Don't joke about it, Miss Dyson. There are quite a few Ozymandiases in this country waiting to be toppled. And you'll see it happen. *We* won't leave it to time to bring them down.

Mr M has been listening to the exchange between Thami and Isabel very attentively.

Mr M (*trying to put a smile on it*) Who is the *we* you speak of with such authority, Thami?

Thami The People.

Mr M (*recognition*) Yes, yes, yes, of course . . . I should have known. 'The People' . . . with a capital P. Does that include me? Am I one of 'The People'?

Thami If you choose to be.

Mr M I've got to choose, have I? My black skin doesn't confer automatic membership. So how do I go about choosing?

Thami By identifying with the fight for our freedom.

Mr M As simple as that? Then I am most definitely one of 'The People'. I want our freedom as much as any of you. In fact, I was fighting for it in my own small way long before you were born! But I've got a small problem. Does that noble fight of ours really have to stoop to pulling down a few silly statues? Where do you get the idea that we, The People, want you to do that for us?

Thami (*trying*) They are not our heroes, teacher.

Mr M They are not our statues, Thami! Wouldn't it be better for us to rather put our energies into erecting a few of our own? We've also got heroes, you know.

Thami Like who, Mr M? Nelson Mandela? (*shaking his head with disbelief*) Hey! *They* would pull *that* statue down so fast –

Mr M (*cutting him*) In which case they would be just as guilty of gross vandalism . . . because that is what it will be, regardless of who does it to whom. Destroying somebody else's property is inexcusable behaviour! No, Thami. As one of The People you claim to be acting for, I raise my hand in protest. Please don't pull down any statues on my behalf. Don't use me as an excuse for an act of lawlessness. If you want to do something 'revolutionary' for me let us sit down and discuss it, because I have a few constructive alternatives I would like to suggest. Do I make myself clear?

Thami Yes, teacher.

Mr M Good. I'm glad we understand each other.

Isabel (*intervening*) So, what's next? Mr M? How about singling out a few specific authors who we know will definitely come up. Like Dickens. I bet you anything you like there'll be questions about him and his work.

Mr M Good idea. We'll concentrate on novelists. A short list of hot favourites.

Isabel Thomas Hardy . . . Jane Austen . . . who else, Thami?

Mr M Put your heads together and make a list. I want twenty names. Divide it between the two of you and get to work. I must be on my way.

Isabel Just before you go, Mr M, I've got an invitation for you and Thami from my mom and dad. Would the two of you like to come to tea one afternoon?

Mr M What a lovely idea!

Isabel They've had enough of me going on and on about the all-knowing Mr M and his brilliant protégé Thami. They want to meet you for themselves. Thami? All right with you?

Mr M Of course we accept Isabel. It will be a pleasure and a privilege for us to meet Mr and Mrs Dyson. Tell them we accept most gratefully.

Isabel Next Sunday.

Mr M Perfect.

Isabel Thami?

Mr M Don't worry about him, Isabel. I'll put it in my diary and remind him at school. (*He leaves.*)

Isabel (*sensitive to a change of mood in Thami*) I think you'll like my folks. My mom's a bit on the reserved side but that's just because she's basically very shy. But you and my dad should get on well. Start talking sport with him and he won't let you go. He played cricket for EP, you know. (*Pause.*) You will come, won't you?

Thami (*edge to his voice*) Didn't you hear Mr M?
'A delight and a privilege! We accept most gratefully.'
(*writing in his notebook*) Charles Dickens . . . Thomas
Hardy . . . Jane Austen . . .

Isabel Was he speaking for you as well?

Thami He speaks for me on nothing!

Isabel Relax . . . I know that. That's why I tried to ask
you separately and why I'll ask you again. Would you
like to come to tea next Sunday to meet my family? It's
not a polite invitation. They really want to meet you.

Thami Me? Why? Are they starting to get nervous?

Isabel Oh, come off it, Thami. Don't be like that.
They're always nervous when it comes to me. But this
time it happens to be genuine interest. I've told you. I
talk about you at home. They know I have a good time
with you . . . that we're a team . . . which they are now
very proud of, incidentally . . . and that we're cramming
like lunatics so that we can put up a good show at the
Festival. Is it so strange that they want to meet you after
all that? Honestly, sometimes dealing with the two of
you is like walking on a tightrope. I'm always scared I'm
going to put a foot wrong and . . . well I just *hate* being
scared like that.

 *A few seconds of truculent silence between the two of
 them.*

What's going on, Thami? Between you two? There's
something very wrong, isn't there?

Thami No more than usual.

Isabel No you don't! A hell of a lot more than usual,
and don't deny it because it's getting to be pretty obvious.
I mean I know he gets on your nerves. I knew that the

first day we met. But it's more than that now. These past couple of meetings I've caught you looking at him, watching him in a . . . I don't know . . . in a sort of hard way. Very critical. Not just once. Many times. Do you know you're doing it?

Shrug of the shoulders from Thami.

Well if you know it or not, you are. And now he's started as well.

Thami What do you mean?

Isabel He's watching you.

Thami So? He can watch me as much as he likes. I've got nothing to hide. Even if I had he'd be the last person to find out. He sees nothing, Isabel.

Isabel I think you are very wrong.

Thami No, I'm not. That's his trouble. He's got eyes and ears but he sees nothing and hears nothing.

Isabel Go on. Please. (*Pause.*) I mean it, Thami. I want to know what's going on.

Thami He is out of touch with what is really happening to us blacks and the way we feel about things. He thinks the world is still the way it was when he was young. It's not! It's different now, but he's too blind to see it. He doesn't open his eyes and ears and see what is happening around him or listen to what people are saying.

Isabel What are they saying?

Thami They've got no patience left, Isabel. They want change. They want it now!

Isabel But he agrees with that. He never stops saying it himself.

Thami No. His ideas about change are the old-fashioned ones. And what have they achieved? Nothing. We are worse off now than we ever were. The people don't want to listen to his kind of talk any more.

Isabel I'm still lost, Thami. What kind of talk is that?

Thami You've just heard it, Isabel. It calls our struggle vandalism and lawless behaviour. It's the sort of talk that expects us to do nothing and wait quietly for White South Africa to wake up. If we listen to it our grand-children still won't know what it means to be free.

Isabel And those old-fashioned ideas of his . . . are we one of them?

Thami What do you mean?

Isabel You and me. The competition.

Thami Let's change the subject, Isabel. (*Takes up his notebook.*) Charles Dickens . . . Thomas Hardy . . . Jane Austen . . .

Isabel No! You can't do that! I'm involved. I've got a right to know. Are we an old-fashioned idea?

Thami Not our friendship. That is our decision, our choice.

Isabel And the competition.

Thami (*uncertain of himself*) Maybe . . . I'm not sure. I need time to think about it.

Isabel (*foreboding*) Oh boy. This doesn't sound so good. You've got to talk to him, Thami.

Thami He won't listen.

Isabel Make him listen!

Thami It doesn't work that way with us, Isabel. You can't just stand up and tell your teacher he's got the wrong ideas.

Isabel Well, that's just your bad luck because you are going to have to do it. Even if it means breaking sacred rules and traditions, you have got to stand up and have it out with him. I don't think you realize what all of this means to him. It's a hell of a lot more than just an 'old-fashioned idea' as far as he's concerned. This competition, you and me, but especially you, Thami Mbikwana, has become a sort of crowning achievement to his life as a teacher. It's become a sort of symbol for him, and if it were to all suddenly collapse . . .! No. I don't want to think about it.

Thami (*flash of anger and impatience*) Then don't! Please leave it alone now and just let's get on with whatever it is we've got to do.

Isabel Right, if that's the way you want it . . . (*Takes up her notebook.*) . . . Charles Dickens, Thomas Hardy, Jane Austen . . . who else?

Thami I'm sorry. I know you're only trying to help, but you've got to understand that it's not just a personal issue between him and me. That would be easy. I don't think I would care then. Just wait for the end of the year and then get out of that classroom and that school as fast I can. But there is more to it than that. I've told you before: sitting in a classroom doesn't mean the same thing to me that it does to you. That classroom is a political reality in my life . . . it's a part of the whole political system we're up against and Mr M has chosen to identify himself with it.

Isabel (*trying a new tack*) All right. I believe you. I accept everything you said . . . about him, your relationship, the situation . . . no arguments. OK? But doesn't all of that only make it still more important that the two of you start talking to each other? I know *he* wants to, but he doesn't know how to start. It's *so* sad . . . because I can see him trying to reach out to you. Show him how it's done. Make the first move. Oh Thami, don't let it go wrong between the two of you. That's just about the worst thing I could imagine. We all need each other.

Thami I don't need him.

Isabel I think you do, just as much as he . . .

Thami (*his anger flaring*) Don't tell me what I need, Isabel! And stop telling me what to do! You don't know what my life is about, so keep your advice to yourself.

Isabel (*deeply hurt*) I'm sorry. I don't mean to interfere. I thought we were a team and that what involved you two concerned me as well. I'll mind my own business in future. (*She collects her things.*) Let's leave it at that then. See you next week . . . I hope! (*Starts to leave, stops, returns and confronts him.*) You used the word friendship a few minutes ago. It's a beautiful word and I'll do anything to make it true for us. But don't let's cheat, Thami. If we can't be open and honest with each other and say what is in our hearts, we've got no right to use it. (*She leaves.*)

SCENE SIX

Thami alone.

Thami (*singing*)
Masiye Masiye Skolweni
Masiye Masiye Skolweni
eskolweni Sasakhaya
eskolweni Sasakhaya (*repeat*)

Gongo Gongo
Iyakhala Intsimbi
Gongo Gongo
Iyakhala Intsimbi.

(*translating*)
Come, come, let's go to school
Let's go to our very own school
Gongo Gongo
The bell is ringing
Gongo Gongo
The bell is calling!

Singing that at the top of his voice and holding his slate under his arm, seven-year-old Thami Mbikwana marched proudly with the other children every morning into his classroom.

Gongo Gongo
The school bell is ringing!

And what a wonderful sound that was for me. Starting with the little farm school, I remember my school bells like beautiful voices calling to me all through my childhood . . . and I came running when they did. You should have seen me, man. In junior school I was the first one at the gates every morning. I was waiting there when the caretaker came to unlock them. Oh yes! Young

Thami was a very eager scholar. And what made it even better, he was also one of the clever ones. 'A most particularly promising pupil' is how one of my school reports described me. My first real scholastic achievement was a composition I wrote about myself in Standard Two. Not only did it get me top marks in the class, the teacher was so proud of me, she made me read it out to the whole school at assembly.

(*his composition*) 'The story of my life so far. By Thami Mbikwana. The story of my life so far is not yet finished because I am only ten years old and I am going to live a long long time. I come from Kingwilliamstown. My father is Amos Mbikwana and he works very hard for the *baas* on the railway. I am also going to work very hard and get good marks in all my classes and make my teacher very happy. The story of my life so far has also got a very happy ending because when I am big I am going to be a doctor so that I can help my people. I will drive to the hospital every day in a big, white ambulance full of nurses. I will make black people better free of charge. The white people must pay me for my medicine because they have got lots of money. That way I will also get lots of money. My mother and my father will stop working and come and live with me in a big house. That is the story of my life up to where I am in Standard Two.'

I must bring my story up to date because there have been some changes and developments since little Thami wrote those hopeful words eight years ago. To start with I don't think I want to be a doctor any more. That praiseworthy ambition has unfortunately died in me. It still upsets me very much when I think about the pain and suffering of my people, but I realize now that what causes most of it is not an illness that can be cured by the pills and bottles of medicine they hand out at the clinic. I don't need to go to university to learn what my people really need is a strong double-dose of that tradi-

tional old Xhosa remedy called *nkululeko* . . . freedom.
So right now I'm not sure what I want to be any more.
It's hard, you see, for us 'bright young blacks' to dream
about wonderful careers as doctors or lawyers when we
keep waking up in a world which doesn't allow the
majority of our people any dreams at all.

But to get back to my composition, I did try my best
to keep that promise I made in it. For a long time . . .
Standard Three, Standard Four, Standard Five . . . I did
work very hard and I did get good marks in all my
subjects. This 'most particularly promising pupil' made a
lot of teachers very happy.

I'm sorry to say but I can't do it any more. I have
tried very hard, believe me, but it is not as simple and
easy as it used to be to sit behind that desk and listen to
the teacher. That little world of the classroom where I
used to be happy, where they used to pat me on the head
and say: 'Little Thami, you'll go far!' . . . that little room
of wonderful promises where I used to feel so safe has
become a place I don't trust any more. Now I sit at my
desk like an animal that has smelt danger, heard something moving in the bushes and knows it must be very,
very careful.

At the beginning of this year the Inspector of Bantu
Schools in the Cape Midlands Region, Mr Dawid
Grobbelaar – he makes us call him Oom Dawie – came
to give us Standard Tens his usual pep-talk. He does it
every year. We know Oom Dawie well. He's been coming
to Zolile for a long time. When he walked into our classroom we all jumped up as usual but he didn't want any
of that. 'Sit, sit. I'm not a bloody sergeant-major.' Oom
Dawie believes he knows how to talk to us. He loosened
his tie, took off his jacket and rolled-up his sleeves. It
was a very hot day.

'*Dis teeter. Nou kan ons lekker gesels.* Boys and girls
or maybe I should say "young men" and "young

women" now, because you are coming to the end of your time behind those desks . . . you are special! You are the elite! We have educated you because we want you to be major shareholders in the future of this wonderful Republic of ours. In fact, we want *all* the peoples of South Africa to share in that future . . . black, white, brown, yellow, and if there are some green ones out there, then them as well. Ho! Ho! Ho!'

I don't remember much about what he said after that because my head was trying to deal with that one word: the future! He kept using it . . . 'our future', 'the country's future', 'a wonderful future of peace and prosperity'. What does he really mean, I kept asking myself. Why does my heart go hard and tight as a stone when he says it? I look around me in the location at the men and women who went out into that 'wonderful future' before me. What do I see? Happy and contented shareholders in this exciting enterprise called the Republic of South Africa? No. I see a generation of tired, defeated men and women crawling back to their miserable little pondoks at the end of a day's work for the white *baas* or madam. And those are the lucky ones. They've at least got work. Most of them are just sitting around wasting away their lives while they wait helplessly for a miracle to feed their families, a miracle that never comes. Those men and women are our fathers and mothers. We have grown up watching their humiliation. We have to live every day with the sight of them begging for food in this land of their birth, and their parent's birth . . . all the way back to the first proud ancestors of our people. Black people lived on this land for centuries before any white settler had landed! Does Oom Dawie think we are blind? That when we walk through the streets of the white town we do not see the big houses and the beautiful gardens with their swimming pools full of laughing people, and compare it with what we've got, what we have to call home? Or does Oom Dawie just think we are very stupid? That in spite of the wonderful education he has given us, we can't use the simple arithmetic of add and subtract, multiply and divide to work out the rightful share of twenty-five million black people?

Do you understand me, good people? Do you understand now why it is not as easy as it used to be to sit behind that desk and learn only what Oom Dawie has decided I must know? My head is rebellious. It refuses now to remember when the Dutch landed, and the Huguenots landed, and the British landed. It has already forgotten when the old Union became the proud young Republic. But it does know what happened in Kliptown in 1955, in Sharpeville on 21 March 1960 and in Soweto on 16 June 1976. Do you? Better find out because those are dates your children will have to learn one day. We don't need Zolile classrooms any more. We know now what they really are – traps which have been carefully set to catch our minds, our souls. No, good people. We have woken up at last. We have found another school . . . the streets, the little rooms, the funeral parlours of the location . . . anywhere the people meet and whisper names we have been told to forget, the dates of events they try to tell us never happened and the speeches they try to say were never made. Those are the lessons we are eager and proud to learn, because they are lessons about *our* history, about *our* heroes. But the time for whispering them is past. Tomorrow we start shouting. *AMANDLA*!

Act Two

SCENE ONE

Isabel and Thami. She has books and papers. Behind a relaxed and easy manner, she watches Thami carefully.

Isabel What I've done is write out a sort of condensed biography of all of them . . . you know, the usual stuff . . . date of birth, where they were born, where they died, who they married . . . etcetera, etcetera. My dad made copies for you and Mr M. Sit. (*Hands over a set of papers to Thami.*) You OK?

Thami Ja, Ja.

Isabel For example . . . (*reading*) Brontë sisters . . . I lumped them all together . . . Charlotte 1816–1855; Emily 1818–1848; Anne 1820–1849 . . . Can you believe that? Not one of them reached the age of forty. Anne died when she was twenty-nine, Emily when she was thirty, and Charlotte reached the ripe old age of thirty-nine! Family home: Haworth, Yorkshire. First publication a joint volume of verse: *Poems by Currer, Ellis and Acton Bell.* All novels published under these *noms-de-plume.* Charlotte the most prolific . . . (*abandoning the notes*) Why am I doing this? You're not listening to me.

Thami Sorry.

Isabel (*she waits for more, but that is all she gets.*) So? Should I carry on wasting my breath or do you want to say something?

Thami No, I must talk.

Isabel Good. I'm ready to listen.

Thami I don't know where to begin.

Isabel The deep end. Take my advice, go to the deep end and just jump right in. That's how I learnt to swim.

Thami No. I want to speak carefully because I don't want you to get the wrong ideas about what's happening and what I'm going to say. It's not like it's your fault, that it's because of anything you said or did . . . you know what I mean?

Isabel You don't want me to take personally whatever it is you are finding so hard to tell me.

Thami That's right. It's not about you and me personally. I've had a good time with you, Isabel.

Isabel And I've had an important one with you.

Thami If it was just you and me, there wouldn't be a problem.

Isabel We've got a problem have we?

Thami I have.

Isabel (*losing patience*) Oh, for God's sake, Thami. Stop trying to spare my feelings and just say it. If you are trying to tell me that I've been wasting my breath for a lot longer than just this afternoon . . . just go ahead and say it! I'm not a child. I can take it. Because that is what you are trying to tell me isn't it? That it's all off.

Thami Yes.

Isabel The great literary quiz team is no more. You are pulling out of the competition.

Thami Yes.

Isabel You shouldn't have made it so hard for yourself, Thami. It doesn't come as all that big a surprise. I've had

a feeling that something was going to go wrong somewhere. Been a strange time these past few weeks, hasn't
it? At home, at school, in the shop . . . everywhere!
Things I've been seeing and doing my whole life just
don't feel right any more. Like my Saturday chats with
Samuel – I told you about him, remember, he delivers
for my dad – well you should have heard the last one.
It was excruciating. It felt so false, and forced, and
when I listened to what I was saying and how I was
saying it . . . oh my God! Sounded as if I thought I was
talking to a ten-year-old. Halfway through our misery
my dad barged in and told me not to waste Samuel's
time because he had work to do, which of course led to a
flaming row between me and my dad . . . Am I changing,
Thami? My dad says I am.

Thami In what way?

Isabel Forget it. The only thing I *do* know at this
moment is that I don't very much like the way anything
feels right now, starting with myself. So have you told
Mr M yet?

Thami No.

Isabel Good luck. I don't envy you that little conversation. If I'm finding the news a bit hard to digest,
I don't know what he is going to do with it. I've just
got to accept it. I doubt very much if he will.

Thami He's got no choice, Isabel. I've decided and that's
the end of it.

Isabel So do you think we can at least talk about it?
Help me to understand? Because to be absolutely honest
with you, Thami, I don't think I do. You're not the only
one with a problem. What Mr M had to say about the
team and the whole idea made a hell of a lot of sense to
me. You owe it to me, Thami. A lot more than just my
spare time is involved.

Thami Talk about what? Don't you know what is going on?

Isabel Don't be stupid, Thami! Of course I do! You'd have to be pretty dumb not to know that the dreaded 'unrest' has finally reached us as well.

Thami We don't call it that. Our word for it is *'Isiqalo'* – the beginning.

Isabel All right then, 'the beginning'. I don't care what it's called. All I'm asking you to do is explain to me how the two of us learning some poetry, cramming in potted bios . . . interferes with all of that.

Thami Please just calm down and listen to me! I know you're angry and I don't blame you. I would be as well. But you must understand that pulling out of this competition is just a small side-issue. There was a meeting in the location last night. It was decided to call for a general stay-at-home. We start boycotting classes tomorrow as part of that campaign.

Isabel Does Mr M know about all of this?

Thami I think he does now.

Isabel Wasn't he at that meeting?

Thami The meeting was organized by the Comrades. He wasn't welcome.

Isabel Because his ideas are old fashioned.

Thami Yes.

Isabel School boycott! Comrades! So our safe, contented little Camdeboo is really going to find out what it's all about. How long do you think it will last?

Thami I don't know. It's hard to say.

Isabel A week.

Thami No. It will be longer.

Isabel A month? Two months?

Thami We'll go back to school when the authorities scrap Bantu education and recognize and negotiate with student committees. That was the resolution last night.

Isabel But when the boycott and . . . you know . . . everything is all over could we carry on then, if there was still time?

Thami I haven't thought about that.

Isabel So think about it. Please.

Thami (*nervous about a commitment*) It's hard to say, Isabel . . . but ja . . . maybe we could . . . I'm not sure.

Isabel Not much enthusiasm there, Mr Mbikwana! You're right. Why worry about a stupid competition. It will most probably be too late anyway. So that's it then. Let's just say we gave ourselves a crash course in English Literature. Could have done a lot worse with our spare time, couldn't we? I enjoyed myself. I read a lot of beautiful poetry I might never have got around to. (*uncertain of herself*) It doesn't mean the end of everything though, does it? I mean, we can go on meeting, just as friends?

Thami (*warily*) When?

Isabel Oh . . . I mean, you know, like any time. Next week! (*Pause.*) I'm not talking about the competition, Thami. I accept that it's dead. I think it's a pity . . . but so what. I'm talking now about you and me just as friends. (*She waits. She realizes.*) So our friendship *is* an old-fashioned idea after all. Well don't waste your time here. You better get going and look after . . . whatever it is that's beginning. And good luck!

Thami starts to go.

No! Thami, come back here! (*struggling ineffectually to control her anger and pain*) There is something very stupid somewhere and it's most probably me but I can't help it . . . *it just doesn't make sense!* I know it does to you and I'm sure it's just my white selfishness and ignorance that is stopping me from understanding *but it still doesn't make sense.* Why can't we go on seeing each other and meeting as friends? Tell me what is wrong with our friendship?

Thami You're putting words in my mouth, Isabel. I didn't say there was anything wrong with it. But others won't see it the way we do.

Isabel Who? Your comrades?

Thami Yes.

Isabel And they are going to decide whether we can or can't be friends!

Thami I was right. You don't understand what's going on.

Isabel And you're certainly not helping me to.

Thami (*trying*) Visiting you like this is dangerous. People talk. U'Sis Pumla – your maid – has seen me. She could mention, just innocently but to the wrong person, that Thami Mbikwana is visiting and having tea with the white people she works for.

Isabel And of course that is such a big crime!

Thami In the eyes of the location . . . Yes! My world is also changing, Isabel. I'm breaking the boycott by being here. The Comrades don't want any mixing with whites. They have ordered that contact must be kept at a minimum.

Isabel And you go along with that.

Thami Yes.

Isabel Happily?

Thami (*goaded by her lack of understanding*) Yes! I go along happily with that!!

Isabel Hell, Thami, this great beginning of yours sounds like . . . (*Shakes her head.*) . . . I don't know. Other people deciding who can and who can't be your friends, what you must do and what you can't do. Is this the freedom you've been talking to me about? That you were going to fight for?

Mr M enters quietly. His stillness is a disturbing contrast to the bustle and energy we have come to associate with him.

Mr M Don't let me interrupt you. Please carry on. (*to Thami*) I'm most interested in your reply to that question. (*Pause.*) I think he's forgotten what it was, Isabel. Ask him again.

Isabel (*backing out of the confrontation*) No. Forget it.

Mr M (*persisting*) Isabel was asking you how you managed to reconcile your desire for freedom with what the Comrades are doing.

Isabel I said forget it, Mr M. I'm not interested any more.

Mr M (*insistent*) But I am.

Thami The Comrades are imposing a discipline which our struggle needs at this point. There is no comparison between that and the total denial of our freedom by the white government. They have been forcing on us an inferior education in order to keep us permanently suppressed. When our struggle is successful there will be no more need for the discipline the Comrades are demanding.

Mr M (*grudging admiration*) Oh, Thami . . . you learn your lessons so well! The 'revolution' has only just begun and you are already word-perfect. So then tell me, do you think I agree with this inferior 'Bantu education' that is being forced on you?

Thami You teach it.

Mr M But unhappily so! Most unhappily, unhappily so! Don't you know that? Did you have your fingers in your ears the thousand times I've said so in the classroom? Where were you when I stood there and said I regarded it as my duty, my deepest obligation to you young men and women, to sabotage it, and that my conscience would not let me rest until I had succeeded. And I have! Yes, I have succeeded! I have got irrefutable proof of my success. You! Yes. You can stand here and accuse me, unjustly, because I have also had a struggle and I have won mine. I have liberated your mind in spite of what the Bantu education was trying to do to it. Your mouthful of big words and long sentences which the not-so-clever Comrades are asking you to speak and write for them, your wonderful eloquence at last night's meeting which got them all so excited – yes, I heard about it! – you must thank me for all of that, Thami.

Thami No I don't. You never taught me those lessons.

Mr M Oh, I see. You have got other teachers, have you?

Thami Yes. Yours were lessons in whispering. There are men now who are teaching us to shout. Those little tricks and jokes of yours in the classroom liberated nothing. The struggle doesn't need the big English words you taught me how to spell.

Mr M Be careful, Thami. Be careful! Be careful! Don't scorn words. They are sacred! Magical! Yes, they are. Do you know that without words a man can't think? Yes, it's true. Take that thought back with you as a present from the despised Mr M and share it with the Comrades. Tell them the difference between a man and an animal is that man thinks, and he thinks with words. Consider the mighty ox. Four powerful legs, massive shoulders, and a beautiful thick hide that gave our warriors shields to protect them when they went into battle. Think of his beautiful head, Thami, the long horns, the terrible bellow from his lungs when he charges a rival! *But it has got no words and therefore it is stupid!* And along comes that funny little, hairless animal that has got only two thin legs, no horns and a skin worth nothing and he tells that ox what to do. He is its master and he is that because he can speak! If the struggle needs weapons, give it words, Thami. Stones and petrol bombs can't get inside those police armoured cars. Words can. They can do something even more devastating than that . . . they can get inside the heads of those inside those armoured cars. I speak to you like this because if I have faith in anything, it is faith in the power of the word. Like my master, the great Confucius, I believe that, using only words, a man can right a wrong and judge and execute the wrongdoer. You are meant to use words like that. Talk to others. Bring them back into the classroom. They will listen to you. They look up to you as a leader.

Thami No, I won't. You talk about them as if they were a lot of sheep waiting to be led. They know what they are doing. They'd call me a traitor if I tried to persuade them otherwise.

Mr M Then listen carefully, Thami. I have received instructions from the department to make a list of all those who take part in the boycott. Do you know what

they will do with that list when all this is over . . .
because don't fool yourself, Thami, it will be. When your
boycott comes to an inglorious end like all the others . . .
they will make all of you apply for re-admission and if
your name is on that list . . . (*He leaves the rest
unspoken.*)

Thami Will you do it? Will you make that list for them?

Mr M That is none of your business.

Thami Then don't ask me questions about mine.

Mr M (*his control finally snaps, he explodes with anger
and bitterness*) Yes, I will! I will ask you all the questions
I like. And you know why? Because I am a man and you
are a boy. And if you are not in that classroom tomorrow
you will be a very, very silly boy.

Thami Then don't call me names, Mr M.

Mr M No? Then what must I call you? Comrade
Thami? Never! You are a silly boy now, and without
an education you will grow up to be a stupid man!

*For a moment it looks as if Thami is going to leave
without saying anything more, but he changes his
mind and confronts Mr M for the last time.*

Thami The others called *you* names at the meeting last
night. Did your spies tell you that? Government stooge,
sell-out, collaborator. They said you licked the white
man's arse and would even eat his shit if it meant
keeping your job. Did your spies tell you that I tried
to stop them saying those things? Don't wait until
tomorrow to make your list, Mr M. You can start now.
Write down the first name: Thami Mbikwana.

He leaves.
A few seconds of silence after Thami's departure.

Isabel makes a move towards Mr M but he raises his hand sharply, stopping her, keeping her at a distance.

Isabel This fucking country! (*She leaves.*)

SCENE TWO

Mr M alone. To start with, the mood is one of quiet, vacant disbelief.

Mr M It was like being in a nightmare. I was trying to get to the school, I knew that if I didn't hurry I was going to be late so I *had to get to the school* . . . but every road I took was blocked by policemen and soldiers with their guns ready, or Comrades building barricades. First I tried Jabulani Street, then I turned into Kwaza Road and then Dlamini Street . . . and then I gave up and just wandered around aimlessly, helplessly, watching my world go mad and set itself on fire. Everywhere I went . . . overturned buses, looted bread vans, the government offices . . . everything burning and the children dancing around, rattling boxes of matches and shouting *Tshisa, Qhumisa! Tshisa, Qhumisa! Tshisa, Qhumisa!* . . . and then running for their lives when the police armoured cars appeared. They were everywhere, crawling around in the smoke like giant dung-beetles looking for shit to eat. I ended up on the corner where Mrs Makatini always sits selling *vetkoek* and prickly pears to people waiting for the bus. The only person there was little Sipho Fondini from Standard Six, writing on the wall: 'Liberation First, then Education.' He saw me and he called out: 'Is the spelling right, Mr M?' And he meant it! The young eyes in that smoke-stained little face were terribly serious. Somewhere else a police van raced past me crowded with children who should have also been at their desks in school. Their hands waved desperately through the bars, their voices called out: 'Teacher! Teacher! Help us! Tell our mothers. Tell our fathers.' 'No, Anela,' I said. 'This is too much now. Just stand here and close your eyes and wait until you wake up and find your world the way it was.' But that didn't happen. A police car came around the corner and suddenly there were children everywhere throwing stones and tear gas bombs falling all around and I knew that I wasn't dreaming, that I was coughing and choking and hanging on to a lamp-post in the real world. No! No!

Do something, Anela. Do something. Stop the madness! Stop the madness!

SCENE THREE

Mr M alone in Number One Classroom. He is ringing his school bell wildly.

Mr M Come to school! Come to school! Before they kill you all, come to school!

Silence. Mr M looks around the empty classroom. He goes to his table, and after composing himself, opens the class register and reads out the names as he did every morning at the start of a new school day.

Johnny Awu, living or dead? Christopher Bandla, living or dead? Zandile Cwati, living or dead? Semphiwe Dambuza . . . Ronald Gxasheka . . . Noloyiso Mfundweni . . . Steven Gaika . . . Zachariah Jabavu . . . Thami . . . Thami Mbikwana . . . (*Pause.*) Living or dead?

How many young souls do I have present this morning? There are a lot of well-aimed stray bullets flying around on the streets out there. Is that why this silence is so . . . heavy? But what can I teach you? (*Picks up his little black dictionary from the table.*) My lessons were meant to help you in *this* world. I wanted you to know how to read and write and talk in *this* world of living, stupid, cruel men. (*helpless gesture*) Now? Oh my children! I have no lessons that will be of any use to you now. Mr M and all of his wonderful words are . . . useless, useless, useless!

> *The sound of breaking glass. Stones land in the classroom.*
> *Mr M picks one up.*

No! One of you is still alive. Ghosts don't throw stones with hot, sweating young hands. (*Grabs the bell and rings it wildly again.*) Come to school! Come to school!

> *Thami appears.*

Thami (*quietly*) Stop ringing that bell, Mr M.

Mr M Why? It's only the school bell, Thami. I thought you liked the sound of it. You once told me it was almost as good as music . . . don't you remember?

Thami You are provoking the Comrades with it.

Mr M No, Thami. I am summoning the Comrades with it.

Thami They say you are ringing the bell to taunt them. You are openly defying the boycott by being here in the school.

Mr M I ring this bell because according to my watch it is school time and I am a teacher and those desks are empty! I will go on ringing it as I have been doing these past two weeks, at the end of every lesson. And you can tell the Comrades that I will be back here ringing it tomorrow and the day after tomorrow and for as many days after that as it takes for this world to come to its senses. Is that the only reason you've come? To tell me to stop ringing the school bell?

Thami No.

Mr M You haven't come for a lesson, have you?

Thami No, I haven't.

Mr M Of course not. What's the matter with me?
Slogans don't need much in the way of grammar, do
they? As for these . . . (*indicating the stone in his hand*)
No, you don't need me for lessons in stone-throwing
either. You've already got teachers in those very
revolutionary subjects, haven't you? (*Picks up his
dictionary, the stone in one hand, the book in the other.*)
You know something interesting, Thami . . . if you put
these two on a scale I think you would find that they
weighed just about the same. But in this hand I am
holding the whole English language. This . . . (*of the
stone*) . . . is just *one* word in that language. It's true!
All that wonderful poetry that you and Isabel tried to
cram into your beautiful heads . . . in here! Twenty-six
letters, sixty thousand words. The greatest souls the
world has ever known were able to open the floodgates
of their ecstasy, their despair, their joy! . . . With the
words in this little book. Aren't you tempted? I was.
(*Opens the book at the fly-leaf and reads.*) 'Anela
Myalatya. Cookhouse. 1947'. One of the first books
I ever bought. (*impulsively*) I want you to have it.

Thami (*ignoring the offered book*) I've come here to
warn you.

Mr M You've already done that and I've already told
you that you are wasting your breath. Now take your
stones and go. There are a lot of unbroken windows left.

Thami I'm not talking about the bell now. It's more
serious than that.

Mr M In my life, nothing is more serious than ringing
the school bell.

Thami There was a meeting last night. Somebody stood up and denounced you as an informer.

Pause. Thami waits. Mr M says nothing.

He said you gave names to the police.

Mr M says nothing.

Everybody is talking about it this morning. You are in big danger.

Mr M Why are you telling me all this?

Thami So that you can save yourself. There's a plan to march to the school and burn it down. If they find you here . . .

Pause.

Mr M Go on. (*violently*) If they find me here *what?*

Thami They will kill you.

Mr M 'They will kill me.' That's better. Remember what I taught you . . . if you've got a problem, put it into words so that you can look at it, handle it, and ultimately solve it. They will kill me! You are right. That is very serious. So then . . . what must I do? Must I run away and hide somewhere?

Thami No, they will find you. You must join the boycott.

Mr M I'm listening.

Thami Let me go back and tell them that we have had a long talk and that you have realized you were wrong and have decided to join us. Let me say that you will sign the declaration and that you won't have anything to do with the school until all demands have been met.

223

Mr M And they will agree to that? Accept me as one of them even though it is believed that I am an informer?

Thami I will tell them you are innocent. That I confronted you with the charge and that you denied it and that I believe you.

Mr M I see. (*studying Thami intently*) *You* don't believe that I am an informer.

Thami No.

Mr M Won't you be taking a chance in defending me like that? Mightn't they end up suspecting you?

Thami They'll believe me. I'll make them believe me.

Mr M You can't be sure. Mobs don't listen to reason, Thami. Hasn't your revolution already taught you that? Why take a chance like that to save a collaborator? Why do you want to do all this for me?

Thami (*avoiding Mr M's eyes*) I'm not doing it for you. I'm doing it for the struggle. Our cause will suffer if we falsely accuse and hurt innocent people.

Mr M I see. My 'execution' would be an embarrassment to the cause. I apologize, Thami. For a moment I allowed myself to think that you were doing it because we were . . . who we are . . . the 'all-knowing Mr M and his brilliant protégé Thami'! I was so proud of us when Isabel called us that. Well, young Comrade, you have got nothing to worry about. Let them come and do whatever it is they want to. Your cause won't be embarrassed, because you see, they won't be 'hurting' an innocent man. (*He makes his confession simply and truthfully.*) That's right, Thami. I am guilty. I did go to the police. I sat down in Captain Lategan's office and told him I felt it was my duty to report the presence in our community of strangers from the north. I told him that I had reason to believe that they were behind the present unrest. I gave the Captain names and addresses. He thanked me and offered me money for the information, which I refused. (*Pause.*) Why do you look at me like that? Isn't that what you expected from me? . . . A government stooge, a sell-out, an arse-licker? Isn't that what you were all secretly hoping I would do . . . so that you could be proved right? (*appalled*) Is that why I did it? Out of spite? Can a man destroy himself, his life for a reason as petty as that?

I sat here before going to the police station saying to myself that it was my duty, to my conscience, to you, to the whole community to do whatever I could to put an end to this madness of boycotts and arson, mob violence and lawlessness . . . and maybe that is true . . . but only maybe . . . because Thami, the truth is that I was so lonely! You had deserted me. I was so jealous of those who had taken you away. *Now,* I've *really* lost you, haven't I? Yes. I can see it in your eyes. You'll never forgive me for doing that, will you? You know, Thami, I'd sell my soul to have you all back behind your desks for one last lesson. Yes. If the devil thought it was worth having and offered me that in exchange – one lesson! – He could have my soul. So then it's all over! Because this . . . (*of the classroom*) . . . is all there was for me. This was my home, my life, my one and only ambition . . . to be a good teacher! (*Indicates his dictionary.*) Anela Myalatya, twenty years old, from Cookhouse, wanted to be that the way your friends wanted to be big soccer stars playing for Kaizer Chiefs! That ambition goes back to when he was just a skinny little ten-year-old pissing on a small grey bush at the top of the Wapadsberg Pass. We were on our way to a rugby match at Somerset East. The lorry stopped at the top of the mountain so that we could stretch our legs and relieve ourselves. It was a hard ride on the

back of that lorry. The road hadn't been tarred yet.
So there I was, ten years old and sighing with relief as
I aimed for the little bush. It was a hot day. The sun right
over our heads . . . not a cloud in the vast blue sky.
I looked out . . . it's very high up there at the top of the
pass . . . and there it was, stretching away from the foot
of the mountain, the great pan of the Karoo . . . stretching away for ever it seemed into the purple haze and heat
of the horizon. Something grabbed my heart at that
moment, my soul, and squeezed it until there were tears
in my eyes. I had never seen anything so big, so beautiful
in all my life. I went to the teacher who was with us and
asked him: 'Teacher, where will I come to if I start
walking that way?' . . . And I pointed. He laughed. 'Little
man,' he said, 'that way is north. If you start walking
that way and just keep on walking, and your legs don't
give in, you will see all of Africa! Yes, Africa, little man!
You will see the great rivers of the continent: the Vaal,
the Zambesi, the Limpopo, the Congo and then the
mighty Nile. You will see the mountains: the
Drakensberg, Kilimanjaro, Kenya and the Ruwenzori.
And you will meet all our brothers: the little Pygmies of
the forests, the proud Masai, the Watusi, tallest of the
tall, and the Kikuyu standing on one leg like herons in a
pond waiting for a frog.' 'Has teacher seen all that?' I
asked. 'No,' he said. 'Then how does teacher know it's
there?' 'Because it is all in the books and I have read the
books and if you work hard in school, little man, you can
do the same without worrying about your legs giving in.'

He was right, Thami. *I* have seen it. It is all there in
the books just as he said it was and I have made it mine.
I can stand on the banks of all those great rivers, look up
at the majesty of all those mountains, whenever I want
to. It is a journey I have made many times. Whenever
my spirit was low and I sat alone in my room, I said to
myself: Walk, Anela! Walk! . . . And I imagined myself at

the foot of the Wapadsberg, setting off for that horizon that called me that day forty years ago. It always worked! When I left that little room, I walked back into the world a proud man, because I was an African and all the splendour was my birthright. (*Pause*). I don't want to make that journey again, Thami. There is someone waiting for me now at the end of it who has made a mockery of all my visions of splendour. He has in his arms my real birthright. I saw him on the television in the Reverend Mbopa's lounge. An Ethiopian tribesman, and he was carrying the body of a little child that had died of hunger in the famine . . . a small bundle carelessly wrapped in a few rags. I couldn't tell how old the man was. The lines of despair and starvation on his face made him look as old as Africa itself. He held that little bundle very lightly as he shuffled along to a mass grave, and when he reached it, he didn't have the strength to kneel and lay it down gently . . . He just opened his arms and let it fall. I was very upset when the programme ended. Nobody had thought to tell us his name and whether he was the child's father, or grandfather, or uncle. And the same for the baby! Didn't it have a name? How dare you show me one of our children being thrown away and not tell me its name! I demand to know who is in that bundle! (*Pause.*) Not knowing their names doesn't matter any more. They are more than just themselves. The tribesmen and dead child do duty for all of us, Thami. Every African soul is either carrying that bundle or in it. What is wrong with this world that it wants to waste you all like that . . . my children . . . my Africa! (*Holding out a hand as if he wanted to touch Thami's face.*) My beautiful and proud young Africa!

More breaking glass and stones and the sound of a crowd outside the school. Mr M starts to move. Thami stops him.

Thami No! Don't go out there. Let me speak to them first. Listen to me! I will tell them I have confronted you with the charges and that you have denied them and that I believe you. I will tell them you are innocent.

Mr M You will lie for me, Thami?

Thami Yes.

Mr M (*desperate to hear the truth*) Why?

> *Thami can't speak.*

Why will you lie for me, Thami?

Thami I've told you before.

Mr M The 'Cause'?

Thami Yes.

Mr M Then I do not need to hide behind your lies.

Thami They will kill you.

Mr M Do you think I'm frightened of them? Do you think I'm frightened of dying?

> *Mr M breaks away from Thami. Ringing his bell furiously he goes outside and confronts the mob. They kill him.*

SCENE FOUR

Thami waiting. Isabel arrives.

Thami Isabel.

Isabel (*it takes her a few seconds to respond*) Hello Thami.

Thami Thank you for coming.

Isabel (*she is tense. Talking to him is not easy*) I wasn't going to. Let me tell you straight out that there is nothing in this world . . . nothing! . . . that I want to see less at this moment than anything or anybody from the location. But you said in your note that it was urgent, so here I am. If you've got something to say, I'll listen.

Thami Are you in a hurry?

Isabel I haven't got to be somewhere else, if that's what you mean. But if you're asking because it looks as if I would like to run away from here – from you! – very fast, then the answer is yes. But don't worry, I'll be able to control that urge for as long as you need to say what you want to.

Thami (*awkward in the face of Isabel's severe and unyielding attitude*) I just wanted to say goodbye.

Isabel Again?

Thami What do you mean?

Isabel You've already done that, Thami. Maybe you didn't use that word, but you turned your back on me and walked out of my life that last afternoon the three of us . . . (*She can't finish.*) How long ago was that?

Thami Three weeks I think.

Isabel So why do you want to do it again? Aren't you happy with the last time? It was so dramatic, Thami!

Thami (*patiently*) I wanted to see you because I'm leaving the town, I'm going away for good.

Isabel Oh, I see. This is meant to be a 'sad' goodbye is it? (*She is on the edge.*) I'm sorry if I'm hurting your feelings but I thought you wanted to see me because you had something to say about recent events in our little community . . . (*Out of a pocket she takes a crumpled little piece of newspaper which she opens with unsteady hands.*) . . . a certain unrest-related . . . I think that is the phrase they use . . . yes . . . here it is . . . (*reading*) '. . . unrest-related incident in which according to witnesses the defenceless teacher was attacked by a group of blacks who struck him over the head with an iron rod before setting him on fire.'

Thami Stop it, Isabel.

Isabel (*fighting hard for self-control*) Oh Thami, I wish I could! I've tried everything, but nothing helps. It just keeps going around and around inside my head. I've tried crying. I've tried praying! I've even tried confrontation. Ja, the day after it happened I tried to get into the location. I wanted to find the witnesses who reported it so accurately and ask them: 'Why didn't you stop it!' There was a police roadblock at the entrance and they wouldn't let me in. They thought I was crazy or something and 'escorted' me back into the safekeeping of two now very frightened parents. There is nothing wrong with me! All I need is someone to tell me why he was killed. What madness drove those people to kill a man who had devoted his whole life to helping them. He was such a good man, Thami! He was one of the most beautiful human beings I have ever known and his death is the ugliest thing I have ever known.

Thami gives her a few seconds to calm down.

Thami (*gently*) He was an informer, Isabel. Somehow or the other somebody discovered that Mr M was an informer.

Isabel You mean that list of pupils taking part in the boycott? You call that informing?

Thami No. It was worse than that. He went to the police and gave them the names and addresses of our political action committee. All of them were arrested after his visit. They are now in detention.

Isabel Mr M did that?

Thami Yes.

Isabel I don't believe it.

Thami It's true, Isabel.

Isabel No! What proof do you have?

Thami His own words. He told me so himself. I didn't believe it either when he was first accused, but the last time I saw him, he said it was true, that he had been to the police.

Isabel (*stunned disbelief*) Mr M? A police spy? For how long?

Thami No. It wasn't like that. He wasn't paid or anything. He went to the police just that one time. He said he felt it was his duty.

Isabel And what do you mean?

Thami Operation Qhumisa . . . the boycotts and strikes, the arson . . . you know he didn't agree with any of that. But he was also very confused about it all. I think he wished he had never done it.

Isabel So he went to the police just once . . .

Thami Yes.

Isabel As a matter of conscience.

Thami Yes.

Isabel That doesn't make him an 'informer', Thami!

Thami Then what do you call somebody who gives information to the police?

Isabel No! You know what that word really means, the sort of person it suggests. Was Mr M one of those? He was acting out of concern for his people . . . you said so yourself. He thought he was doing the right thing! You don't murder a man for that!

Thami (*near the end of his patience*) Be careful, Isabel.

Isabel Of what?

Thami The words you use.

Isabel Oh? Which one don't you like? Murder? What do you want me to call it – 'an unrest-related incident'? If you are going to call him an informer, then I am going to call his death murder!

Thami It was an act of self-defence.

Isabel By who?

Thami The People.

Isabel (*almost speechless with outrage*) What? A mad mob attacks one unarmed, defenceless man and you want me to call it –

Thami (*abandoning all attempts at patience, he speaks with the full authority of the anger inside him*) Stop, Isabel! You just keep quiet now and listen to me. You're always saying you want to understand us and what it means to be black . . . well if you do, listen to me carefully now. I don't call it murder, and I don't call the people who did it a mad mob, and yes, I do expect you to see it as an act of self-defence – listen to me! – blind and stupid but still self-defence. He betrayed us and our fight for freedom. Five men are in detention because of Mr M's visit to the police station. There have been other arrests and there will be more. Why do you think I'm running away? How were those people to know he wasn't a paid informer who had been doing it for a long time and would do it again? They were defending themselves against what they thought was a terrible danger to themselves. What Anela Myalatya did to them and their cause is what your laws define as treason when it is done to you and threatens the safety and security of your comfortable white world. Anybody accused of it is put on trial in your courts and if found guilty they get hanged. Many of my people have been found guilty and have been hanged. Those hangings *we* call murder!

Try to understand, Isabel. Try to imagine what it is like to be a black person, choking inside with rage and frustration, bitterness, and then to discover that one of your own kind is a traitor, has betrayed you to those responsible for the suffering and misery of your family, of your people. What would you do? Remember there is no magistrate or court you can drag him to and demand that he be tried for that crime. There is no justice for black people in this country other than what we make for ourselves. When you judge us for what happened in front of the school four days ago just remember that you carry a share of the responsibility for it. It is your laws that have made simple, decent black people so desperate that they turn into 'mad mobs'.

Isabel has been listening and watching intently. It looks as if she is going to say something but she stops herself.

Say it, Isabel.

Isabel No.

Thami This is your last chance. You once challenged me to be honest with you. I'm challenging you now.

Isabel (*faces him*) Where were you when it happened, Thami? (*Pause.*) And if you were, did you try to stop them?

Thami Isn't there a third question, Isabel? Was I one of the mob that killed him?

Isabel Yes. Forgive me, Thami. Please forgive me! But there is that question as well. Only once! Believe me, only once – late at night when I couldn't sleep. I couldn't believe it was there in my head, but I heard the words . . . 'Was Thami one of the ones who did it?'

Thami If the police catch me, that is the question they will ask.

Isabel I'm asking you because . . . (*an open, helpless gesture*) . . . I'm lost! I don't know what to think or feel any more. Help me. Please. You're the only one who can. Nobody else seems to understand that I loved him.

This final confrontation is steady and unflinching on both sides.

Thami Yes, I was there. Yes, I did try to stop it. (*Thami gives Isabel the time to deal with this answer.*) I knew how angry the people were. I went to warn him. If he had listened to me he would still be alive, but he wouldn't. It was almost as if he wanted it to happen. I think he hated himself very much for what he had done, Isabel. He kept saying to me that it was all over. He was right. There was nothing left for him. That visit to the police station had finished everything. Nobody would have ever spoken to him again or let him teach their children.

Isabel Oh Thami, it is all so wrong! So stupid! That's what I can't take – the terrible stupidity of it. We needed him. All of us.

Thami I know.

Isabel Then why is he dead?

Thami You must stop asking these questions, Isabel. You know the answers.

Isabel They don't make any sense, Thami.

Thami I know what you are feeling. (*Pause.*) I also loved him. Doesn't help much to say it now, I know, but I did. Because he made me angry and impatient with his 'old-fashioned' ideas, I didn't want to admit it. Even if I had, it wouldn't have stopped me from doing what I did, the boycott and everything, but I should have tried harder to make him understand why I was doing it. You were right to ask about that. Now . . .? (*a helpless gesture*) You know the most terrible words in your language, Isabel? Too late.

Isabel Ja.

Thami I'll never forgive myself for not trying harder with him and letting him know . . . my true feelings for him. Right until the end I tried to deny it . . . to him, to myself.

Isabel I'm sorry. I . . .

Thami That's all right.

Isabel Are the police really looking for you?

Thami Yes. Some of my friends have already been detained. They're pulling in anybody they can get their hands on.

Isabel Where are you going? Cape Town?

Thami No. That's the first place they'll look. I've written to my parents telling them about everything. I'm heading north.

Isabel To where?

Thami Far, Isabel. I'm leaving the country.

Isabel Does that mean what I think it does?

Thami (*nods*) I'm going to join the movement. I want to be a fighter. I've been thinking about it for a long time. Now I know it's the right thing to do. I don't want to end up being one of the mob that killed Mr M – but that will happen to me if I stay here. I know I'm doing the right thing. Believe me.

Isabel I'll try.

Thami And you?

Isabel I don't know what to do with myself, Thami. All I know is that I'm frightened of losing him. He's only been dead four days and I think I'm already starting to forget what he looked like. But the worst thing is that there's nowhere for me to go and . . . you know . . . just be near him. That's so awful. I got my father to phone the police but they said there wasn't enough left of him to justify a grave. What there was has been disposed of in a 'Christian manner'. So where do I go? The burnt-out ruins of the school? I couldn't face that.

Thami Get your father or somebody to drive you to the top of the Wapadsberg Pass. It's on the road to Cradock.

Isabel I know it.

Thami It was a very special place to him. He told me that it was there where it all started, where he knew what he wanted to do with his life . . . being a teacher,

being the Mr M we knew. You'll be near him up there.
I must go now.

Isabel Do you need any money?

Thami No. *Sala Kakhule,* Isabel. That's the Xhosa
goodbye.

Isabel I know it. Auntie taught me how to say it. *Hamba
Kakhule,* Thami.

Thami leaves.

SCENE FIVE

*Isabel alone. She stands quietly, examining the silence.
After a few seconds she nods her head slowly.*

Isabel Yes! Thami was right, Mr M. He said I'd feel
near you up here. He's out there somewhere, Mr M . . .
travelling north. He didn't say where exactly he was
going, but I think we can guess, can't we?

I'm here for a very 'old-fashioned' reason, so I know
you'll approve. I've come to pay my last respects to
Anela Myalatya. I know the old-fashioned way of doing
that is to bring flowers, lay them on the grave, say a
quiet prayer and then go back to your life. But that
seemed sort of silly this time. You'll have enough flowers
around here when the spring comes . . . which it will. So
instead I've brought you something which I know will
mean more to you than flowers or prayers ever could.
A promise. I am going to make Anela Myalatya a
promise. You gave me a little lecture once about wasted
lives . . . how much of it you'd seen, how much you
hated it, how much you didn't want that to happen to
Thami and me. I sort of understood what you meant at
the time. Now, I most certainly do. Your death has seen
to that. My promise to you is that I am going to try as

237

hard as I can, in every way that I can, to see that it doesn't happen to me. I am going to try my best to make my life useful in the way yours was. I want you to be proud of me. After all, I am one of your children, you know. You did welcome me to your family. (*A pause.*) The future is still ours, Mr M.

Isabel leaves the stage.

End.

PLAYLAND

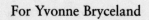

For Yvonne Bryceland

The Arts and Society

*Edited extracts from a talk delivered at
Rhodes University in 1991 in which Fugard
explores the relationship between the two.*

There are as many ways and reasons for writing a play
as there are individual playwrights. All I can talk about
with any authority is my own personal experience. Just
of late there has been an attempt on the part of certain
political groupings in the country to tell artists what they
should be doing, what their social obligations are, and
how they should go about discharging them. I believe
very strongly that artists should be left to look after
themselves in this regard. When it comes to the arts,
nobody has the right to make rules for another.

So let me start off by saying this: I am more in love
with my craft as a playwright – more passionately committed to theatre and excited by its extraordinary power,
its extraordinary imaginative freedom, than I have ever
been and I think one of the main reasons for this is the
powerful dynamic that exists in South African theatre.

Talking to audiences overseas, particularly in America,
I have claimed for South Africa an almost unique
dynamic in terms of the relationship between the event
on the stage and the political and social reality out in
the streets. I personally cannot think of another country
where there is as direct and electrifying a relationship
between the two, where the drama on the streets is being
so immediately reflected by the drama on the stage.

Not even in Eastern Europe where even more
dramatic political change has taken place is theatre as

directly in touch with the events out on the streets as is the case in our country.

This dynamic, which was virtually non-existent when I did my first plays in Johannesburg thirty-five years ago, is, I repeat, one of the main reasons for the depth and strength of my commitment to the medium.

One small point in parenthesis. Don't let what I have just said leave you with the impression that now, on the brink of my sixtieth birthday, I pick up my pen and sail with confidence into the writing of a new play.

I am in fact at work on a new play at the moment [*Playland*] and I still find myself terribly intimidated by the reality of blank paper. None of my past experience in writing plays helps me deal with what I describe as the 'inquisition of blank paper' when I face up to it at the outset of a new work.

Now in spite of all I have said about the exciting, committed energy of our theatre, I must also tell you that I find myself very frustrated by the label 'political playwright' which I have ended up with.

I can understand how it happened. There is a very obvious political spin-off to the plays I write. But then my work is not unique in that regard. I don't think it is possible to tell a South African story accurately and truthfully and for it *not* to have a political spin-off.

I believe we live in one of the most highly politicized societies in the world. In other countries people take their politics seriously enough, but they don't talk, argue, dream, live it, to the extent we do. The South African reality is surely unique in that regard.

When I take stock of an ordinary day in my life, I can't find any area of my living which politics has not invaded; I can't find any area of experience in which the political issues, the political realities do not, in some way or another, have a resonance. They are there in the most intimate relationships I have with other human beings, and most pertinently of course in the relationship I have with myself.

Nevertheless, even though I can understand how I have ended up with that label I still find it very frustrating because I think it creates an expectation that gets in the way of people receiving the play I have written. Even more seriously, I think, in the way that it tries to take away certain freedoms from me as a writer.

If people are sitting in an audience for one of my plays waiting for a political message, they are going to be very disappointed. I am a storyteller, not a political pamphleteer, and because of their misguided anticipation they will, in all likelihood, not get the story I am trying to tell.

This has happened with some frequency in my career, particularly on the part of the critics who, quite frankly, are too often the laziest members of the audience. They are the ones who came up with the label in the first place. They keep me pigeonholed because it solves a lot of problems for them. Pigeonholing a writer gives you the comfortable illusion that you know who and what he or she is.

You see, the only way to stay alive creatively as a writer is to constantly generate for yourself new challenges, to try to break out of the mould of old habits and formulae, turn corners and go in new directions. I am very conscious of this because I have felt the need for it at several critical periods in my writing life.

I have seen a few fellow playwrights of my time die creatively because they were incapable of generating new challenges for themselves. You undergo profound emotional and intellectual changes as an individual in the living of your life, and your writing has to keep up with this. If it doesn't, you will end up 'imitating' yourself, or worse than that, imitating a self that no longer exists. What was at first a deeply felt personal truth becomes a hollow formula, repeated now simply to stay in the good books of the critics who liked it when it first appeared. I could not go back at this point and write a play like *The Blood Knot,* the play in which I discovered my voice for the first time.

A very changed Athol Fugard is writing the new play, yet so many critical definitions of my work are still the old ones generated by *The Blood Knot.*

A personal example of what I am talking about came with my play *A Place with the Pigs,* which I *know* is a very good play, possibly one of my best, and will one day confound the critics who did not think so. But it was seemingly not about South African politics and that was enormously disconcerting both to the critics and to the audiences. A play about a Russian soldier who deserted the front line and hid in a pigsty for thirty-seven years? What has happened to Fugard? I acted in the premiere productions in the United States and South Africa and I could literally hear the audience scratching its head and asking, 'When is he going to start talking about what we expect him to talk about?'

That is a very severe limitation when you're a writer. It's a particularly severe limitation in theatre because theatre is a very immediate medium. Judgements are passed very quickly, too quickly, in my opinion . . . and the success or failure of a play that has taken nine months to write is decided overnight. It's not like a novel which can lie around and be taken up and reassessed and brooded on and thought about. The notices are out there the next day and regrettably South African audiences are now also allowing the critics to do all their thinking for them.

I said earlier that I think of myself as a storyteller, that I don't preach political sermons. In all the writing that lies behind me not once has an idea been the provocation that led to the writing of a new play.

The genesis of a new work has always been something that I have experienced personally, or something that I have seen happen to other people as I have gone about the business of living my life, or even something that I've read in a newspaper. Somehow or other there have always been the faces of people involved, the realities of actual lived lives.

Obviously there is an intellectual content to a good story as well. Ideally you should leave the theatre with both head and heart excited. What I am talking about is the *genesis* of new work on my side and for me that has always been an image of a particular individual or a group of individuals, something that they had done or something that was done to them.

And what is more, they are usually desperate individuals – human desperation is the real substance of theatre. Nobody has ever written a good play about a group of happy people who started off happy and who were happy all the way through. Whether it's *Antigone* or *Mother Courage* or some of those extraordinary disembodied voices which come out of Samuel Beckett's universe, we are talking about human desperation – that is the substance of drama – and in South Africa if you have found a desperate individual, nine times out of ten you have also found a desperate political situation.

I end up writing a play when that external event, that thing I read in the newspaper, that incident I saw on the street or that little thing that happened to me, coincides with what I can only describe as a build-up of subconscious pressure within myself to the point where it needs release.

When I look back on my writing life I am conscious of how leading up to the writing of every new play there has been – without my necessarily being aware of it at first – the build-up of a certain kind of psychic pressure inside me which has intensified with time and which finally becomes so acute that I need a story into which I can release it.

The Swedish poet Tranströmer has a line to the effect that when the external event coincides with the internal reality the poem happens. That is how it works for me as a playwright.

What I have also discovered is that it doesn't work if I try to use something that is immediately around me, some image from the day that I've just lived or from a day past or from a month past – somehow it only works when the image is one that has lain around in my life gestating for a long time, more often than not for years. The seminal images of my new play go back all of twenty-five years in my notebooks.

I am an addicted keeper of notebooks. When I see things which I think might be useful to me in the future they go into my notebook and that is where I always look when I realize that I am pregnant again.

I am not always aware of the nature of the pressure that has built up in me and what is really involved when I suddenly take up an image and develop it into a play. Awareness of what was actually going on in my subconscious usually only comes some time after the event.

A good example of all of this is my play *The Road to Mecca*. About seven or eight years ago, having known about her for at least fifteen years, I suddenly found myself thinking about a play based on the life and work of Helen Martins of Nieu-Bethesda. What I realize now is that my hidden agenda in writing that play was an attempt to understand the genesis, nature and consequences of a creative energy.

One of the great fears of my life has been the possible drying up of my creative energy. What would I do if I ever found that I could not write again and there was still a lot of time left to live?

I once said in an interview that the only truly safe place I have ever known in this world, in this life that I have lived, was at the centre of a story as its teller. I speak to you with a measure of authority and confidence tonight only because when I go back to Port Elizabeth I go back to my desk where I am writing a new play and because of that I know who I am, what I am, where I am and why I'm there. All the whys, whos, whats and wheres of my life are taken care of when I am writing.

I go through a terrible kind of limbo existence between one act of storytelling and another. I have only once experienced that indescribable hell called writer's block when you just can't get it down on paper, and although it was many years ago, that once was enough. It is a form of anguish that still frightens me when I think about it now. Dealing with that fear was, I now believe, one of the main reasons for writing *The Road to Mecca*.

It is not a biographical play about the real Helen Martins. The Miss Helen of my *The Road to Mecca* is actually a self-portrait. It was only after I had written the play that I realized what I had been trying to do. I used the symbolic vocabulary of the play to understand my own personally dreaded moment of darkness – the extinction of my creativity.

What happens when all the candles go out? What Miss Helen realizes of course is that to be a true master you have got to know not only how to light them, but also how to blow them out. This recognition has, I think, been the inspiration behind some of the most moving works of art. When you listen to Strauss's four last songs or Mahler's *Das Lied von der Erde* you are in fact in the presence of artists who have recognized the need for renunciation. The affirmation in my play is Miss Helen's recognition and acceptance of that necessity.

Characters

Martinus Zoeloe
Gideon le Roux
'Barking Barney' Barkhuizen, *voice off*

Playland was first performed on 16 July 1992 at the Market Theatre, Johannesburg, presented by Mannie Manim Productions, with the following cast:

Martinus Zoeloe John Kani
Gideon le Roux Sean Taylor
'Barking Barney' Barkhuizen Bill Flynn

Director Athol Fugard
Designer/Assistant Director Susan Hilferty
Lighting Mannie Manim
Sound Mark Malherbe
Production Manager Wesley France
Stage Manager Melanie Dobbs
Deputy Stage Manager/Sound Operator Christo Boshoff
Deputy Stage Manager Haccius Mokopakgos
Wardrobe Hazel Maree
Production Assistant Debbie Falb

Playland was first performed in England at the Donmar Warehouse, London, on 25 February 1993, with the following cast:

Martinus Zoeloe John Kani
Gideon le Roux Sean Taylor
'Barking Barney' Bill Flynn

Associate Director and Designer Susan Hilferty
Sound Designer Mark Malherbe
Lighting Designer Mannie Manim
Tour Manager Wesley France

Scene One

*A small travelling amusement park encamped on the
outskirts of a Karoo town. A large sign with the name
playland is prominently positioned. There is also an
array of other gaudy signs advertising the various
sideshows and rides – the Big Wheel, the Wall of Death,
the Ghost Train and so on. They are all festooned with
coloured lights which will be switched on when the night
gets under way. Battered speakers of a PA system at the
top of a pole.*

*Foreground: the night-watchman's camp. A broken
car from one of the rides with a square of canvas
stretched over it to provide shelter from sun and rain,
and a paraffin tin brazier.*

Time: the late afternoon of New Year's Eve, 1989.

*Gideon le Roux saunters on. Casually but neatly
dressed for a warm Karoo evening. He is stopped by
the sound of an angry voice with laughter and heckling
from other voices. Martinus Zoeloe walks on from the
opposite side. Old overalls, and a rolled-up balaclava
on his head.*

Martinus Ja! Ja! Go on. Laugh as much as you like but
I say it again: I'll see all of you down there in Hell. That's
right. All of you. In Hell! And when you wake up and
see the big fires and start crying and saying you sorry
and asking forgiveness, then it's me who is laughing.

*Gideon stands quietly smoking a cigarette and
listening to the harangue. Martinus is not aware of
his presence.*

Ja! That day it is Martinus who has a good laugh. You
tell lies and cheat and drink and make trouble with the
little girls and you think God doesn't know? He knows!
He sees everything you do and when the Big Day of
Judging comes he will say to you, and you, and specially
you: Hey! You fucked the little girls in Cradock and gave
them babies; you fucked the little girls in Noupoort and
gave them babies – what you got to say for yourself?
And you got nothing to say because it's true and that's
the end of it. And all the times you *verneuk* the *baas*
with the tickets and put the money in your pockets, he
knows about that as well. And also the generator petrol
you are stealing and selling in the location. Baas Barney
swear at me, but I know it's you. I see you there by the
petrol drums when you think nobody is looking. So
voetsek to all of you! (*He sees the white man for the first
time.*)

Gideon (*applauding*) That's it my friend. That's what
I like to hear. Somebody who is not afraid to speak his
mind. So you tell them. You tell them loud and clear.

Martinus Joburg skollies. All of them. All they know is
to make trouble for other people.

Gideon Then go make some for them. Ja. Report them
to your baas. Don't let them get away with it. You got
to speak up in this bloody world. It's the only way to put
an end to all the nonsense that is going on. Everywhere
you look – bloody nonsense! People think they can get
away with anything these days. There's no respect left
for nothing no more.

Martinus That one with the skeel oog, he's the one. The
first time I see him there in Beaufort West, when he
comes looking for work, I knew! Skelm! And I warn
Baas Barney. That one is trouble I tell him. But he
wouldn't listen. So now we have it.

Gideon Then to hell with your Baas Barney as well! That's what I say. If he won't listen then too bad. You tried your best. My advice to you is just carry on and do your job and to hell with everything else. What is your job here?

Martinus Watchman and handyman.

Gideon Night-watchman for Playland. That sounds OK.

Martinus Night and day watchman.

Gideon All the time?

Martinus All the time. I watch everything all the time.

Gideon So when do you sleep?

Martinus I don't sleep.

A silence settles between the two men. Gideon tries again.

Gideon Bloody hot again today, hey? On the news they said it was thirty-six degrees in the shade here by us. In the shade, mark you! (*hollow laugh*) I like that. I felt like phoning them and asking, is that now supposed to be a joke or what? Over by De Aar it was forty-one. Can you imagine? Chickens was dying of heat stroke. De Aar! (*Shakes his head.*) God knows this dump is bad enough, but De Aar! No man, that's a fate worse than death. They say there's a ou bollie there who fries his breakfast eggs on his motorcar bonnet in summer. Says he uses multi-grade instead of margarine.

Hollow laugh. No response from Martinus.

Anyway that's how bad it is. Couple of months ago they offered me a transfer there with a pay rise. I turned it down flat. (*Pause.*) By the way, what's your name?

Martinus Martinus.

Gideon Martinus. That's a good one.

Martinus Martinus Zoeloe.

Gideon That's sommer a bakgat name, man! Martinus Zoeloe. B. G. Buitengewoon. So listen, Martinus, when do things get going around here? You know, the lights and the music and everything. When do you people switch on?

Martinus Seven o'clock.

Gideon (*looking at his watch*) Hour to go, then five more and it's hip-hip-hooray time hey! Goodbye 1989, welcome 1990! And 'bout bloody time too. Hell, this year now really went slowly, hey? I thought we'd never get here. Some days at work it was so bad I use to think my watch had stopped. I check the time and I see it's ten o'clock. Two hours later I check it again and it's only half-past ten.

Hollow laugh. Nothing from Martinus.

Didn't look as if it was going to be so bad in the beginning. I got my discharge at the end of February and it looked as if things were going to be O.K. – you know, being home, being alive . . . (*hollow laugh*) . . . and everything. I mean, shit man, there I was waking up in my own bed again with my old ma bringing me a cup of condensed milk coffee the way I use to dream about it up there on the Border. Ja, March was also all right. I had some good times. Even April. But then . . .! Shit-a-brick! June, July, August, September – fucking nothing, man! All of them. Just nothing. And I tried. Believe me I tried, but I just couldn't get things going again. Every day I wake up and say to myself, 'Come on now Gid, get your arse in gear and let's get things going today' . . . but that's as far as it gets.

Like my pigeons. I use to be crazy about pigeons. Me
and my dad. Just before he died we had over a hundred
of them in a hok there in the backyard. Tumblers,
Pouters, Homers, Racers, Fantails – we had them all.
This was the time they use to flock – you know, all come
together and fly around before settling into the hok for
the night. Hell that was a beautiful sight, man. Aerial
manoeuvres of the Karoo Squadron we use to call it.
All the time in formation, round and round in the sky!

You would think they was following orders the way
all them would suddenly swerve and change direction . . .
(*He laughs at the memory.*) Then after my dad died . . .
I don't know . . . somehow it just wasn't the same any
more without him. I kept them going and all that – fed
them and cleaned the hok – but my heart wasn't in it the
way it use to be when he was also there. Then one
morning I go to feed them and – *Here!* – a wild cat or
something had got into the hok in the night and gone
mad! Half of them were lying around in pieces, man –
dead as fucking freedom fighters . . . I had to pull the
necks of another ten of them that was still alive they was
in such a bad way. That did it. I sold the rest of them
and I thought that was the end of it. Not a damn! I'm
sitting up there on the Border one day – and this is now
years later, remember – and I suddenly find myself
thinking about them and how lekker it would be to start
up again – buy a few breeding pairs, fix up the hok and
watch them fly at sunset. From then on that was all I use
to think about. You got to have something to think
about up there man, otherwise you go mad. I'm not
joking. I've seen it happen. Anyway, the truth of the
matter is I haven't done a bloody thing about it since I've
been back. The old hok is still standing there on three
legs, ready to fall over, full of spider webs. I don't know
what it is, man, but I just can't get things going again.
I'm not bosbefok or anything like that. The doctors have

given me some pills for my nerves and to help me sleep, but otherwise I'm O.K. Ai! It's just . . . I don't know. Like tonight. I was ready to just sit at home with my ma and fall asleep in front of the television again. Can you believe it? New Year's Eve? That's when I thought to myself, 'No man, this has now gone far enough. Get out Gideon le Roux. Get among the people. Join in. Grab some fun. Look for romance!' So here I am ladies! Don't all rush at once. (*hollow laugh*) Anyway . . . that is going to be my resolution tonight when midnight comes: No bloody miseries next year! I don't care how I do it, but 1990 is going to be different. Even if it kills me, I'm going to get things going again.
You got yours ready?

Martinus What?

Gideon Your New Year's resolution.

Martinus What is that?

Gideon Midnight, man. When 1990 comes. You give up smoking or something like that.

Martinus I don't smoke.

Gideon Then something else. Drinking.

Martinus I don't drink.

Gideon Well there must be something you want to give up.

Martinus No.

Gideon Okay. So you're perfect. Good luck to you. (*A hip flask of cane spirit appears out of a pocket.*) That means I don't have to offer you a dop hey! (*hollow laugh*) Last year I gave up drinking. It lasted about ten minutes because then I needed a drink to give up smoking, and then I needed a drink *and* a cigarette to

give up wanking – and that's not the capital of China,
my friend! And so it went. Every dop was another
resolution . . . that lasted ten minutes! Base Camp
Oshakati! That was quite a party. Talk about your
friends going to Hell – if you had seen me and my
buddies that night you would have sent the lot of us
there as well.

*Another silence. Both men stare at the horizon where
a Karoo sunset is flaring to a dramatic climax.*

How about that, hey!

Martinus Ja, it's starting now.

Gideon It might have been a useless bloody year, but it's
certainly going out in style. I mean, look at it! It's right
around us. That's sommer a cinerama sunset for you.

Martinus Ja, it's going to be a big one tonight.

Gideon We use to get them like that up in South West.
From one end of the sky to the other – red, red. I'm
telling you man, it looked like the end of the world had
come. And believe me there was a couple of times when
it also felt like that.

Martinus The Day of Judgement.

Gideon That's a good one. I like it. Days of Judgement!
Ja, for a lot of men that's what they turned out to be.
And they were good men. My buddies! But that's the
way it was. One day you're swapping jokes with him,
the next day you're saying prayers for him . . . and
wondering if it's your turn next. (*Pause.*) I can remember
sitting there in the bush one day. It was about this time –
late, late afternoon, nearly getting dark. That sky wasn't
just red my friend, it was on fire! And you could smell it
too. Smoke, burning rubber, ammo, dust, bush . . .
everything! We'd had a big contact with SWAPO that

day, and we weren't expecting it. They caught us
napping. Jesus it was rough. Anyway, it was klaarstaan
time again – sunset, sunrise, SWAPO's favourite times for
a hit – and one of my buddies comes and parks next to
me there in the trench. I say to him, 'We're alive,
Charlie. We're alive.' And Charlie says, 'You know Gid,
I'm not so sure any more that that's the good news.'
I always remember that. Because he was right. It always
only got worse.

Martinus (*gesturing at the sunset*) I watch it every night.
Every time it is different and I see different things.

Gideon Free bioscope!

Martinus Last night it was like gold.

Gideon I didn't see it last night.

Martinus (*pointing*) That way, on the road to Beaufort
West. Big, big piles of the gold that makes them all mad
in Johannesburg. Mountains of gold!

Gideon How about that hey? Mountains of gold! We'd
all be millionaires.

Martinus And then sometimes nothing happens. The sun
goes down slowly, slowly, and then it's gone. And then
the light goes away slowly, slowly, and then it's also
gone, and it's dark and the stars are shining.

Gideon They say it's just the dust in the atmosphere
what does it. You know . . . the colours and the clouds
and everything. But even so it still makes you think,
doesn't it? Like over there, that big one. Doesn't it look
like they finally dropped the atomic bomb on De Aar?
I mean look at it. That's the atomic bomb cloud. What
do they call it again? Ja, the mushroom cloud!

Martinus Tonight I see the fires of Eternal Damnation.

Gideon Hell, that's a heavy one.

Martinus That's right, Hell!

Gideon Well, I suppose if you believe in that Bible stuff it could be, but speaking for myself . . . (*Shakes his head.*) . . . no thank you. I had the Bible shoved down my throat since I was small and I'm gat-full of it now man. I've got a bad dose of religious indigestion.

Martinus Hell Fires on the Day of Judgement!

Gideon Don't get yourself all excited my friend, I've told you, it's just dust in the atmosphere what does it. What they call an optical illusion.

Martinus (*laughs*) It's coming!

Gideon What?

Martinus The Day of Judgement. For everybody.

Gideon You've been listening to the dominees, haven't you?

Martinus And when that day comes, everybody will stand there and one by one *He* will call our names.

Gideon Ja, ja. I know. Time to meet your Maker and all the rest of it. And for the sinners it's down to the old devil and his braaivleis, and for the others it's up to the singing angels for a happy ending. I don't want to spoil it for you, Martinus, but it happens to be fairy stories my friend, stupid fairy stories, and I've heard them all. If you want to believe them, that's your business. I don't. So if you don't mind, keep them to yourself please. This is supposed to be Playland, not Sunday School. I came here to have a little bit of fun, so let's keep it that way. Okay?

Another laugh from Martinus.

Martinus Ja, that's the way it is. Playland is Happyland! Pretty lights and music. Buy your ticket for the Big Wheel and go round and round and forget all your troubles, all your worries.

That's why they all come. I know. I watch them. Fifteen years I've been with Playland now, and all that time I am watching the people. Noupoort, Cradock, Hanover, Beaufort West, Laingsburg, Colesberg, Middelburg . . . all the places here in the Great Karoo. They pray for rain but they wait for Playland and the happiness machines. And when we switch on the lights and the music, they come. Like moths they come out of the night – the old uncles with the fat aunties, the young boys and the pretty girls, even the little children. They all come to play because they all want to forget.

But it's no good. You can try to forget as hard as you like but it won't help, because all the things you did are written down in the Big Book, and when the day comes you will stand there and He will read them to you. And then what you got to say?

Gideon Plenty, my friend.

Martinus Ja?

Gideon Oh ja! To start with, the so-called 'Big Book'. Just stop now for a moment and try to imagine just how big that book has got to be if what everybody is doing wrong down here is written in it. Ja. You ever thought about that? There's a lot of people in this world, Mr Martinus Zoeloe, and a hell of a lot of 'doing wrong' going on all the time. And also who the hell is writing it all down? They'll need more than shorthand up there if they want to keep up with what's going on down here, that I can tell you.

Martinus holds up the five fingers of one hand and the thumb of the other.

Martinus (*unperturbed*) Number Six is the big one.

Gideon Number Six what?

Martinus The Ten Commandments. Number Six, 'Thou shalt not kill'. That's the big one. Not even your enemy. Not even the man you hate more than anything in the world. If you steal something you can always give it back. If you tell a lie, you can always still tell the truth. But when you kill a man you take his life and you can't give that back. He's dead, and that's the end of it.

Gideon (*agitated*) So why you telling me all this?

Martinus It's in the Bible.

Gideon (*sharply*) I know it's in the Bible. What I'm asking is why you telling me. You think I'm stupid or something? I learnt all about the commandments in Sunday School thank you very much. So just keep your sermons to yourself, O.K.? If you want to play dominee go preach to those skollie friends of yours.

And anyway, everybody knows there's times when you got to do it.

Martinus What?

Gideon Number Six.

Martinus No.

Gideon Yes there is! What about self-defence?

Martinus shakes his head.

Or protecting women and children?

Martinus shakes his head again.

What about Defending Your Country Against Communism?

Martinus (*doggedly*) Aikona!

263

Gideon (*beside himself with frustration*) Those are all times when it's all right to do it! Even the bloody dominees say so. I've heard them myself. Sermons up in the Operational Area.

Martinus (*implacable*) No. The Bible says 'Thou shalt not kill thy neighbour'.

Gideon So who the hell is talking about neighbours? I'm talking about criminals and communists! No man, this little discussion of ours is now getting out of hand. (*restraining himself*) Listen Martinus, I don't want to start a bad argument between us so let me tell you again, and this is now really for the last time, O.K.? I am gat-full of the Bible. I don't need another dose of it. Do I make myself clear?

You've now really got it on the brain, haven't you? Don't you ever talk about anything else?

Martinus Like what?

Gideon Like anything, for God's sake. Rugby. Women. Even bloody politics would be better. Talk ANC if you like – all that one-man-one-vote kak – but just change the record for God's sake! (*another drink*) Somebody I would have liked you to meet is Ou Tollie – he was the Bushman tracker with our unit. He knew what the score was. Never use to join us for church services – just sit there on one side under a thorn-bush and watch us singing our hymns, saying our prayers, and the dominees sermonizing about Heaven and Hell and all the rest of it. So one day I asked him what he thought about things. You know what he said? 'When we die, we die. The wind blows away our footprints and that is the end of us.' Ou Tollie! Ja, he knew what the score was.

They been up there you know. Right round the earth, to the moon and back . . . they even getting ready now to go to Mars . . . and what's more they also got pictures

of everything up there, and guess what, my friend . . .
there's no sign of your Heaven and Hell anywhere! Put
that in your old Bantu pipe and smoke it. Ja! Science, my
friend, science! There's a thing up there called a satellite
that is going all the way to the End of the World and it's
taking pictures all the time and sending them back and
all you can see is outer space . . . miles and miles of
bugger all. It's almost as bad as the Karoo up there.
So I don't know where you think your angels are flying
around, but it's certainly nowhere up in the big blue sky,
that I can tell you.

Martinus listens calmly.

And finally my friend, just in case you haven't noticed,
I would like to point out that the Fires of Eternal
Damnation have now gone out, so where the hell is
the party?

Martinus stares at him blankly.

It's quarter past seven man. Nearly twenty past.

Martinus So?

Gideon So, where's the lights and music? You told me
things get going at seven o'clock.

Martinus That's right.

Gideon Well for God's sake I'm telling you it's past
seven o'clock. (*He shows his watch.*) Look for yourself
if you don't believe me.

Martinus shrugs his shoulders indifferently.

Now what the hell is that supposed to mean?

Martinus Maybe the generators is broken down again.
There's lots of trouble with the generators. Last month in
Noupoort, two nights the generators broke down.

Gideon So what must we do?

Martinus Wait. They will try to fix it.

Gideon (*huge disbelief*) I don't believe it! We get ourselves all nicely dressed up, drive for bloody miles to get
here, and now we must just stand around and wait like a
lot of bloody sheep while they *try* to fix the generators.
How long does it take them?

Martinus Sometimes they fix it quick. Sometimes it takes
a long time. Sometimes they can't fix it and must send
away for spare parts.

Gideon And then?

Martinus Nothing.

Gideon Nothing what?

Martinus Then nothing happens tonight. Everybody
must go home. Last month in Noupoort . . .

Gideon To hell with what happened last month in
Noupoort. I'm not remotely interested in Noupoort's
troubles. They can drop an atomic bomb on that dump
as well as far as I'm concerned.

Pause. Martinus calm, Gideon agitated.

No man. This is about as much nonsense as a man can
take. What a bloody year. No doubt about it now . . .
the worst one of my entire life. With all my willpower
I hang on until we get to the last arsehole day of it, then
I make a special effort and pull myself together and get
out of the house, and where do I land up?

A broken-down Playland! And now you tell me I must
just go back home if they can't fix the generator? No, my
friend. Oh no! You can maybe sell that bullshit to those
railway japies in Noupoort, but nobody is going to buy
it over here. We weren't born yesterday. If you want to

call yourselves Playland you better prove it tonight, otherwise good old Baas Barney will start the New Year with more than just his generators broken.

The PA system suddenly crackles into life with static and feedback whine.

Barney (*a voice over the PA system*) Testing, testing, one, two, three, four, testing. Can you hear me, Martinus?

Martinus (*shouting back*) I can hear you, Baas Barney!

Barney Loud and clear?

Martinus Loud and clear, Baas Barney.

Barney All right, Jackson – switch on.

The lights of Playland start flickering and after a few false starts they come on and stay on.

Martinus (*a good laugh at Gideon*) There . . . look! Listen! Pretty lights and music! Go forget your troubles white man. Playland is open and waiting for you.

Gideon leaves.

Scene Two

Barney Hello everybody, hello and hello again. Welcome to Playland. This is your Master of Ceremonies, your old friend 'Barking Barney' Barkhuizen promising you a sensational, a spectacular evening of fun and thrills to end the year. We've got a wonderful programme lined up and to start the ball rolling, here is a special New Year's Eve offer: Buy nine tickets for any of the rides and you get one free – and remember, hang on to your ticket stubs because you could be the winner of one of our fabulous prizes. There's a draw every hour on the hour! So what are you waiting for? Let's rock out the old and roll in the new . . . One, two, three and away we go . . .!

An energetic piece of rock and roll music sets the tone and tempo of the evening. Playland is now in full swing. From the speakers at the top of the pole a pastiche of old pop songs, rock and roll and Boere-musiek. Interspersed with these is Barney's voice making announcements about the various sideshows and rides, lucky ticket numbers, lost children and so on and, continuously, the squeals and shrieks of laughter and terror from people on the rides.

(*interrupting a pop song*) Hold everything everybody. Your attention please. This is a very special announcement. She is blonde, she is beautiful, she is Marie du Toit and she is eighteen years old today. So come on everybody . . . (*singing*) 'Happy birthday to you . . .' (*and so on*)

More pop music.

Your attention please. Your attention. Please check your
ticket stubs because if you are the holder of number
eight-zero-four-six, I repeat . . . eight-zero-four-six . . .
you have just won yourself and your partner the famous
gut-buster platter at the Happy Rustler Steakhouse.
Come to the information desk for your voucher. Our
next draw will be for a fashion perm at Maison Capri,
so hurry up and buy your tickets for the Big Wheel,
the Whip . . .

More pop music.

This is the lost property department speaking . . . will
the parents of little Willie Liebenberg please come to the
caravan next to the Wall of Death . . . the parents of
little Willie Liebenberg please . . .

More pop music.

Your attention please, your attention! This is an
emergency announcement. Will anyone with an empty
and rumbling stomach please report immediately to the
stall next to the Rifle Range. We have a sizzling stack of
our famous Karoo burgers and Boere dogs in need of
urgent gastromedinomical attention. I repeat, anyone . . .

More pop music.
*Gideon is in the middle of all this, trying too hard
to have a good time. He tells jokes, tries to sing
along with the music, and wisecracks about the PA
announcements, creating an image of forced and
discordant gaiety.*

Scene Three

*Later. The night-watchman's camp. Martinus alone.
Gideon returns. Liquor and desperation give a new,
aggressive edge to his behaviour. He wears a silly paper
hat and carries a noise-maker.*

Gideon (*singing*)
   . . . baby don't you know I love you so
   Can't you feel it when we touch
   I will never never let you go
   I love you Oh so much.

. . . but I don't mean you poephol! (*hollow laugh*) How
you doing there, Marty?

Martinus You back.

Gideon Ja me. Who else? Your old friend Corporal
Gideon le Roux.

Martinus Corporal?

Gideon That's it. Two stripes. But listen, forget about
the rank. Just call me Gid. I been thinking about it you
see and what do you say we must just let bygones be
bygones? I want us to be buddies. Me and you. Gid and
Marty. Okay?

Martinus Okay.

Gideon (*holding out his hand*) Put it there.

   They shake.

So then tell me, how is things with you, Marty?

Martinus (*humouring him*) I'm doing all right, Gid.

Gideon Then why you looking so sad, man? I'm sitting
up there on top of the big wheel, admiring the view,
looking down and seeing everything and everybody and
there, in the corner, all by his lonely self, I see my buddy,
poor old Marty. Everybody else was having such a good
time but you were just sitting there looking so sad. Cheer
up man! It's not the end of the world yet, just the end of
a totally useless bloody year – and we're nearly there
Marty! Two more hours to go and then it's Happy
New Year!

Martinus You having a good time, hey, Gid?

Gideon You bet. I'm having myself one hell of a good
time. I've tried everything out there – the Lucky
Fishpond, shooting wooden ducks with a pellet gun,
ping-pong balls in the clown's mouth . . . you name it,
I've done it. And all the rides as well. Just between you
and me, the Ghost Train is now really bloody stupid –
kids' stuff you know . . . But the Big Wheel . . .! Three
times man. Round and round and up and down.
Whoopee! And you know something, it is just like you
said – I've forgotten all my troubles. How about that!
My sick ma, my stupid job, the stupid bloody foreman
at my stupid bloody job, my stupid bloody car that
I already know won't start when I want to go home –
you've got to give me a push, O.K.? – I've forgotten
them all! And I'm not finished. I'm going back for more.
I want to go round and round and up and down until
I even forget who the bloody hell I am! (*hollow laugh*)
How's that?

Martinus That's very good, Gid. But then why you here?

Gideon Why am I here? That's a very good question.

Martinus The Big Wheel is over there. There's nothing
for you here.

Gideon Oh yes there is! You! My buddy. You are here so that's why I am here. First thing you learn up there in the bush. Don't ever desert a buddy.

Martinus You won't forget your troubles if you sit here with me.

Gideon Hey hey hey! Marty. Why you talking like that man? If I didn't know you so well I would say you was trying to get rid of me. You're not trying to do that are you . . . because if you were, then you hurt my feelings man. Eina! You hurt my feelings bad! (*hollow laugh*)

It's only a joke. Hell Marty, listen, as one buddy to another let me give you a gentle word of advice. Lighten up a little bit man. You know, try a little smile or a chuckle now and then. It can be very heavy going with you sometimes.

Anyway, jokes aside now, if you want to know the truth, the whole truth and nothing but the truth so help me God, I came back here because I got something for you. A present. Ja. I mean it when I say I was thinking about you out there. You ask the others that were up there on the Border with me – Ou Charlie, or Stan, or Neelsie – all of them. They'll tell you Corporal Gideon le Roux was always thinking of his buddies. Because that is the way I was brought up – to think about others.

So I've got a wonderful present for you. It's going to make you very happy. It's better than a hundred rides on the Big Wheel because it won't just help you forget your troubles, it's going to get rid of them for you . . . and for keeps, my buddy. That's a money-back guarantee. You ready for it? It's a New Year's resolution that I made up specially for you to deal with all your problems. When midnight comes, you must stand to attention . . . (*He gets Martinus standing to attention, removes his balaclava and puts his paper hat on Martinus's head.*) . . . raise your right hand and say, 'I, Martinus Zoeloe, do

solemnly swear that my New Year's resolution for 1990
is . . . No More Dominees! No More Sermons from the
Dominees! No More Bible Stories from the Dominees!
No More Bullshit from the Dominees! Hallelujah and
Amen!' (*a big hollow laugh*)

How's that, Marty? I'm telling you man, that is the
answer to all your problems, because that is where they
come from – those black crows up there in the pulpit
taking advantage of simple-minded people like you. You
make that your resolution tonight and I promise you my
friend that in 1990 you will be a happy man.

Martinus Like you.

Gideon Ja, like me. Well? I'm waiting, Marty.

*Martinus studies Gideon in silence for a few seconds
then goes up to him and puts the paper hat back on
his head. He retrieves his balaclava and returns to
his seat.*

Is it my imagination, Marty, or do you now not really
care too much for my present? Hey? I know you are not
the excitable sort but even so, can't you try to squeeze
out a little 'Thank you, Gid'? Haai Marty, I can see you
want to break my heart tonight. Why my buddy? What
have I done? That heart is full of good feelings for you.
Don't hurt it. That's not the way buddies treat each
other.

Martinus You make jokes about your heart, but you
must be careful with it. Because *He* can see into it.

Gideon Who? Chris Barnard? (*Laughs.*) Joke Marty!
Joke.

Martinus All the secrets you hide away there – the big
ones, the bad ones – it's no good because *He* knows
them.

Gideon Marty . . . I've got a horrible feeling you are starting again.

Martinus He knows them all. Ja! Like a skelm in the night looking for your money under your mattress, *He* comes when you are sleeping and *He* finds them and looks at them.

Gideon Ja! There you go again – more bloody dominee talk.

Martinus It's not dominee talk.

Gideon Yes it is. I know the sound of dominee talk like I use to know the sound of a good cabbage fart from my dad.

Martinus *He* told me so himself.

Gideon Who?

Martinus *Him.*

Gideon Him?

Martinus Ja.

Gideon Oh I see. This is now the Big Baas himself we're talking about.

   Martinus nods.

He spoke to you.

Martinus Ja.

Gideon God.

Martinus God Almighty.

Gideon He came around here and had a little chat with you.

Martinus It was in a dream. He talked to me in a dream.

For a few seconds Gideon is speechless.

Gideon (*defeated*) No. No! That's it. I give up. I surrender. I'm waving the white flag, Marty.

Martinus (*imperturbable as ever*) I dreamed that I was praying like the dominee said I must. I was kneeling and telling *Him* that I was sorry for what I did and wanted forgiveness. And then I heard Him. 'It's no good, Martinus. I can see into your heart. I can see you are not sorry for what you did.' So I said 'That's true, God. I am not sorry.' And He said 'Then I can't forgive and you must go to Hell. All the people who are not sorry for what they did will go to Hell.'

Gideon Just like that.

Martinus Ja.

Gideon And then you woke up.

Martinus Ja.

Gideon And you believed it.

Martinus Ja.

Gideon And now you also want me to believe it.

Martinus Ja.

Gideon Hell Marty, you're asking for a lot tonight. First it's the Bible stories I must believe and now it's your dreams . . .! (*beginning to lose patience again*) What's the matter with you man? You can't believe them like they was real, like they was something that really happened to you. A dream . . . is just a bloody dream. It's what goes on in your head when you are sleeping, when your eyes are closed. Like when you imagine things. Don't you even know the difference between that and what is real? Must I also now explain that to you?

Martinus says nothing. Gideon pursues the subject with morbid persistence.

Real is what you can believe because you can touch it, and see it, and smell it . . . with your eyes wide open. Next time you sit there in the bush and have a boskak, have a good look at what you leave there on the ground, because that is what real means. When you can show me Heaven and Hell like I can show you shit, then I'll listen to the dominees and believe all their Bible stories. (*Cane bottle reappears.*) And let me just also say that for somebody who is so certain he is on his way to Hell, you seem to be taking things very easy, buddy boy. According to your Bible that is a fairly serious state of affairs you know. It's not like going to gaol. When you get down there, you stay down there. There's no such thing as getting time off for good behaviour. It's a one-way ticket my friend. Suffering and agony non-stop. And for ever. But if you got no problems with that, then O.K. Good luck to you. (*Takes a swig from his bottle.*) What did you do, Marty? What's the charge the Big Baas is going to read out of the Big Book when the Big Day comes? Must have been a good one if he's given you a one-way ticket for it. Come on man you can tell me. I know how to keep a secret. We're buddies now, remember. Buddies always share their secrets Marty.

Still no response from Martinus. Gideon continues in a conspiratorial whisper.

It was Number Six wasn't it? The Big One. You killed somebody, hey. That's why the Big Baas is so the hell in with you. (*elated laughter*) Ja, I knew it man. I'm telling you, the moment I saw you I smelt it. I said to myself 'Be careful Gid. There's something about that bugger.'

Martinus Go back to Playland, Gid. Go ride the Big Wheel.

Gideon (*more laughter, he continues greedily*) Not a damn. I'm having a good time here with you. So come on, man. Spill the beans. What happened? Housebreaking and theft? Armed robbery? No. You don't look like that sort. You're not one of those skollies. Something else . . . wait a bit, wait a bit, I've got it! Your woman. Right? You caught your woman with another man! How's that?

Martinus Leave me alone.

Gideon (*laughter*) Looks like I'm getting hot. Who got it Marty? Your woman? The man? Both of them? (*still more laughter*) How did you do it? Knife? Did you get away with it?

Martinus I'm telling you again, leave me alone.

Gideon Come now, Marty, don't take it personally. I'm only trying to help. All I want is to help you deal with your problems.

Martinus You got no help for me. So go!

Gideon (*brutally*) No!

Martinus What do you want here?

Gideon The fucking truth. That's what I want. You killed somebody. It's written all over you man. Think I'm blind? And I want to know who it was.

Martinus I'm telling you nothing.

Gideon Oh yes?

Martinus Yes! Nothing!

Pause. Gideon backs out of the developing confrontation.

Gideon Okay, if that's the way you want it. I reckon that's the end of buddies then.

Martinus Yes! So go back to your own people.

Gideon What people? That fucking herd of Karoo Zombies out there grazing on candy floss? My people? Shit! Any resemblance between me and them is purely coaccidental. You try to talk to them, exchange a few friendly words and they look at you as if you were a fucking freak or something. Playland! Ja, that's where they belong. Two rand to shoot wooden ducks with a pellet gun. We weren't shooting wooden ducks with pellet guns up there on the Border, my friend. While that crowd of fat arses were having joyrides in Playland we were in Hell. Ja! For your information you don't have to wait for Judgement Day to find out what that word means. Hell is right here and now. I can take you to it. It's called the Operational Area and it's not everlasting bonfires either. It's everlasting mud and piss and shit and sweat and dust. And if you want to see the devil I can show you him as well. He wears a khaki uniform, he's got an AK47 in his hands.

Martinus SWAPO.

Gideon Ja, that's his name. And he wasn't shooting at wooden ducks either.

Martinus Did you kill him?

Gideon The devil? (*hollow laugh*) Ja. I killed him. How else do you think I'm here? That's the only way you stayed alive. The Law of the Jungle! That's what we use to say. Kill or be killed . . . and don't think about it.

Martinus (*pointing at Gideon and laughing triumphantly*) Number Six! You also. Number Six! I'll see you in Hell, Corporal Gideon le Roux.

Gideon (*with all the vulgarity he can muster*) Fuck you!

Martinus (*his laughter cut short*) Hey!

Gideon That's right. I'll say it again. Fuck you! You can shove Number Six right up your arse. And don't point your fucking finger at me again. It's rude, my boy.

Martinus Haaikona!

Gideon Haaikona yourself. I'm telling you to mind your own business, Martinus Zoeloe. The secrets in my heart have got nothing to do with you or anybody else.

Martinus (*restraining himself*) Okay. I mind my own business. And you also. The secrets in my heart got nothing to do with you. So go. There is nothing for you here. This is my place.

Gideon Your place?

Martinus Ja. My place. This is the night-watchman's place. I am the night-watchman. You go somewhere else.

Gideon Don't you tell me to go! This is still a free country. You people haven't taken over yet. (*His bottle is empty. He hurls it away and leaves.*)

Scene Four

Later. Gideon is back in the bright lights and loud music of Playland. He is a dark, brooding presence watching the world with smouldering resentment. Everybody is getting ready for the arrival of the New Year.

Barney (*attempting an American accent*) Good evening ladies and gentlemen and welcome to this Karoo Broadcasting Corporation New Year's Eve Special. I am your KBC host for the evening – 'Barking Barney' Barkhuizen – speaking to you live from Cape Karooveral where the space shuttle Playland is waiting on the launching pad . . . primed and ready for her blast-off into 1990. According to the countdown clock there is now only three minutes left before ignition so get ready folks to wave 1989 goodbye. The weather forecast continues to be favourable – for the launch and for romance – starry skies and a balmy breeze. Mission control informs us that the countdown is proceeding smoothly so it looks as if we're all set for another successful launch at the stroke of midnight.

And now there is only two minutes to go. An expectant hush is settling over the large crowd gathered here to participate in this historic event. Looking at the closed- circuit television monitors I can see that all the astronauts in Playland are putting away the last of their Karoo burgers and Boere dogs and are now buckling up and bracing themselves for the G-forces that are going to spin them off into Playland's 1990 Orbit of Happiness. One minute to go! We've still got the green light on all systems. The tension is unbearable ladies and gentlemen

as the countdown clock ticks its way through the
last seconds of 1989. On everybody's lips, the same
whispered prayer, Thank God it's over. Twenty seconds
left as we line up for the final countdown . . . and here
it comes . . .!!

Ten – nine – eight – seven – six – five – four – three –
two – one – zero!!!

We have a launch! We-have-a-launch! Yes, ladies and
gentlemen, Playland has lifted off into 1990 . . .

*The New Year arrives with an explosion of sound –
voices singing, voices cheering, motor car hooters,
sirens, fireworks . . . a cacophony that imperceptibly
begins to suggest the sound of battle. Gideon's
contribution is to make as much 'Happy New Year'
noise as he can, ending up with the singing of 'Auld
Lang Syne'. This gets progressively more violent and
finally degenerates into a wild, wordless animal sound.
When he stops, all is silent. He hears nothing except
his breathing and his heart beating.*

Gideon Easy Gid . . . you're alive! . . . easy does it . . .
you're alive . . . it's over . . . it's all over and you're
alive . . .

The sounds of Playland fade back in.

Scene Five

*Later. The night-watchman's camp. Martinus is alone.
Midnight has come and gone and all that is left of the
celebrations are a few distant and receding sounds of
revelry. The last piece of music – 'Goodnight Sweetheart'
– is playing over the PA system.*

Barney (*now a tired, off-duty voice*) Okay everybody,
that's it. Cash up and bring your ticket rolls and money
to the caravan. Give it a few more seconds Jackson and
then you can start to switch off. And Martinus, make
sure everything is locked up properly tonight. We're
too near that damned location for my liking. They've
got to give us a better site next time otherwise we're not
coming here again. New Year's Eve and we only had half
the crowd we had at De Aar last month. This lot should
go over there for a few lessons in how to have a good
time. *Here,* it was hard going tonight. (*a long and
audible yawn*) Ek is moeg, kêrels. Ek is moeg!

> *A few more seconds and then the music is cut off
> abruptly and Playland's illuminations start to go out.
> Gideon returns yet again to Martinus. He stands
> silently. Martinus is getting ready for his night shift –
> old overcoat and kierie.*

Martinus It's finished, white man. It's all over for
tonight. Time for you to go home now. You heard what
the music said, 'Goodnight Sweetheart. It's time to go.'
(*He laughs.*) Ja, everybody is sad when the happiness
machine stop and the lights go out. But don't worry.
You can come again tomorrow. Your Playland is safe.

Martinus will watch it for you. Martinus will watch all
your toys and tomorrow you can come and play again.

But now it is my time! Now night-watchman
Martinus Zoeloe is in charge.

Ja! You want to know about me, white man. Okay.
I tell you this. I know how to watch the night and wait
for trouble. That is my job. While all the sweethearts are
lying in bed with their sweet dreams, that is what I am
doing – watching the night and waiting for trouble.
I do it well. A long time ago I learnt how to sit with
the ghosts and look and listen and wait – and that time
I was waiting for Big trouble, white man . . . bigger
trouble than a few drunk location skollies looking for
mischief. So they can come and try their nonsense. I am
ready for them!

*He brandishes his kierie in traditional style and then
sets out on his rounds. Gideon blocks his path.*

Gideon Where you going?

Martinus To do my job.

Gideon No.

Martinus No what?

Gideon You're not going anywhere.

Martinus Why not?

Gideon Because I say so, that's why. You stay right
where you are. Don't think you can just switch off the
fucking lights and tell me to go home, because I'm telling
you it's not over.

Martinus It is, white man. Look! There's nobody left.
I tell you Playland is finished for tonight.

Gideon Fuck Playland! I'm talking about you and me.
That's what it's all about now. You and me. Nice and

simple. No complications. You and me. There's things to settle between us, and now is the time to do it. Right now . . . right here.

Martinus There is nothing between you and me.

Gideon laughs.

What do you want from me, white man? All night you keep coming back. For what? If you want to make trouble go do it with your own people.

Gideon Fuck them as well. I'm not interested in them. It's you I want. I want to make some nice trouble with you.

Martinus Why? What did I do to you? Nothing!

Gideon (*another wild laugh*) Nothing?

Martinus Yes! I sit here. I mind my own business and then you come. You come again and again. I didn't call you. I do nothing to you.

Gideon Nothing, Swapo?

Martinus My name is not Swapo.

Gideon It is now. I'm calling you Swapo. If you're not my buddy, that's who you are.

Martinus My name is Martinus Zoeloe.

Gideon Martinus Zoeloe se gat! Name? What the fuck are you talking about? You haven't got a name. You're just a number. Number one, or number two, number three . . . One day I counted you twenty-seven fucking times. I bury you every night in my sleep. You're driving me mad, Swapo. And you call that nothing?

Martinus (*disturbed by Gideon's violent ramblings*) Haai, haai! You are mad. I'm not talking to you no more.

*He makes another determined move to leave. Gideon
blocks his path again.*

Gideon I said no.

Martinus Let me go.

Gideon No. I told you, you're not going anywhere.
I haven't finished with you.

Martinus (*rising anger*) To hell with you. I've finished
with you. Get out of my way.

Gideon Make me. Go ahead. Make me. (*He starts
pushing Martinus back.*)

Martinus Don't do that.

Gideon (*another push*) I'll do any fucking thing I like.

Martinus I warn you, white man.

Gideon (*another push*) About what, black man? Warn
me about what? You trying to scare me? Don't flatter
yourself. There's fuck-all you can say or do that will
scare me. But if you want to try something, go ahead.

*The two men are on the brink of real physical
violence.*

So what are you waiting for? Come, let's see what you
can do.

Martinus (*breaking away*) No Martinus! Stop! (*He
makes a supreme effort to control himself. He returns
and confronts Gideon.*) Gideon le Roux! I say your
name. Please now, listen to me. I put down my kierie.
I tell you nicely, I don't want to make trouble with you.
Don't you make trouble with me. Leave me alone.
Because if we make trouble for each other tonight, then
I know what happens.

Gideon Oh yes?

Martinus Yes! I will do it again. S'true's God. I do it again.

Gideon What?

Martinus Number Six.

Gideon Good old Number Six! So I was right. You did kill somebody.

Martinus I killed a white man.

Gideon You bullshitting me? You still trying to scare me?

Martinus Andries Jacobus de Lange, the Deceased. I killed him.

Gideon You're telling the truth. (*laughter*) How about that! It gets better and better. In fact, it's fucking perfect. (*More laughter out of a violent, dark elation.*) I knew it. I knew it all along. The moment I saw you I knew there was something . . . you know . . . between us – me and you. And there it is. You killed a white man. Now we can get down to real business.

Martinus No! There is nothing between you and me.

Gideon (*laughter*) Oh yes there is. (*singing*)
    I will never, never let you go
    I love you Oh so much!

Who was he? The white man?

Nothing from Martinus.

Listen, Swapo, there's a lot of shit we got to clean up tonight, so you better start talking. What happened?

Martinus My woman, she worked for him. For his wife and children. The housework and the washing.

Gideon You see! I knew it! I knew there was a woman in it.

Martinus It was in Port Elizabeth. I had a job in the cement factory there. I was saving money to get married. Thandeka, my woman, was living at the white people's house. On Sundays she comes to visit me in the location. And so it was until one day when she comes to me I see that she is unhappy. I asked her what was wrong but she wouldn't tell me anything. Then another time when she comes she was crying and I asked her again and then she told me. She said the white man was coming all the time to her room in the backyard and trying to get into bed with her. She always said no to him and pushed him out. But then one night he beat her and forced her to get into the bed with him.

Gideon And then?

Martinus I killed him.

Gideon How? How did you do it?

Martinus A knife.

Gideon Ja! You bastards like the knife, don't you?

Martinus I sent my woman away. I waited in her room. When the white man opened the door and came in I had my knife ready and I killed him.

Gideon Just like that.

Martinus Just like that.

Gideon Did he fight?

Martinus Yes, but he wasn't strong, so I killed him quickly. He's in Hell. He didn't even have time to pray to God.

Gideon Number Six!

Martinus Number Six. And I'm *not* sorry. When the judge asked me if I was, I told him. I told him that if

287

I saw that white man tomorrow I would kill him again.
So then he sentenced me to death and my woman to
fifteen years. He wouldn't believe her when she told him
what the white man did to her. He said that we killed
him because we wanted to rob the house.

Gideon Why didn't they hang you?

Martinus They nearly did. I sat in the death cell six
months waiting for the rope. I was ready for it. But
when there was just three days to go the white man's
wife went to the judge and told him that my woman
was telling the truth. She told him that her husband had
forced other servants to get into his bed. So then they
changed my sentence to fifteen years. They let my woman
go free. I never saw her again. That is my story.

Gideon Story my arse! It's a fucking joke man. A bad
joke. You killed that poor bugger just for that? Just for
screwing your woman? (*laughter*)
   You people are too funny. Listen my friend, if screwing
your woman is such a big crime, then you and your
brothers are going to have to put your knives into one
hell of a lot of white men . . . starting with me! Ja.
What's the matter with you? Were you born yesterday?
We've all done it. And just like you said, knocked on
that door in the backyard, then drag her on to the bed
and grind her arse off on the old coir mattress. That's
how little white boys learn to do it. On your women!
   And you want to know something else, Swapo? They
like it from us! Your woman was crying crocodile tears.
I bet you anything you like she had a bloody good time
there with the *baas* humping away on top of her.

   *Martinus rigid, every muscle tense as he tries to
   control the impulse to throw himself at Gideon.*

Now do you understand what I'm saying? If you want

to kill that white man again, now's your chance. He's
standing right here in front of you. (*Gideon waits.*)
Come on! What you waiting for? Try to make it two.
You got nothing to lose, Swapo. You already got your
one-way ticket. You can't go to Hell twice.

You think you're big stuff don't you because you
killed one white man? That's your score. One! And now
you think you can maybe make it two. One . . . two.
(*laughter*) What a bloody joke! You're an amateur, man.
What you did was child's play. I was with the pros and
for ten years we were up there on the Border sending
your freedom fighting brothers to Hell, and I'm not
talking about one or two. We were into double figures,
man. One amazing bloody day I did the rounds and
counted twenty-seven of them that we'd blown away to
Kingdom Come. Ja! Twenty-fucking-seven. Do you have
the remotest idea what that means? What it feels like to
count twenty-seven dead men? You had to have a strong
stomach for it my friend. Those brothers of yours were
full of shit, and I don't mean their politics. I mean the
real stuff. They started stinking even before the sun had
cooked them up a bit, because when that happened,
when they'd been in the oven for a couple of days, as
we use to say, then I'm telling you, you didn't eat meat
for a week. (*speaking with manic intensity*) That was
the first thing I use to do you see. When it was all over –
the shooting and screaming – all that fucking noise like
the world was coming to an end, when suddenly it was
quiet like now, I would take a deep breath, say to myself
'You're alive, Gid', then walk around and count.
I always wanted to know how many there were, you see.
Even before the OC asked for a body count I was out
there doing it. You could take your time you see, walk
around slowly and carefully and do it properly like my
pa use to do when he counted his cabbages in the
backyard. The Oubaas was crazy about cabbages, man,

'specially the way my ma use to cook it for him, in a pot with nice pieces of fat mutton. It made him fart like an impala ready for takeoff, but he had to have his cabbage. So every morning it was 'Come Gideon, let's go count our blessings,' and I would hold his hand and walk next to him and say nicely after him 'One cabbage, two cabbage, three cabbage . . .' that's how I learnt to count. Even before I was in school man I knew how to count my blessings. But now it wasn't cabbages any more, it was 'One Swapo, two Swapo, three Swapo . . .' My very first time I counted there was eight of them. Shit man, that was something new for me. The only dead person I had ever seen was my pa when we all said goodbye to him in his coffin and now suddenly there I was counting eight of them – lying all over the place, some of them with pieces missing. Then for a long time it looked as if fifteen was going to be the record until that follow-up when we ambushed a whole bloody unit . . . and when it came time to count . . .! Twenty-fucking-seven of them! I couldn't believe it man. A new record! 'Twenty-seven Swapo cabbages in the garden, Sir!'

He salutes. Martinus just stares at him.

So where's your sense of humour? That's a joke. Didn't you get it? Swapo cabbages. I counted the dead men like my pa use to count his fucking cabbages. So don't just stand there and stare at me like a bloody baboon. Laugh!

Martinus No.

Gideon (*rage*) What do you mean 'No'? It's a bloody good joke man. 'Twenty-seven Swapo cabbages in the garden, Sir!'

Martinus Then why don't you laugh?

Gideon You want to hear laughter? I'll give you fucking

laughter. (*He makes a violent and grotesque attempt at laughter that spirals away into the sound of his pain and torment. He is left totally defeated.*)

Martinus (*after a pause*) No, you are not laughing. (*He speaks quietly, calmly.*) What is the matter with you, white man? What is it you are doing tonight? You come here to me, but I don't want you. I tell you so, but you come back. You come back again and again. You make bad trouble between us. You try to make me kill you and now you tell me you are laughing at dead men but I can see it is a lie. Why? Why are you telling me that lie? Why are you trying so hard to make me believe it?

Gideon denies nothing

I remember once when I also tried very hard to tell a lie. It was when I was still small. I broke the window in our house in the location. I was very frightened because my father was a very cross man. So when he came home from work I told him that the other boys playing in the street had done it. I tried very hard to make him believe it. It was no good. He could see my lie and so I got the hiding. When it was finished and I had stopped crying, he said to me, 'That was for breaking the window. Now you get another one, a good one, for telling me a lie and trying to hide what really happened.' Is that why you are doing it? Are you hiding something away like little Martinus? (*disturbed by the direction his thoughts are taking*) Aikona! Aikona Martinus! Suka! Leave it now. Go to work. Leave him. His nonsense is not your business. (*He tries to leave.*) Fuck you, white man! I'll see you in Hell. Hey! I said fuck you, white man!

No reaction from Gideon. Martinus returns.

Okay. I am going to ask you, but you must tell me no more lies. What is the true feeling inside you?

Gideon Leave me alone.

Martinus No, you must tell me now. You must speak the truth. What is the feeling you got inside you?

Gideon Feeling? I've got fucking feelings for Africa, man. Which ones do you want? Bad feelings, sick feelings, hate feelings?

Martinus Inside you now. Your feelings about what you did. The dead men. Twenty-seven dead men.

Gideon No! Leave me alone. I say fuck you to you as well. Go do your work. Go do anything you like – just go. You're right, there's nothing between you and me.

Pause. Martinus decides. He sits.

Martinus Listen to me now. I am going to tell you something else. When I was sitting in the death cell, waiting, the prison dominee came to visit me. Dominee Badenhorst. He came to me every day with his Bible. He read to me about the Commandments – specially Number Six – Thou Shall Not Kill. He said to me, 'Martinus, you have sinned. You have killed a man. But if you pray and ask God for Forgiveness and he looks into your heart and sees that you are really sorry, then he will forgive you.'

Then I said to him, 'But I am not sorry.' Then he said, 'Then you will go to Hell, Martinus.'

'I can't help it, Dominee,' I said, 'then I will go to Hell, but I can't feel sorry.'

He wouldn't believe me. 'No,' he said, 'that is not so. You are a good man, Martinus. Look deep into your heart. I know you are sorry for what you did.'

'Listen, Dominee,' I said, 'I say it to the Judge and now I say it to you also – if I saw that white man tomorrow, I would kill him again. It would make me very very happy to kill him again.'

The dominee was very sad and prayed for me. There in the cell, on his knees, he prayed to God to make me feel sorry. But it is no good. I still don't have that feeling. All the years I was in gaol, and all the years I sit here by the fire, I ask myself, 'What is it that makes a man feel sorry? Why doesn't it happen inside me?' Baas Joppie – he was the prison carpenter, I was his handlanger – he was sorry. He killed his father and he was so sorry for doing it he cried all the times he told me about it. And Jackson Xaba – they hanged him – guilty four times for rape and murder, he told me also he was sorry. But me . . .? (*He shakes his head.*) The dominee said that if I looked deep into my heart I would find that feeling. I try. I look inside. When I sit here every night I look inside and I find feelings, strong feelings for other things. When I remember Thandeka and I wonder where she is, I feel a big sadness inside me. Or when I just sit by the fire when it is cold and the tea is hot, that makes me feel good inside. Bread and meat, good! Rain! Rain falling in this dry Karoo – very good! I even find feelings for dead dogs. But for him – Andries Jacobus de Lange, the Deceased, the man I killed – *No!*

And now there is you. (*again shaking his head in disbelief*) You have got that sorry feeling for what you did, for the men you killed, haven't you?

Gideon tries to wave him away.

When did it come? When you killed them? Later? When you counted them?

Gideon What difference does it make when it happened? It happened! (*a voice shorn of all deception*) I was too revved up at the time to feel anything. When you're in the middle of something like that and you've got your finger on the trigger of that R3, there's only one thought in your head: You're alive, Gid! Keep it that way, man.

Stay fucking alive. The only thing going on inside you is a sort of wild feeling, but I mean like really wild man. And anyway because it was a follow-up we didn't even rest, so there wasn't time to think about anything. We just kept on going after them.

We came back that way a few days later. Hell, man, it was terrible. A man starts smelling bad the minute he's dead, but when he's been lying out in the sun for a few days . . .! Believe me I wasn't exaggerating when I said you can't eat your food afterwards. Me and another chap was detailed to take the bodies and dump them in a big hole. Oh boy! First we had to load them on to the back of the lorry, one by one – we had to wear gloves and masks it was so bad – then we drove over to the hole. When we got there I see this old woman come out of the bush and stand there and watch us. She didn't do anything or say anything – she just stood there watching.

So we back the lorry up to the hole and started . . . He grabs the hand, I grab a leg, drag it to the edge and then . . . into the hole. First you kind of try to do it nicely you know, because after all they was human beings, but by the time you get halfway through you just don't give a damn any more – it's hot and you're feeling naar so you just chuck them in. All the time I was doing this I had a strange feeling that it reminded me of something, but I couldn't remember what it was. And the old woman was still standing there watching us. I couldn't take it any more so I started shouting and swearing at her, telling her to go away, and while I was doing that suddenly it came to me, the thing I was trying to remember.

It was the time we was on holiday at Mossel Bay – me and my mom and my dad. I was still just a little outjie in a khaki broek. Every day me and my dad would take his fishing rod and go down to the rocks. He would put on some bait and throw out and then wait for a big one.

My job was to catch him the small fishes in the rock pools for him to use as bait. So one day I catch this lekker fat little fish and I'm all excited and I start to cut it up and then – *Here!* man, hundreds of little babies jump out of its stomach on to the rock. Just so big . . . (*indicating with his fingers*) . . . little babies man! – they already has little black dots where their eyes was going to be – jumping around there on the rock. And the mother fish also, with her stomach hanging open where I had cut her, wagging her tail there on the rock. And I looked down at all of this and I knew man, I just knew that what I had done was a terrible sin. Any way you look at it, whether you believe all that stuff about Heaven and Hell and God Almighty or not it makes no difference. What I had done was a sin. You can't do that to a mother and her babies. I don't care what it is, a fish or a dog or another person, it's wrong!

So then what the hell was going on man? There I was on the back of that lorry doing it again, only this time it was men I was sommer throwing into that hole. Maybe one of them was that woman's son. Maybe I had killed him. That did it. Something just went inside me and it was snot and tears into that face mask like I never cried in my whole life, not even when I was small. I tore off the mask and gloves and got off the lorry and went over to where the old woman had been standing, but she was gone. I ran into the bush to try and find her, I looked and called, but she was gone. That's where they found me the next day. They said I was just walking around in a dwaal.

Martinus What did you want with the old woman?

Gideon I wanted to tell her about that little boy. I wanted to tell her that he knew what was right and wrong. I don't know what happened to him, what went wrong in his life, but he didn't want to grow up to be a man throwing other men into a hole like rotten cabbages. He didn't want to be me. And when I had told her all that, I was going to ask her for forgiveness . . . but she was gone.

A silence between the two men. Martinus finally understands.

Martinus So that is it. That is why you keep coming back tonight. Forgiveness.

Gideon Ja.

Martinus For twenty-seven dead men.

Gideon Ja.

Martinus How many did you kill?

Gideon Doesn't make any difference, man. You killed one, you killed them all.

Martinus Number Six twenty-seven times! And you say there was also other times?

Gideon Ja.

Martinus No! That's too big for me, white man. I'm just a night-watchman. Go ask God for that forgiveness.

Gideon Forget about Him, man. He's forgotten about us. It's me and you tonight. The whole world is me and you. Here! Now! (*anger and bitterness*) Do you think I wanted it to be this way? Do you think that if I could have chosen the other person in my world tonight it would be you? No such luck. We've got no choices, man. I've got you and you've got me. Finish and klaar. Forgive me or kill me. That's the only choice you've got.

Martinus If I forgive you, then I must forgive Andries Jacobus de Lange, and if I forgive him, then I must ask God to forgive me . . . and then what is left? Nothing! I sit here with nothing . . . tonight . . . tomorrow . . . all my days and all my nights . . . nothing!

(*violent rejection*) No! It's too late to talk forgiveness
to me. It's like you say, it's all finish and klaar now.
We've done what we've done. Number Six – you and
me. So leave it alone. We go to Hell and that is the end
of it. (*Pause. It is Martinus's moment of defeat.*) Haai
white man! Why did you bring me so much trouble
tonight? Forgive you or kill you! What do I know about
forgiveness? Nothing. My heart knows how to hate
Andries Jacobus de Lange. That is all it can do. But kill
you? No. I don't know if I can do it again.

I know I have only killed one man, but I have done it
too many times. Every night when I sit here I wait again
in that little room in the backyard. I wait again in the
dark with my knife, I wait for him and when he comes I
kill him – again and again – too many times.

Gideon Ja. I know what you're saying. It burns you out,
hey? Kill somebody and sooner or later you end up like
one of those landmine wrecks on the side of the road up
there on the Border – burnt-out and bloody useless.

So where the hell did it go wrong, man? Because it
wasn't meant to be like this. Isn't that so? I mean, did
you want to spend your whole life like you just said –
hating one man and spooking with him every night in
that little room where you killed him?

Martinus No. I wanted to do other things with my life.

Gideon I didn't want to spend mine hating myself. But
look at me. That's all I do now. Everything else is just
pretending. I try to make it look as if I'm getting on with
things like everybody else: I wake up, go to work, joke
with the other ous, argue with the foreman, go home, eat
supper, watch TV with my ma . . . but it's all a lie man.
Inside me I'm still at that hole outside Oshakati. That's
where I go every bloody night in my dreams – looking
for that old woman in the bush . . . and never finding her.

(*parodying himself*) 'You're alive, Gid!' What a bloody joke. I'm as dead as the men I buried and I'm also spooking the place where I did it.

Pause. First light of the new day.

It's getting light. Hell, have we been talking that long?

Martinus Ja, we've been talking long.

Gideon I can see you now. Yessus, you're an ugly bugger.

Martinus You too.

Gideon This is about the time when me and my dad use to wake up, get dressed and then go open the hok and let them out – even in winter – early morning, just before sunrise. Then we would go back into the kitchen and make our coffee and take it out into the backyard and watch them flying around. Sometimes they was up there in the sunlight, while we were still in the shadows! It always made us laugh. I don't know why, but we would just stand there, drink our coffee, watch the dawn manoeuvres of the Karoo Squadron . . . and laugh our bloody heads off. And there were no lies in that laugh. It was for real. That was how we felt inside. So . . .

Martinus is silent.

That's it then. New Day. New Year. Did I wish you Happy New Year last night?

Martinus No.

Gideon Well better late than never as they say. Happy New Year to you and . . . what else? . . . Ja, thanks for the chat.

An awkward, hesitant moment between the two men. Gideon starts to leave.

Martinus (*impulsively and with conviction*) To hell with it! I have got something to say.

Gideon What?

Martinus I also want to see them. Those pigeon-birds. Flying round up there like you say. I also want to see that.

Gideon What are you saying, man?

Martinus I am saying to you that when Playland comes back here next time – Christmas and New Year – I want to do it like you said . . . look up in the sky, watch the pigeon-birds flying and drink my tea and laugh!

Gideon Do you mean that?

Martinus I am saying it to you because I mean it. To hell with spooking! You are alive. So go home and do it. Get some planks, find some nails and a hammer and fix that hok. Start again with the pigeon-birds. (*Pause.*) Do you hear what I am saying, Gideon le Roux?

Gideon I hear you, Martinus Zoeloe.

Martinus Do you understand what I am saying?

Gideon Ja, I think so. And you also hey. Get out of that little room, man. Let old Andries spook there by himself tonight. Do you understand me, Martinus Zoeloe?

Martinus Ja, I understand you.

Gideon Good. And to prove that you are alive and not a spook come give me a push, man. I know that bloody tjorrie of mine is not going to start again. Been giving me trouble all bloody week. I don't know what is wrong with it. Been into the garage two times already this month . . .

> *They walk off together.*
> *End.*

VALLEY SONG

To the memory of Barney Simon

Characters

The Author, in his early sixties
Abraam Jonkers, 'Buks', in his seventies
Veronica, his granddaughter, seventeen years old

Note

The role of the Author and Buks
must be played by the same actor.

Valley Song was first performed in London at the Royal Court Theatre on 31 January 1996, in association with Mannie Manim Productions and Patricia Macnaughton, with the following cast:

The Author and **'Buks'** Athol Fugard
Veronica Esmeralda Bihl

Director Athol Fugard
Designer/Associate Director Susan Hilferty
Original Music Didi Kriel
Lighting Designer Mannie Manim
Sound Mark Malherbe
Company Manager Leigh Colombick
Deputy Stage Manager Barbara Grafe

A bare stage.

Enter the Author. He comes down and speaks directly to the audience.

Author (*a handful of pumpkin seeds*) Genuine Karoo pumpkin seeds. Ja. 'Ware Karoo Pampoen saad!' This is the so-called 'Flat White Boer' variety – that's the actual name! – Flat White Boer pumpkin. You know them – those big, round, white beauties – you sometimes still see them on the roofs of little farm cottages when you drive through the Karoo – well, this is how they start out. One of these, together with a little prayer for rain, in a hole in the ground. And in a good year, when you get that rain, this little handful could give you up to a hundred of those beauties!

Now is not the time to plant them. In my village, in the Sneeuberg mountains, the soil is still bone-dry and rock-hard with frost – our winters are a long and serious affair! So you put them away in a little tin – with a lid – the mice get very hungry in winter! – and you put the tin on a shelf in the kitchen or the garage or wherever you keep your other seeds – cabbage, carrot, beetroot, beans, onion, peas, mealies . . . they all do well in the Valley – and you wait for spring. Because when that comes . . .! (*a little laugh*) . . . when old Spitskop has got his head in the clouds again, when the Valley has had its first rain and the danger of a late frost is passed, and that wonderful smell of damp earth is mingled with the fragrance of roses and pine trees, when the world is rowdy again with birdsong and bleating lambs and noisy children, that's when you take those little tins down from the shelf and go out to your vegetable akkers and start planting.

Imagine a spring day like that and these seeds in the hands of old Abraam Jonkers – in the Village we all just call him 'ou Buks'. He's out there in his akkers behind the derelict old Landman house with his spade, planting – a little stab at the ground and then a seed, stab at the ground and a seed – it's a well-rehearsed action. He's planted a lot of pumpkin seeds in the course of his seventy-six years. And there's nothing haphazard about what he's doing either. When the young plants come up he wants to see them standing shoulder to shoulder in lines as straight as those the Sergeant-Major drilled them into on the Sonderwater Parade Ground during the Second World War. Buks was a corporal in that famous old Coloured regiment, the Cape Corps, and was stationed up in the Transvaal guarding Italian prisoners-of-war. He's in fact thinking about those days as he drops the seeds into the ground. One of the prisoners became a good friend of his and taught him a couple of Italian songs. He's trying very hard to remember one of them – they are now the only souvenirs he's got left of that time. Everything else – badges and brass buttons, discharge papers and scraps of his old uniform, even his old army kitbag – either lost or disintegrated with time. Only the song is left and even that has mouldered away to only half the memory it used to be. It went something like this:

In the course of the song he moves into the character of Buks.

Buks
   Lae donder mobili
   En soo moretsa
   da da de da da da

*Veronica enters. She carries Buks' lunch – bottle of
tea, sandwiches and an enamel mug.*

Veronica Oupa! Oupa!

Buks (*ignoring her and trying again*)
Lae donder mobili
En soo moretsa
da da de da da da

Veronica Oupa! Are you deaf?

Buks (*turning to her and bellowing-out in good
sergeant-major style*) A . . . ten . . . tion!

Veronica obeys.

By the left – Quick march! Left-right, left-right, left-
right . . .

Veronica marches.

Plato-o-o-n halt!

*Veronica stops, staying rigidly at 'Attention' while
Buks carries out an inspection.*

What do you want, Private?

Veronica It's lunch-time, Corporal. (*She salutes.*)

Buks No, Veronica . . . your other arm!

Veronica Sorry, Corporal. (*She salutes again.*)

Buks That's better. Platoon dismissed!

Veronica Tell me the truth now, Oupa, were you a real
soldier?

Buks I don't know. What's a 'real' soldier? I was just an
ordinary soldier.

Veronica You know man, Oupa, like on TV. With a gun
and all that.

Buks I had a gun. When I went on guard duty I had a real gun with real bullets . . . and all that.

Veronica But did you ever shoot anybody with it?

Buks No. I've told you before I was guarding Italian prisoners and none of them tried to escape.

Veronica Well then, you certainly didn't win the war, did you?

Buks No. I certainly didn't. The other men did that – the ones up north. I just marched up and down the fence with my gun on my shoulder and Carlo Tucci on the other side trying to teach me the words of Italian songs. (*another attempt at his Italian song*)

Veronica What's it mean?

Buks I don't know. He told me but I've forgotten.

Veronica I'm going to make a song about you. I'll call it 'The Army Man'.

Buks Good. I like that. But you must remember in your song that I was a corporal . . . two stripes!

Veronica (*singing*) My Oupa was a corporal. Left, left-right, left-right.

Buks Come. Give me some tea.

> *Veronica lays out lunch – pours tea into an enamel mug.*

Veronica (*a 'recitative' mixture of song and speech*) Nearly fresh brown bread and delicious first-grade Langeberg Kooperasie Smooth Apricot Jam.

Buks Who says so?

Veronica The jam tin label says so. Eerste Graad. Langeberg Kooperasie.

Buks (*tasting his tea*) How much sugar did you put in?

Veronica The usual, Oupa. Three spoons for every mug.

Buks (*he tastes again*) What is happening to all the sweetness in the world?

Veronica What do you mean, Oupa?

Buks I don't know. I don't know what I mean. But put in an extra spoon tomorrow. That Whiteman was back here again early this morning looking at the house and the land . . . our akkers.

Veronica So?

Buks I'm just saying. That's three times now.

Veronica That doesn't mean anything. Stop worrying about it, Oupa. Every few months there's another car full of white people driving around the village and looking at the old houses and talking about buying, and what happens? . . . They drive away in the dust and we never see them again. You watch and see: it will be just the same with this lot . . . nothing will happen!

Buks This one looks serious, my child. He even had the keys to get into the house.

Veronica Did he say anything to you?

Author No. Just greeted me. Then walked around – like a Whiteman! – and looked at everything.

Veronica Well, I still say you are worrying for nothing.

Buks Anyway, worry or not there's nothing we can do about it, hey. If he buys the land he can tell me take my spade and my wheelbarrow and go and that's the end of the story.

Veronica Don't say that, Oupa! That will make it come true!

Buks You're right. Let's talk about something else. So what mischief were you up to this morning, my girl?

Veronica Nothing, Oupa. Nothing . . . nothing . . . nothing . . . nothing! There's no good mischief left in this place. I've used it all up. Anyway, I'm not looking for mischief anymore.

Buks I see. So what are you looking for then?

Veronica Adventure and romance!

Buks That's now something new. Since when is this?

Veronica Since a long time, Oupa.

Buks Well, I don't know how much adventure and . . . what was it?

Veronica Romance.

Buks I don't know how much of that you are going to find around here.

Veronica So then what, Oupa?

Buks What do you mean?

Veronica What is there for me? I'm bored.

Buks Open your eyes and look around you.

Veronica They're open, Oupa . . . wide open . . . and what do I see? Always just the same old story. Nothing happens here, Oupa.

Buks Nothing happens? Haai, you young people! (*Out of a pocket comes a handful of pumpkin seeds.*) Veronica. Come here. What are these?

Veronica Pumpkin seeds.

Buks No. That's what people call them but that is not what they really are. They are miracles. A handful of

312

miracles, Veronica! Every year, in these akkers . . .
thousands of miracles. And you say nothing happens
here?

Veronica Ja, I know all that, Oupa, but a girl can't make
adventure and romance out of pumpkin seeds.

Buks Veronica! Veronica! What's got into you lately?
You're as restless as a little dwarrelwindjie out there in
the veld. What's the matter with you?

Veronica I don't know, Oupa. Yes, I do. I'm Veronica
Jonkers and I want to sing!

Buks So?

Veronica So Oupa asked me and I'm telling you. I want
to sing.

Buks So sing. Nobody is stopping you.

Veronica No. Oupa doesn't understand.

Buks Then you must explain to me.

Veronica I want to sing to lots of people.

Buks But you already do that. In Church. At the School
Concert. You know how much everybody likes your
singing and all the nice songs you make.

Veronica That's not enough.

Buks Not enough? I hear you. The whole village hears
you. God hears you. And that is not enough?

Veronica I don't mean it that way, Oupa. But I don't just
want to sing hymns and the same old school songs to the
same old people . . . over and over again.

Buks But you don't. Every time I listen there's a new
song coming out of you.

Veronica You mean the ones I make up myself?

Buks Ja. And let me tell you my girl those are the best songs I ever heard.

Veronica Oupa is just saying that to make me happy.

Buks If it makes you happy that's good – but I'm saying it because it's the truth.

Veronica I made a new one this morning when I was cleaning the house.

Buks There, you see! That's what I mean.

Veronica So do you want to hear it?

Buks But of course.

Veronica Are you ready?

Buks (*getting 'ready' . . . putting down his mug and folding his arms*) Yes.

Veronica It's called: 'Railway Bus O Railway Bus'.

Buks Railway Bus?

Veronica Yes. But you must say it two times with a 'O' in between. 'Railway Bus O Railway Bus'.

Buks The Railway Bus that used to come from Graaff-Reinet?

Veronica Yes, yes, yes! Wait for the song, Oupa. Then you'll understand. (*Sings.*)

> Railway Bus O Railway Bus
> Why don't you come no more?
> I want to travel fast
> On the smooth tar road
> Far away, Far away.
> Railway Bus O Railway Bus
> I want to climb on board,
> I want to see Big Cities,

322

And strange places
Far away, Far away –

(*Breaks off abruptly when she sees her song is disturbing her Oupa.*) What's the matter, Oupa?

Buks No. I don't want to hear it.

Veronica Why?

Buks Because I don't like it. Don't sing it to me again.

Veronica But why? What's wrong with it.

Buks The Railway Bus is not a nice thing for a song. Sing me one of your other songs . . . about the school or our house, or that nice one about when it rains. Ja. Sing me that one.

Veronica I don't feel like singing that song, Oupa.

A hurt, estranged silence settles in between the two of them. Veronica starts to leave.

I'm going now, Oupa.

Buks Veronica . . .

Veronica Yes, Oupa?

Buks Come back. Come sit here.

She returns to his side.

I'm not cross with you, my child. I'm not cross with your song. I'm not even cross with the old Railway Bus . . . but it brings back memories . . . memories of things I've tried all these years to forget. That is why your song upset me.

Veronica Are they memories about my mother, Oupa?

Buks Ja . . . about her mostly. If that Railway Bus hadn't been there and made it so easy for her, who knows?

315

Maybe she would still be alive and sitting here with us today. That is how she ran away. And that is how you came back – in your Ouma's arms, wrapped in a blanket. Haai!

Veronica Oupa has told me so little.

Buks Because I've tried so hard to forget.

Veronica You promised you would tell me everything one day when I was old enough. I think I'm old enough now, Oupa.

Buks I was working here on the akkers when I got a message that your Ouma had phoned from Graaff-Reinet to say I must meet the bus. I thought she was bringing back your mother, you see. We didn't know anything about there being a baby. After she ran away we waited and waited but we didn't hear anything for a whole year. Then when the hospital in Johannesburg phoned they just said we must come quickly because your mother was very sick. So your Ouma went. I waited here. Then I got the message that I must meet the bus and like I said I thought she was bringing Caroline back. But instead it was you. By the time your Ouma got to the hospital, your mother was already dead. Betty never saw her daughter again.

Veronica She ran away with her boyfriend, didn't she?

Buks Who told you that?

Veronica Other children, Oupa. They hear what their parents say about me.

Buks What else do you know?

Veronica His name. Harry Ruiters.

Buks That's right.

Veronica Is he my father?

Buks No! (*Pause.*) I don't know. (*Pause.*) Maybe he is.

Veronica What was he like?

Buks Don't think about him, Veronica! He was a rubbish, a good for nothing rubbish who led your mother into sin. He made trouble in the village from the day he was born – fighting and stealing. Ja. The first time they caught him breaking into the shop he was too young to go before the magistrate so they gave him a good hiding at the police station and sent him home. It didn't help anything. A few years later they caught him again and this time he was old enough to go to court. They were waiting for his case to come up when he ran away with your mother.

Veronica And my mother? Tell me about her.

Buks It hurts me to talk about her.

Veronica I'm sorry, Oupa, but it feels like I know nothing about her.

Buks What did you want to know?

Veronica Anything. You say she looked like me?

Buks Oh yes. So much it almost frightens me.

Veronica Why 'frighten' Oupa?

Buks No, that's the wrong word. Surprise. I meant to say surprise.

Veronica Did she like singing?

Buks Yes, but not like you. (*a small smile and a shake of the head*) . . . definitely not like you.

Veronica (*eagerly*) You remember something else?

Buks Yes, but it's not about Caroline, it's about you. After your Ouma got off the bus and we were walking home – I was carrying her suitcase and she was carrying you – you started to cry. And I thought . . . Oh heavens, this child is going to be difficult, I can hear that right now. And I said so to your Ouma. But she said: No, Buks. She's not crying. She's singing.

Veronica Ouma said that?

Buks She did. She's singing, Buks, she said. Look for yourself. And I did . . . and so waar! . . . I could see she was right. You know the way a baby squashes and wrinkles up its face when it's crying, like a dirty old handkerchief you've been sneezing in the whole summer, well that wasn't what I saw. Your eyes were open, your face was smooth and this funny little noise was coming out of your mouth . . . Betty was right! You were singing.

Veronica laughs and claps her hands with happiness.

And so it was from then on. Your Ouma always used to say to me: 'If that child ever stops singing, Abraam Jonkers, then you must know there is something wrong with the world.' That was your Ouma. Betty Bruintjies. She loved you, my girl.

Veronica I haven't got a picture of her in my head. All I can remember is a soft voice and a pair of strong hands . . . beautiful hands! . . . I think they're Ouma's.

Buks Of course they're hers. After she died the only other hands that washed you and fed you were mine, and they're not beautiful.

Veronica Yes, they are!

It is a moment of deep union between the old man and the young girl.

Oupa, I'm not going to sing that song again.

Buks No. Sing it if it makes you happy.

Veronica No. I'm not going to if it upsets you.

Buks What will upset me is if you don't have a nice supper waiting for me tonight when I get home. What have you got?

Veronica (*more recitative*) Glenryck Maalvis Chilli-chilli en Sneeuberge aartappel en wortels . . .

Buks So what are you doing sitting here? Go home and cook.

Veronica Right, Corporal. (*She salutes.*)

Buks The other arm, Veronica!

Veronica (*salutes again and then goes marching off, singing her latest song*)
> My Oupa was a soldier
> But he didn't win the war.
> Put a pampoen on the
> left-right left-right left-right.
>
> He had a gun and bullets
> But he didn't know what for.
> Put a pampoen on the
> left-right left-right left-right.

Buks So, Betty . . . what do you think? (*A pause . . . he remembers.*) 'Speak, woman, I can see there are thoughts in your head!' (*Shakes his head.*) Ja, if only it was still like that and we could sit down at the kitchen table tonight and talk about things the way we used to. More and more I feel so useless . . . so by myself . . .! There's nobody I want to talk to anymore – only Veronica, and I can't put my worries on those young shoulders, 'specially when she is one of them. Am I saying the right things to her, Betty? Doing the right things?

You can see for yourself she is happy. She is singing more than ever – even making her own songs now. And obedient. She listens to me. When I tell her to do something she does it. But I can also see she is starting to get restless. She's nearly as old now as Caroline was when she ran away. And she looks so much like her, Betty, it really does frighten me. Just yesterday she was standing in the street laughing and teasing a young man, her hands on her hips just the way her mother used to do it. I thought I was seeing a ghost. Because it was Caroline standing there! So waar! I nearly called her name. Sometimes it happens in the house as well, when she's sweeping, or doing the washing . . . I see Caroline! But then she starts singing and I remember . . . No! It's Veronica. It's my grandchild.

And now there is also this Whiteman looking at the house and the land. He is going to buy, Betty, I know it. And then what do I do? I know what you want to say . . . Have faith in the Lord, Abraam Jonkers . . . and I do . . . it's just that He's asking for a lot of it these days. And He's not making me any younger! I feel too old now for all these worries. Every day there's a new one. I don't know anymore . . . is it me or is it the world that's gone so skeef. I wake up in the morning and I lie there and listen to the birds and Veronica singing, or I can smell the rain that fell in the night, and I think to myself . . . Ja! This is now going to be a good day and my heart fills up with happiness again the way it used to when you were lying there next to me . . . but there's a leak somewhere Betty, because at the end of it . . . there's nothing left . . . it's all gone. (*Shaking his head.*)

Anyway, Betty . . . where was I? Ja! I got the pumpkin seed in, I led water to the potatoes – those onions also need some but there wasn't any left for them. I'll get Veronica to say a little prayer for rain tonight – her prayers are very strong! And if you want to give us some help up there, Betty, that would also be very nice.

Veronica (*coming forward and speaking to the audience*)
So like my Oupa said I must, I go home and I cook
supper. I also see that there is hot water ready for him to
wash himself when he comes home. And a clean shirt.
He always wears a clean shirt for supper. Then we eat
and after I wash the dishes we go for a walk and visit
somebody or maybe somebody comes and visits us and
if it's summertime we take the kitchen chairs and go sit
outside under the bluegum tree where it's nice and cool
and we talk and talk. The last thing that happens is that
we go and sit at the table again and I read to my Oupa
from the Bible. Oupa can't read. He only went as far as
Standard One in school. Then we say good-night because
now it's supposed to be bedtime you see. Night, Oupa.
Moenie vergeet om die kers dood te blaas nie. I say
'supposed to be' because I got other ideas. As soon as
I hear my Oupa snoring – he sleeps in the bedroom and
I sleep in the kitchen – I get up and go quietly out of the
house and when I'm outside I run like hell to old Mrs
Jooste's house – the big white one there on the corner in
Martin Street. That old Boerevrou doesn't know it but
she's my best friend. You see she drinks whisky and
watches TV until late, late at night. And she's always got
the curtains open so if I stand on a box or something
I can look over her head and see the whole TV. But the
best thing of all is that that old Boerevrou likes music –
doesn't matter what kind – fast slow, hop skip en jump,
Boeremusik, tiekie-draai — but that's what she looks
for . . .!

> *She grabs her apple box and, standing on it, gives us
> the scene . . . mimicking the pop star she sees on the
> screen. Mike in hand she sings to an audience of
> thousands . . . she sings loudly in a very soft voice. At
> the end of her song there is a small round of applause
> from the Author who has been watching from the*

shadows. Veronica gets a fright, grabs her apple box and starts to run away.

Author Don't run away!

Veronica You gave me a fright, Master!

Author I'm sorry. I didn't mean to.

Veronica How long has Master been watching?

Author A long time.

Veronica So?

Author So what?

Veronica So did you like what you heard?

Author Yes. Very much.

Veronica Then why didn't you show it?

Author But I did. I clapped.

Veronica That's not enough. (*showing him how to do it*) You must clap your hands and stamp your feet and shout and scream . . . Veronica! Veronica! . . . and then I come out again you see and sing some more. That's the way they're going to do it one day.

Author When you're famous.

Veronica That's right. In Johannesburg and Durban and Cape Town . . . Veronica! Veronica! Give us more! We want to hear Veronica!

Author So then come on. Sing some more.

Veronica Just like that?

Author Why not?

Veronica (*to the audience*) Listen to him! He wants the famous Veronica to sing for him just like that? (*back to Author*) It will cost you a lot of money, 'Master'.

Author How much?

Veronica For one ticket?

Author Yes.

Veronica (*taking a chance*) Twenty-five rand. If you bring your girlfriend you must pay fifty rand.

   Laughter.

You laugh now but wait and see. One day it will happen.

Author Go on. I want to hear more.

Veronica I'll be on TV. Ja. Then you can stand here on the stoep and loer through the window and watch me singing. I'll be wearing a beautiful shiny green dress – that's my colour – and green shoes with high, high heels and long gloves that go all the way up to my elbow and a fancy hairstyle with sparkles in it. You wait and see, my boy. You wait and see.

Author So that's your dream.

Veronica Yes. Anything wrong with it?

Author No. But it's a big one.

Veronica Of course. That's the only way to do it.

Author Really?

Veronica Oh yes. What's the use of a little dream. A dream must be big and special. It much be the most special thing you can imagine for yourself in the whole world. Don't you have dreams like that?

Author Not any more, but I used to.

Veronica There you see. You've got to dream big. It's like my friend Alfred Witbooi – he told me he's dreaming about getting a job so that he can buy a bicycle. So I straight away saw this big, black shiny new bicycle with a loud ringatingaling bell and all that, but he said No, he just wanted to buy Baasie Koopman's old second-hand bicycle. I was so cross with him! No, Alfred! I said. Wake up! You're not dreaming properly – it must be a brand-new bicycle with a bell and a lamp, and a pump and a red light in the back and everything else.

Author I think Alfred is being sensible.

Veronica No. Alfred's a bangbroek.

Author Come on, Veronica. That's not fair. You know how hard it is to find work here in the Valley. If he tries to save up enough for a new bicycle he could spend the rest of his life waiting for it.

Veronica No, he won't. If he dreams properly he'll get it.

Author How do you dream 'properly'?

Veronica You must see it and believe it. Alfred must see the bicycle like he was watching it on TV, he must see himself sitting on it and riding around the village ringing the bell and waving at everybody and then he must believe that is what is going to happen. He must believe that as hard as he can.

Author It doesn't always work that way, Veronica.

Veronica Yes, it does!

Author A lot of my big dreams didn't come true and I saw them very clearly.

Veronica Then that's because you didn't believe them hard enough.

Author I think I did.

Veronica No, you didn't . . . otherwise they would have come true. Anyway I don't want to argue anymore. Don't spoil it for me!

Author Okay, okay. I'll stop.

Veronica So then come on. I want to dream some more. Come on! (*clapping her hands and stamping her feet, etc.*) I showed you how to do it.

Author (*clapping his hands and stamping his feet, etc.*) Veronica! Veronica! We want Veronica!

Veronica (*once again mike in hand and talking to an audience of thousands*) Thank you . . . thank you . . . and now all you beautiful people I am going to sing you one of my very own songs . . . number one on the hit parade! . . . 'Wake up and dream properly, Alfred Witbooi' (*sings*)

> Wake up and dream properly, Alfred Witbooi,
> Don't waste your life on a second-hand dream.
> Dream it now,
> Dream it new,
> That bicycle
> Was meant for you.
> Wake up and dream properly Alfred Witbooi . . .

Author (*to the audience*)

> 'The Earth is the Lord's, and the fullness thereof;
>   the world and they that dwell there in.
> For He has founded it upon the seas, and established
>   it upon the floods.
> Who shall ascend into the the hill of the Lord? Or
>   who shall stand in the holy place?
> He that hath clean hands and a pure heart, who hath
>   not lifted his soul into vanity, nor sworn deceitfully.
> He shall receive the blessing from the Lord and
>   righteousness from the God of his salvation.'

Psalm 24.

> *Buks and Veronica stand side by side and sing a hymn. Veronica's voice rings out pure and clear.*

Die Heiland is gebore!
– so klink die engelstem;
en sang van hemelskare
ruis soet oor Betlehem.
Uit liefde tot die wereld
Het God sy Seun gegee;
wie in Hom glo – sal lewe,
want Hy bring heil en vree.
Amen

At the end of the hymn Veronica positions the apple box for her Oupa in the shade of the old bluegum tree outside their house.

Veronica (*with all the conviction she can muster*) I don't believe it! It's not going to happen! Come on now, Oupa. I can't do it by myself. You must also be strong. So say it with me: I don't believe it! It's not going to happen! Oupa!!

Buks It doesn't work like that, Veronica. If we want to believe it or not that is what Stella said. She says she heard him say so with her own two ears. She came by this way 'specially to tell me. She said she was cleaning there in the municipal office on Friday afternoon when the Whiteman came in and spoke to Mrs Kruger. She heard him say: 'I want to buy the old Landman house and the land.' Those were his words.

Veronica Well then, maybe she heard wrong.

Buks Stella hear wrong? She's got the biggest ears in the whole village . . . 'specially when she's listening to someone else's business.

Veronica Well, even if she is right none of our people is going to try and push in there with him. Everybody knows those are your akkers.

Buks It's not our people I'm worried about, it's him, the Whiteman. If he buys the house and the land he's going to get a piece of paper that tells him those akkers are his. He can tell me to go anytime he likes and get somebody else to work for him.

Veronica It makes me so mad. It's just not right.

Buks Come now, Veronica . . .

Veronica No, Oupa! You mustn't accept it just like that.

Buks There's nothing we can do.

Veronica Yes, there is.

Buks What?

Veronica We can tell the Government.

Buks What do you mean?

Veronica A petition Oupa. We write a petition.

Buks What's that?

Veronica It's like a letter, Oupa. And in it we tell the Government just how things are with us here in the Valley. And we must get all of our people to sign it.

Buks And then what happens?

Veronica Then the Government comes here and changes things. They're doing it in lots of other places now, Oupa – taking the land and giving it back to the people.

Buks You think those groot Kokkedoore are going to worry about me and my few akkers? Anyway, I don't think they even know where the village is. You told me yourself once that you couldn't find us on the map.

Veronica That was the school map, Oupa! Don't be silly now. The Government doesn't sit down with a school map and try to find all the places where it must do things. It already knows where everybody is. We had the elections here didn't we? . . . just like all the other places in the country.

Buks No! Leave the Government out of it. Every time they stick their nose in your business you got to pay something. I know what I'm talking about, my child. Government is trouble. I'll be very happy if they don't know where we are.

Veronica Well, God certainly knows where the village is so I'm going to pray to Him to do something.

Buks That's better . . . but God also helps those who help themselves. I think maybe I must go try to speak to the Whiteman myself . . . I see his car is still standing there in front of the Guest House.

Veronica What are you going to say to him, Oupa?

Buks Tell him about myself and those akkers – if he'll listen . . . Ask him, nicely, if I can carry on there.

Veronica I hate to see Oupa like this.

Buks Like what?

Veronica Like you are now. All worried and down and . . . I don't know . . . upset.

Buks I also don't like it, but what can I do? Anyway he doesn't look so bad. He greeted me nicely the last time when they came to look at the house. And, as Stella said, maybe there is also a good side to this business. If he does buy the house and fixes it up and comes to live here in the village, who knows, maybe there's a chance for you in there.

Veronica (*alarmed*) What do you mean, Oupa?

Buks Work, my girl. For you. Ja! Stella is right. They're going to need somebody to clean the house and do the washing.

Veronica No, Oupa!

Buks No? I think you are old enough for it now, Veronica.

Veronica (*panic*) Yes, I know I am but . . . No, no, no! (*A few seconds of surprised silence at her outburst. She is desperate and flustered.*) I know Oupa means good for me . . . and I'm very grateful . . . but No! . . . Oupa mustn't just . . . decide like that . . . what I mean is you promised, Oupa, that when the time came we would talk about these things first . . . yes you did! . . .

Buks Veronica?

Veronica What I'm trying to say, Oupa, is that I also got ideas . . . other ideas about what I want to do . . . about my future and everything . . . so Oupa mustn't decide just like that . . .

Buks You're talking too fast for me. I don't understand what you are saying. Speak so that I can understand you.

Veronica I don't want to do housework, Oupa.

Buks But you do it in here every day, Veronica.

Veronica This is different, Oupa. This is our house. I'm doing it for us. I don't want to do it for other people. I don't want to do it for a living. 'Specially that house.

Buks What is wrong with getting work there? Your Ouma cleaned that house.

Veronica Exactly, Oupa! That's what I been trying to say. Isn't it supposed to be different now.

Buks What must be different?

Veronica Everything. Our lives and . . . and everything. Isn't that why there was an election. Oupa voted in it . . . and all that talk that was going on about how things was going to change and be different from now on. Well, this doesn't look like it. Here we are carrying on and talking just like the 'klomp arme ou kleurlinge' we've always been, frightened of the Whiteman, ready to crawl and beg him and be happy and grateful if we can scrub his floors . . .

Buks Veronica? Where does all this nonsense come from? Who's been giving you these ideas?

Veronica Nobody. I don't need other people to give me ideas. They're my own. And it's not nonsense, Oupa . . .

Buks Veronica! (*It takes him a few seconds to control his anger before he can speak coherently.*) Okay – now you listen to me very carefully, my child. I've never talked to you like this before and I don't ever want to talk to you like this again. You wouldn't be alive today, standing there insulting the memory of your Ouma . . .

Veronica No! I didn't!

Buks (*ignoring her*) . . . insulting the memory of your Ouma, if that 'arme ou kleurling' hadn't gone to the city and rescued you. Ja. You would most probably be lying in the same grave as your mother if Betty Bruintjies hadn't climbed into that vervloekte railway bus and found you and brought you back here. Broken hearted as she was she nursed you and gave you a start in life. Ja, it's true she scrubbed floors in that Landman house, went down on her hands and knees and scrubbed and polished, but if you can walk through your life with even half of the pride that that woman had in herself and her life, then you will be a very lucky girl. As for this 'arme ou kleurling' . . . you're right – I've done a lot of crawling and begging in my life and and I am ready to do it again for those few akkers. You want to know why, Veronica? So that I can grow food there for you to eat, just as I grew food there for your mother and your Ouma to eat, and as my father grew food there for me to eat.

Veronica (*struggling to hold back tears*) I'm sorry, Oupa.

The Author leaves the role of Buks and talks to the audience.

Author Stella was being a little premature in telling Buks that the Whiteman had decided to buy the Landman house and land. At that point I was still only thinking about it. The price wasn't bad but the house itself, like all the other derelict and abandoned old houses in the village, was in a terrible condition with plaster falling off the walls, rotten floorboards, broken windows, a roof that leaked in a dozen places. I could see that it would cost quite a bit to have it made habitable once again. But at the same time the thought of owning a little piece of the Karoo – where I was born – complete with vegetable akkers, vines at the kitchen door, an established orchard and a real working windmill, was very appealing.

On that Sunday I was loading up my car for the drive back to Port Elizabeth when the old man – still in his Sunday suit – came down the road pushing his wheel-barrow. It was piled high with vegetables – half a dozen pumpkins, beetroot, potatoes, a small sack of walnuts . . . He parked it in front of me, took off his hat and spoke . . . 'nicely' . . .

Buks Morning, Master . . .
Master remembers me? . . . at the Landman house . . .
That's right, Master . . . that's right . . .
Abraam Jonkers . . . Jonkers . . . that's right, Master, but everybody here in the village just calls me Buks . . .
Seventy-six, Master, this next birthday . . .

No, no, that's not old, not here by us. I still do a full day's work . . . yes, Master . . . I'm out there on the lands before sunrise and if Master doesn't believe me here is my evidence . . . look . . . (*the barrow load of vegetables*)
Ja, the earth is like a woman, Master, and it's us old men that know how to make her happy . . . Ja, if you look after her she will feed you . . .
No . . . I'm not selling them . . . they are for you, Master . . . yes . . .
Master . . .! I hear that Master is going to buy the Landman house . . . that's what I heard . . .
Oh, I see . . . Master is still thinking about it . . .
I was just asking because if Master does buy it I was wondering what the Master's plans was going to be and if I could carry on there with my few akkers.
I see, Master . . . yes, I see . . . but if Master does decide . . . all right, Master . . . we'll talk then, because I was also going to tell Master that if Master does buy it and fixes up the house nicely and comes to live here in the village I got a young granddaughter who . . .
Okay . . . Okay, Master . . . we'll talk then . . .
Where does Master want me to put the vegetables . . . there by the car? Okay, Master. Thank you, Master.

Author That wheelbarrow-load of vegetables did it. I mean, come on now, how could I pass up the chance to own a piece of my native Karoo earth that would allow me to brag and boast about 'my own pumpkins', 'my own beetroot', 'my own potatoes'. And the timing was perfect! I had ended up sick and tired of the madness and desperate scramble of my life in the make-believe world of Theatre. I wanted to return to 'essentials', to the 'real' world and here was my chance to do it. During the three and a half-hour drive back to PE, a vision of a new life unfolded before me. I could see myself sitting on my stoep after a day of good writing – all prose now, no more nonsense from actors and producers and critics – sitting there on my stoep watching the sun set and admiring my land, finally at peace with myself. In my imagination Buks' little peace offering of vegetables grew into a huge stack of pumpkins, little mountains of beet-root and onions, sacks of the famous Sneeuberg potatoes. By the time I reached home I had made up my mind. I wrote out a cheque for the modest sum they wanted for the house and land, and after the usual formalities between lawyers, I finally had it in my hand . . . The Title Deed! The land was mine!

Or was it? Had my few thousand rand really bought me ownership of that land? Remember the Psalm? 'The Earth is the Lord's, and the fullness thereof.'

I would have felt a lot better if God had countersigned that Title Deed. Because you see, Buks put his first seed into that soil when he was only a few years old . . . when his father went to work for old Landman. Jaap Jonkers. That was his father's name. And it was Landman himself who told Jaap that he must lay a few akkers for himself and grow vegetables there for his family.

That old house that was standing there empty and falling apart when I first saw it, Landman and Jaap built it with their own hands. Just the two of them! And then when Jaap died in the great flu epidemic, the young Buks stepped into his father's shoes and husbanded that land. And that's how it has been ever since. His life is rooted now as deeply in that soil as the old walnut tree next to the windmill. When it's like that between you and a piece of land, you end up being a part of it. Your soul wilts and withers with the young plants during the droughts. You feel the late frosts as if it was your skin that had been burnt black. And when it rains you rejoice and your heart swells with sweetness like the fruit on the trees. But Buks doesn't have a piece of paper with his name on it which says all these things, and so he has to come begging to me because I've got a piece of paper with my name on it which said that those akkers are mine.

Veronica (*to the audience, her mood dark and defiant*) I hate those akkers. Yes. Hate them. I know that's a big sin – to hate the Earth what God created – but I can't help it. That's the way I feel and that's what I want to say. If I was my Oupa I would rather let us go hungry than plant another seed in that ground. I mean it.

It gives us food, but it takes our lives. Oh yes, it does! That's why my mother ran away. I just know it. She didn't want her life to be buried in that old house the way my Ouma's was. If ever anybody sees a spook in that house it will be my Ouma . . . scrubbing the floors. And my Oupa also – he'll spook those akkers one day. You'll see.

He's like a slave now to that little piece of land. That's all he lives for, and it's not even his. He talks about nothing else, worries about nothing else, prays for nothing else . . . 'Come, Veronica, let us hold hands and pray for rain.' 'Come, Veronica, let us hold hands and pray that there is no late frost.' 'Come, Veronica, let us hold hands and pray that the bees don't sting the young pumpkins.'

Well, what about me? I'm also a living thing, you know. I also want to grow. What about: Come, everybody, let us hold hands and pray that the bees don't sting the young Veronica. (*She grabs her apple box and jumps onto it ready to launch into another TV session.*)

Author No, Veronica!

Veronica Why not? I want to dream.

Author I know you do but . . . haven't you heard? She's dead. Look! The curtains are closed. The house is in darkness. Yes. Dead. Sophie Jacobs found her lying on the kitchen floor when she came to clean the house. She was lying there stiff and cold with a broken whisky glass in her hand. Sister Pienaar thinks it was a heart attack and that she was lying there the whole night. They called the ambulance from Graaff-Reinet but it was too late. She was dead.

Veronica is stunned.

Another white spook in the village. There's supposed to be quite a few of them already, you know. Do you believe in ghosts? I'm not sure if I do or if I don't. I must admit I get a little scared when I walk around late at night. I almost imagine I can see them – at the windows of the old houses – pale, frightened white faces looking out at a world that doesn't belong to them anymore. I'm going to be one of them one day. So Veronica Jonkers, it looks like your dreaming times in Martin Street are over, doesn't it.

Veronica No.

Author They're not?

Veronica No.

Author How are you going to do it? Wait for her ghost to open the curtains and turn on the TV set for you?

Veronica There are other ways.

Author So you're not going to stop?

Veronica No.

Author But the same dream?

Veronica Yes!

Author You're famous! You're a TV star!

Veronica (*defiantly*) Yes! Yes! All of that. And more . . . I'm also rich and I'm beautiful . . .! Why don't you want me to dream?

Author I don't want to stop you dreaming but also I don't want you to be hurt.

Veronica By what?

Author Your dreams.

Veronica They can't hurt me.

Author Oh yes, they can. Believe me, I know what I'm talking about. It's a very special hurt — the big dream that didn't come true. It's like your friend Alfred and that old second-hand bicycle he wants to buy. If he doesn't get it it won't be too bad. The world is full of old second-hand bicycles. There'll be another chance one day. But if he takes your advice and starts dreaming – hard! – about a shiny brand-new one and believes – with all his might – that he is going to get it, and then doesn't because the only work he can find are occasional odd jobs that don't even pay enough for him to feed his family . . . That's a recipe for bitterness.

And you're not dreaming about bicycles, Veronica. You're dreaming about your life!

Veronica That's right, and that life isn't over like yours maybe is. If your dreams didn't come true that's your bad luck not mine. Maybe you are ready to be a ghost, I am not. You can't see into the future. You don't know what is going to happen to me.

Author That's true. I don't. But what I do know is that dreams don't do well in this Valley. Pumpkins yes, but not dreams – and you've already seen enough of life to know that as well. Listen to me, Veronica – take your apple box and go home, and dream about something that has a chance of happening – a wonderful year for your Oupa on his akkers with hundreds of pumpkins – or dream that you meet a handsome young man with a good job . . .

Veronica You're wasting your breath.

Author Okay, let's leave it at that. But for your sake I hope you don't remember tonight and what I've said to you in ten years time if like all the other women in the village you are walking barefoot into the veld every day with a baby on your back to collect firewood.

Veronica Never!

Author Because you know what you'll be dreaming about then, don't you? . . . That I've given you a job scrubbing and polishing the floors of my nicely renovated old Landman house.

Veronica Never! Now you listen to me. I swear on the Bible, on my Ouma's grave, that you will never see me walk barefoot with firewood on my head and a baby on my back – you will never see me on my knees scrubbing a Whiteman's floor. (*Veronica leaves the scene. With a demure smile she comes forward and talks to the audience.*) 'More Meneer 'More Mevrou. My name is Veronica and I live here in the village. Would you like to hear a very nice song? I made it myself. Yes, I promise you it's a very, very nice song. It's called: 'The windmill is turning around and around'. Can I sing it for you? (*Composes herself and sings.*)

> The wind is blowing
> And the windmill is turning
> Around and around,
> Around and around.
>
> The water is flowing
> And everything is growing
> In the ground in the ground,
> In the ground in the ground.

Tomatoes and onions,
Cabbages and beans,
Quinces and peaches,
That's what summer means.

Potatoes and carrots,
Pumpkins and peas,
Apples and walnuts,
As much as you please. (*With one final smile of innocence and purity she holds out her hand for a reward.*)

Dankie Mevrou.

She gets it and pockets it and then turns around and walks into a scene with her Oupa. There is a bucket of water and a towel for Buks to wash himself. This is a scene of secrets.

Oupa hear about the business at the Post Office?

Buks No. Tell me.

Veronica There was a bad argument between Mrs Oliphant and old Brigadier Pelser.

Buks What happened?

Veronica It was already past twelve o'clock, you see, and Mrs Oliphant was closing up the Post Office when the Brigadier walked in to do some business there. So Mrs Oliphant said to him, No, he must come back tomorrow because now the Post Office is closed. But the Brigadier said, 'How can the Post Office be closed?' because the door was open and she was behind the counter. So Mrs Oliphant said, 'Look at your watch and you will see that it is past twelve o'clock which is closing-time.' But he just stood there and said he wasn't going until he had done his business. So Mrs Oliphant said to him, 'This is no longer the old South Africa, Brigadier' and she went next door to the police station and got the Police Sergeant to go back with her and tell the Brigadier to leave. By now there was a lot of our people waiting outside to see what would happen, and when the Police Sergeant came out with the Brigadier they all clapped their hands and laughed at him. He got into his bakkie and slammed the door and drove away very fast like it was a racing car. People had to jump out of the way!

Buks And then?

Veronica That's all, Oupa.

Buks Who told you all this?

Veronica I heard it first from Rosie but then Mrs Oliphant told me the whole story herself.

Buks I see. Were you at the Post Office?

Veronica Yes. (*Pause.*) Oupa?

Buks Yes.

Veronica Mrs Oliphant also said that Oupa's got a letter for me. She says she gave it to you yesterday.

Buks That's right. She came past this way to ask me to go and look at her windmill. It's not throwing water the way it should. And she said there was a letter for you. Have you been writing letters?

Veronica Just to my friend Priscilla.

Buks That's nice. Why didn't you tell me about it?

Veronica I didn't think Oupa would be interested. It wasn't an important letter. Just silly talk, you know, and news about the village. (*She waits.*) So can I have it please, Oupa?

> *Buks takes the letter out of a jacket pocket and hands it to her.*

It's open.

Buks That's right.

Veronica Who opened it?

Buks I did.

Veronica Why, Oupa?

Buks I wanted to know what it said.

Veronica But Oupa can't read.

Buks I asked JanMei to read it for me.

Veronica What does the letter say, Oupa?

Buks I don't know – JanMei couldn't read it. He said the writing was too hard for him to read. You tell me what it says, Veronica.

Veronica (*stalling while she scans the letter quickly*) Yes, it's from Priscilla. You remember her, Oupa – Priscilla Meintjies – she was at school with me. We used to play together. Oupa always said you liked her. Then her father died in that motor-car accident and she and her mother and her brothers left the village and went to Johannesburg.

Buks Ja, I remember them. Read the letter, Veronica.

Veronica (*trying to fabricate an 'innocent' letter*) Dear Veronica, How are you keeping? I hope you and your Oupa are happy and well. Please send him our love from all of us. I miss you and all my friends very much. Johannesburg is a very nice place. (*She falters and stops. She is too terrified and ashamed to keep up the lie.*)

Buks Veronica, I think you are lying to me. That isn't what the letter says is it? Answer me child.

Veronica I'm not a child anymore, Oupa.

Buks Just answer me! Look me in the eye, Veronica! I don't think that is what the letter says.

Veronica Yes.

Buks Yes, what?

Veronica Yes, I am lying to you, Oupa.

Her dishonesty leaves Buks speechless for a few seconds.

I'm sorry. Please forgive me, Oupa. I didn't mean to tell Oupa a lie but I got frightened . . . and suddenly it was coming out . . . and I couldn't stop myself . . .

Nothing from Buks.

I said I'm sorry, Oupa!

Still no response.

Anyway, Oupa had no right to open it.

Buks Don't try to tell me about my rights, Veronica! This is my house. I got all the rights I need in here. For as long as you sleep under this roof and eat my food . . .

Veronica Okay, Oupa, then here – take it. (*She holds out the letter.*) You can have it. Go back to Mrs Oliphant and ask her to read it for you. Or the School Principal. Or the Dominee when he comes on Sunday. Let the whole village see how you open my letters and spy on me. Take it, Oupa!

Buks Veronica? What has happened to you? Why are you doing this to me?

Veronica (*ashamed of herself, she relents, opens the letter again and this time reads it truthfully*) 'Dear Veronica, I got your letter and goodness gracious what a surprise it was! Anyway, I asked my mother like you said and she said I must write and tell you that you can certainly come and stay here with us. I sleep on a double pull-out sofa in the lounge so there is plenty of room for

you as well. So come quickly. You will like Eldorado
Park. It's a crazy place. There are a lot of crazy things
here in Johannesburg and I will show them to you. And
you don't have to worry about finding work here also.
There's plenty of jobs here in Johannesburg, 'specially for
a clever good-looker like you. Are you still so crazy
about singing? Write me another letter and tell me when
you are coming. Give my love to everybody, 'specially
Diedericks. Is he still so handsome as ever? Totsiens for
now. Your ever loving friend Priscilla.'

Buks You've been making plans to go to Johannesburg?

Veronica Please try to understand, Oupa.

Buks You also want to run away from me like your
mother?

Veronica Please, Oupa . . . please listen! I was going to
tell Oupa, but first I wanted to know where I was going
and that there was somewhere I could stay so that Oupa
wouldn't worry about me. I wasn't going to just run
away and disappear.

Buks I knew it! I knew there was something going on
behind my back.

Veronica You're not listening to me, Oupa.

Buks That's right. I'm not listening to you because you
tell me lies, Veronica. That's how it started with your
mother. Lies and Secrets. And then stealing.

Veronica No.

Buks Yes. Your mother. From me – her own father. You
keep asking me about her, well here's the truth. She was
a thief. Ja, my own daughter but I must say it . . . a
thief! She knew where I hid my money and then one day,
without even so much as a goodbye to your Ouma, she

took it all and ran away to Johannesburg. I promised
your Ouma that I would never tell you, but she didn't
know that one day you would be like that as well.

Veronica No! No! I would never steal from Oupa.
Never! Never!

Buks So how were you going to Johannesburg?

Veronica I got my own money.

Buks Your own money?

Veronica is silent

What do you mean 'your own money'?

Veronica Money I save, Oupa.

Buks From where?

Veronica From what the White people give me.

Buks You ask them for money?

Veronica No. I earned it. I sing my songs for them and
they pay me. (*misinterpreting Buks' silence and thinking
she can bring him over to her side*) It's true. They all like
my singing. They say I got a good voice and that I must
go somewhere where there is a singing teacher so that
I can take lessons and make it better. That's why I wrote
to Priscilla. And you heard what she said in her letter,
Oupa . . . there's plenty of jobs in Johannesburg so I'll be
able to get work and pay for my singing lessons – because
if I become a very good singer, Oupa, I can make lots of
money. People who sing on the TV and the radio get
paid a lot of money. Just think, Oupa! You can even
come up there as well then if you want to . . . forget
about those old Landman akkers and come and live in
Johannesburg in a proper house with a big garden . . .
(*She takes a chance . . . fetching the tin with her savings,*

opening it and placing it trustingly on the table in front of her Oupa.) Look, Oupa – I nearly got half the price of a train ticket already.

I'm doing it because I want Oupa to be proud of me. I want to give you something back for all you've given me. But I can't do that if I stay here. There's nothing for me in this Valley. Please try to understand what it is like for me. I'll die if I got to live my whole life here.

Buks' devastation turns to rage. He grabs the tin and hurls it out into the night.

No, Oupa! No! It's mine!

Buks Devil's money.

Veronica It's not. I earned it. I earned it properly.

Buks I'm telling you it's Devil's money! That's where it comes from. Devil's money. He's trying to get you the way he got your mother. But this time I'm ready for him. Now you listen to me very carefully, Veronica. Don't let me ever catch you begging money from the White people again. And you can also forget all about Johannesburg. This family has already got one grave up there. There won't be another one. Whatever you might think, you are still a child and I am your Oupa. If you try to run away I'll have the police after you. I mean it. And I'll tell them to lock you up until you come to your senses.

Author (*to the audience*) The Psalm in Church the next Sunday was number one hundred and twenty-one:

> 'I will lift up mine eyes unto the hills from whence
>   cometh my help. My help cometh from the Lord,
>   which made heaven and earth.
> He will not suffer thy foot to be moved: He that
>   keepeth thee will not slumber.
> The Lord is thy Keeper: the Lord is thy shade upon
>   the right hand. The sun shall not smite thee by day

nor the moon by night. The Lord shall preserve
thee from all evil. He shall preserve thy soul.
The Lord shall preserve thy going out and thy coming
in from this time forth, and even for evermore.'

*A darkly silent Veronica comes and stands beside her
Oupa for the Church service, but this time she doesn't
sing. Buks doggedly sings the hymn through to the end.*

Buks (*singing*)

Ek sal die Here loof
Ek sal his Here loof
Met al my hart
Sal ek hom Loof.

Ek sal die here dien
Ek sal die here dien
Met al my hart
Sal ek hom dien.

Ek sal die here dank
Ek sal die here dank
Met al my hart
Sal ek hom dank.

They separate.

Buks You didn't sing.

Veronica No.

Buks Did you pray?

Veronica No.

Buks Why? Is it because of me?

She doesn't answer.

Are you trying to hurt me?

She still doesn't answer.

Did you listen to the Psalm in Church, Veronica? 'I will lift up mine eyes unto the hills . . .' Come do that with me. Look at them . . . all around us, and Spitskop over there waiting for the first snow of winter. Do you see it?

Veronica I see it.

Buks And? Is that all ? Do you just 'see it'? Look again.

Veronica I'm looking.

Buks Don't you sometimes stop and stand still and look at all of them and think how small you are? I do. And then I think: God made them. Ja! All these mountains that stand around and guard the village, He put them down here. That's how big He is. Everything . . . everything you can see with your eyes, or touch with your hands . . . He made it.

The bluegum tree where we sit for shade when the house is too hot, the pretty flowers you like so much, the rain that falls, the birds that sing . . . and your voice, so that you can also sing . . . all of it comes from God. That's how full of love he is for us. Our Church is His house – that is where God lives and that is where we thank Him for all the love He gives us.

What you do in there has got nothing to do with me, or Alfred, or Rosie or Mrs Oliphant or anybody else. It's for Him. He wants to hear that beautiful voice he gave you. He wants to hear you sing and listen to your prayers.

Veronica (*shaking her head*) I can't, Oupa. You've killed the song in me. I can't sing. I can't pray. (*Pause.*) Is Oupa finished?

> *Buks doesn't answer. He stands very still. Veronica waits a few more seconds then leaves.*

Author (*to the audience*) Another late night walk in the village. This time it is winter – a Sneeuberg winter! . . .

bitterly cold and deathly still. Not even a location dog is
barking. A full moon has flooded the Valley with light –
it is almost as bright as day. I can see everything around
me – and very clearly! Trees, houses, fences, the mountains in the distance – but they are all cold and colourless,
drained of their life as if that world has bled to death.
I see a figure coming down the road towards me. I step
into the shadows of a pine tree. It is Buks! His little
woollen cap is pulled down low over his ears, his hands
buried deep in the pockets of his old jacket as he
shuffles slowly past. That is what he has been reduced
to . . . walking those roads late at night like a ghost.
After all, what is there left of his life? First he lost
Caroline – his only child – buried somewhere in an
unmarked grave – he would have made a simple wooden
cross for it if she had died in the village – then he lost
Betty – he made a cross for that grave – he might also
lose his land – and now Veronica – her love and her
songs – her beautiful Valley songs that filled their little
house and his life with laughter and music – they are
now as silent as a grave.

All he's got left is one last little question: What did I
do wrong?

It leads him back, all the way back to the memory of
a day when he was still a young boy. He and his father
were working together on the land. It was very hot and
they had sat down in the shade of a tree to eat a bunch
of grapes which his father had picked. It was late summer.
They were the sweetest grapes he had ever tasted, and he
said so. His father, Jaap Jonkers, laughed and then asked
the little boy 'Do you know who made the grapes so
sweet for us?' Little Abraam knew the answer: 'The
Almighty did.' Jaap patted his son proudly on the back.
'That's right, Abraam, and if you grow up to be a good
man, then God will make the days of your life even
sweeter than those juicy korrels in your mouth.' They

went back to work, but it was so hot it wasn't long before they had to sit down in the shade again. This time the young boy had a question. 'What must I do to be a good man, Pa?' Jaap thought about this question for a long time, so long in fact his son was beginning to think his father hadn't heard him, but then he finally spoke. 'You will live your life in three places Abraam – these akkers, our house and the Church. The rest is unimportant. Here, on the land, you must work, and work hard, my boy, in your house you must love, love everybody who lives under that roof with you and also your neighbour, and in the Church you must have faith and worship the Almighty and thank Him for all His blessings.'

His father's words come back to him again and again now as he haunts the sleeping village. A sense of injustice, of betrayal, begins to rankle and fester in his soul. He was given a promise of days as sweet as Hanepoot grapes, but instead they have ended up as bitter as aloe juice. Because he has tried – Every day! – Just as his father had said he must, he has tried to be a 'good man'. And Betty is his witness. She shared twenty-five years of that life with him. She saw! When Caroline was born he came running home from the akkers where he was planting and she saw him go down on his knees next to her bed, and thank God for the blessing of a child. They had waited seven years for it. When his prayer was finished he made the little bundle in Betty's arms a promise: 'You will never want for food or love in this house.'

The Author moves into the character of Buks.
Veronica comes forward and stands listening to her
Oupa.

Buks You will never want for food or love in this house. And did I not keep that promise, Betty? Was there even one day that she went hungry under this roof. And not just food. Everything else. I sweated my life into those akkers so that she could have everything she needed. I tried to teach her what is right and what is wrong the way my father taught me. We stood together in Church on Sunday and praised the Lord and thanked Him for his blessings.

And I love her. Oh, Betty . . . there is so much love for her inside me I don't know what to do with it. Could I have done more?

Veronica Oupa?

Buks now sees Veronica.

Buks Caroline . . .?

Veronica No . . .

Buks You've come back?

Veronica No . . .!

Buks Betty! Betty! She's come back!

Veronica No . . . no . . .!

Buks Please . . . don't go! . . . I must talk to you – please – I must know – Why? – What did I do wrong? – Help me, Caroline – That's all I want, just to know what I did wrong?

Veronica No, Oupa! It's me . . . Veronica . . .

Buks stops.

. . . your grandchild. Caroline is dead, Oupa. Ouma is also dead. Yes, both of them. Dead a long time ago. There is just you and me left . . . Oupa and Veronica. (*Desperate to help him back to reality, she breaks her silence and sings.*)

You plant seeds
And I sing songs,

We're Oupa and Veronica.
Yes, Oupa and Veronica.
You work hard
And I dream dreams,
That's Oupa and Veronica.
Yes, Oupa and Veronica.

Summer into autumn,
Winter into spring,
Planting seeds and singing songs,
It's Oupa and Veronica.
Yes, Oupa and Veronica.

Buks Veronica . . .?

Veronica That's right. Say it again, Oupa.

Buks Veronica. I thought . . .

Veronica I know Oupa – you thought I was Caroline.

Buks I thought she had come back.

Veronica She can't, Oupa. She's dead.

Buks That's right. My child is dead. We waited for her.
Every day. Right up to the day when we got the message
from the hospital, we waited for her to come back –
Betty here in the house, me on the akkers – waiting.
Sometimes I would stop working and go to the gate and
look down the road and I imagined I could see her
coming with my bottle of tea and bread.
　At night we sat in here and went on waiting. There
was a deep shame between us – your Ouma and me –
I could see it in her eyes and she saw it in mine . . . the
same question: What did we do wrong? Every night, in
this room, at this table, trying to live with that question.
And when your Ouma had cried herself to sleep I used to
get up and go out and walk and ask it again . . . What
did we do wrong? Because we loved her.

Veronica I know that, Oupa. I know she knew it to. You didn't do anything wrong, Oupa. You didn't do anything wrong with me either . . . but I know my time is also coming.

Buks What do you mean?

Veronica You must let me go, Oupa, otherwise I will also run away from you.

Buks No! You mustn't do that! I will let you go. But explain it to me. I want to understand.

Veronica Can Oupa explain to me how a little seed becomes a big pumpkin?

Buks No.

Veronica You said to me once it was a miracle.

Buks That's right.

Veronica You give it water and skoffel out the weeds and it just grows. Isn't that so?

Buks Yes, that is so.

Veronica I think it is like that with me and my singing, Oupa. I also can't tell you how it happens. All I know is that when I sing, I'm alive. My singing is my life. I must look after it the way Oupa looks after his vegetables. I know that if I stay here in the Valley it will die. Does Oupa understand now?

Buks No . . . but that doesn't matter. I'm frightened for you.

Veronica I'm not.

Buks It's a bad world out there, Veronica. Ja. Look at what happened to your mother.

Veronica It won't happen to me, Oupa. You have made

me strong. All that you have taught me has made me strong. Will you give me your blessing, Oupa?

Buks Come here.

She does.

God bless you, my child.

Veronica I love you, Oupa. (*She leaves, singing.*)

> You're breaking my heart
> Valley that I love.
> You're breaking my heart
> When I say Goodbye.
>
> You gave me a start
> Valley that I love.
> But now we must part
> 'Cause I'm on my way.
>
> I'll sing all your songs
> Valley that I love.
> So that people will know
> How beautiful you are.
>
> The dream I've got
> Is leading me away.
> But Valley that I love
> I'll come back one day.

Author So you're going to do it?

Veronica Yes.

Author Johannesburg?

Veronica Yes. The School Principal is giving me a lift to Bellevue. Then I catch the train.

Author Are you excited?

Veronica Yes! But I'm also a little frightened. And sad.
Are my eyes red?

Author A little.

Veronica I had a big cry when I said goodbye to my
Oupa. So did he.

Author So then don't go.

Veronica No!

Author Come on, Veronica. Think of your poor Oupa.
He's only got a few years left. Make them happy ones.
Go back and tell him that you've changed your mind . . .

Veronica No, I can't do that! It isn't something I can
change my mind about. I have to go.

Author You make it sound like an order . . . 'Go To
Johannesburg Veronica Jonkers . . . And Sing!'

Veronica Yes! Don't laugh at me. That is what it feels like.

Author I know. I wasn't laughing at you, I was laughing
at myself.

Veronica Then you understand?

Author Oh yes.

Veronica My Oupa didn't. I tried to explain it to him
but he didn't understand.

Author I would have been surprised if he had. You are
all he's got left in the world. How can he understand
losing that?

Veronica He's not losing me! I told him I'm going to
write to him every week. And the School Principal
promised he will read my letters to him. And I'll come
back to visit him whenever I can.

Author And did that cheer him up?

Veronica No.

Author I always had a feeling that you would do it, you know.

Veronica I don't believe you.

Author No. It's true. The very first time I saw you dreaming on your apple box I had a feeling that one day you would be saying goodbye to the Valley.

Veronica Then why did you make it so hard for me? Always laughing and teasing me and trying to stop me? You're still doing it.

Author I was testing you.

Veronica Testing me?

Author Yes.

Veronica Like in the tests at school?

Author Sort of.

Veronica And did I pass?

Author Oh yes. You're strong. I think you've got what it takes. But I must be honest with you, there's a selfish part of me that wanted you to fail that test.

Veronica Why?

Author A lot of reasons.

Veronica Such as?

Author Like your Oupa, I don't want to see you go. It means the Valley is changing and that selfish part of me doesn't want that to happen. It wants it to stay the unspoilt, innocent little world it was when I first

354

discovered it. On all the late night walks that are left in my life, I want to find little Veronica Jonkers dreaming on her apple box outside Mrs Jooste's house. You see the truth is that I am not as brave about change as I would like to be. It involves letting go of things and I've discovered that that is a lot harder than I thought it was.

And then on top of all that, I am also jealous.

Veronica Of what?

Author You. Your youth. Your dreams. The future belongs to you now. There was a time when it was mine, when I dreamt about it the way you do, but not anymore. I've just about used up all of the 'Glorious Future' that I once had. But it isn't something you give up easily. I'm trying to hold onto it the way your Oupa wanted to hold onto you.

Veronica (*shaking her head*) You old men!

Author That's right. And take my advice . . . Be careful of us!

Veronica It's time for me to go.

Author Good luck.

They salute each other.

The other arm, Veronica!

Veronica Thank you. (*She starts to leave.*)

Author Wait! Can you hear it?

Veronica What?

Author Listen. 'Veronica. Veronica. We want Veronica!'

Veronica Now I'm excited again. (*She leaves the stage.*)

Author And Buks? How do we leave him? Slumped in defeat and misery as we last saw him? I don't think so.

355

That is what Buks himself would describe as a dishonourable discharge from life and Buks is an honourable old soldier. The truth is there was enough life left in him to yield to one last temptation . . . and I was the Devil who did it!

I found him in his house, sitting at the little kitchen table. He asked me 'nicely' to sit down but I said: No, I'm in a hurry . . . and so should you be! Come on, Buks. Onto your legs. Didn't you hear the rain last night? I'm telling you, rain down at my end of the village came down so hard it sounded like that Sonderwater Military Band of yours was practising on the tin roof.

Think of it, Buks. Another spring has come and we are still here! Still strong enough to go out there and plant! Tell me the truth now, Buks, think back to your young days and tell me . . . Did a woman ever smell as good as the Karoo earth after a good rain? Or feel as good? (*another sly laugh*) Ja, the ground is soft and wet and waiting. And look what I've got for you! (*a handful of shiny, white pumpkin seeds*) Pumpkin seeds! Imagine it Buks. An akker full of shiny, flat, white, Boer pumpkins as big as donkey-cart wheels! (*The Devil laughs and starts to leave.*) Come . . . (*Looks back and beckons once more.*) Come . . . that's it! . . . COME!

Blackout.